Galen Grimes

SAMS
Teach Yourself
Upgrading and
Fixing PCs
in 24 Hours

THIRD EDITION

SAMS

201 West 103rd St., Indianapolis, Indiana, 46290 USA

Sams Teach Yourself Upgrading and Fixing PCs in 24 Hours, Third Edition

Copyright © 2002 by Sams Publishing

International Standard Book Number: 0-672-32304-4

Library of Congress Catalog Card Number: 2001096858

Printed in the United States of America

First Printing: November 2001

03   02   01   4   3   2   1

Trademarks

Warning and Disclaimer

ACQUISITIONS EDITOR
Betsy Brown

DEVELOPMENT EDITOR
Jonathan Steever

MANAGING EDITOR
Charlotte Clapp

PROJECT EDITOR
Carol Bowers

COPY EDITOR
Alice Martina Smith

INDEXER
Erika Millen

PROOFREADERS
Rowena Rappaport
Suzanne Thomas

TECHNICAL EDITOR
Dallas G. Releford

TEAM COORDINATOR
Amy Patton

INTERIOR DESIGN
Gary Adair

COVER DESIGN
Aren Howell

PRODUCTION
Susan Geiselman
Rebecca Harmon

Contents at a Glance

Contents

About the Author

Galen A. Grimes has been working with computers since 1980 when he purchased his first PC, an Apple II+. Since then, he has worked on PCs using DOS, Windows (3.1/95/NT 4.0/2000/Me/XP), and UNIX, and has programmed in about a dozen different programming languages including C/C++, Assembler, Pascal, BASIC, and xBase. Galen has a master's degree in Information Science from the University of Pittsburgh, and is currently an assistant professor in the School of Information Sciences and Technology at the McKeesport campus of Penn State University.

Galen has worked as an author for Que and Sams for the past nine years and has written the following titles:

- *Sams Teach Yourself MS FrontPage 2000 in 10 Minutes*
- *Sams Teach Yourself Upgrading and Fixing PCs in 24 Hours*
- *Sams Teach Yourself Upgrading and Fixing PCs in 24 Hours*, Second Edition
- *10 Minute Guide to PC Upgrades*
- *Teach Yourself Netscape Communicator in 24 Hours*
- *10 Minute Guide to Netscape with Windows 95*
- *10 Minute Guide to the Internet with Windows 95*
- *10 Minute Guide to Novell NetWare*
- *10 Minute Guide to Lotus Improv*
- *First Book of DR DOS 6*
- *10 Minute Guide to the Internet and World Wide Web*, Second and Third Editions

Galen has co-authored the following titles:

- *10 Minute Guide to Netscape Communicator*
- *PCs Cheat Sheet*
- *Windows 3.1 Hyperguide*
- *24 Hour Netnews*

Galen has been a contributing author to these titles:

- *Special Edition Using Netscape 2*
- *Special Edition Using CGI*
- *Special Edition Using the World Wide Web*
- *Special Edition Using Netscape 3*
- *Netscape Navigator 3 Starter Kit*
- *WWW Plug-ins Companion*
- *Special Edition Using Netscape Communicator 4*
- *Internet Starter Kit*
- *PCs Cheat Sheet*
- *The Complete Idiot's Guide to Buying a PC ("Home LANs")*
- *Surf the Internet the Lazy Way*

And Galen has developed and provided technical editing assistance on these titles:

- *Sams Teach Yourself Microsoft Internet Explorer 5 in 10 Minutes*
- *Sams Teach Yourself Act! 2000 in 10 Minutes*

Although originally born and raised in Texas, Galen makes his home now in a quiet, heavily wooded section of Monroeville, Pennsylvania, a suburb of Pittsburgh, with his wife Joanne and an assortment of deer, raccoon, squirrels, possums, groundhogs, chipmunks, and birds, which are all fed from their back door. Besides working with computers and surfing the Internet, Galen spends his time playing golf, bicycling, dabbling in amateur astronomy, gardening, cooking, and refining the art of "couch-potatoing." Each fall, he and his wife Joanne are transformed into two of the most enthusiastic football fans for Penn State's Nittany Lions (see http://www.psu.edu/sports/).

Galen can be reached either by e-mail at gag5@psu.edu and galen@felixnet.com or through his Web sites at http://www.felixnet.com/ and http://www.mk.psu.edu/faculty/grimes/index.htm.

Dedication

To Drs. Margaret Signorella, Nancy Herron, Sandra Gleason, and Curtiss Porter, for all the encouragement and mostly for all the support you have given me, and I hope you will continue to give me, as I pursue more scholarly writings and activities.

Acknowledgments

To everyone at Sams—especially Betsy Brown and Carol Bowers for their tireless work at keeping me on schedule. A special thanks to Jon Steever, Dallas Releford, and Alice Martina Smith (a.k.a. AMS). Your comments and suggestions during the final editorial process not only helped make this a much better book but occasionally had me rolling on the floor and laughing out loud. Their work and ideas made a tremendous contribution to this book.

My thanks also go out to Karen Walsh, Kim Cofer, Tony Reitz, and Matt Wynalda for the countless hours they slaved over the manuscript weeding out the errors, and for the countless suggestions they made, which ultimately helped produce a better product.

Tell Us What You Think!

As the reader of this book, *you* are our most important critic and commentator. We value your opinion and want to know what we're doing right, what we could do better, what areas you'd like to see us publish in, and any other words of wisdom you're willing to pass our way.

You can e-mail or write me directly to let me know what you did or didn't like about this book—as well as what we can do to make our books stronger.

Please note that I cannot help you with technical problems related to the topic of this book, and that because of the high volume of mail I receive, I might not be able to reply to every message.

When you write, please be sure to include this book's title and author as well as your name and phone or fax number. I will carefully review your comments and share them with the author and editors who worked on the book.

E-mail: consumer@samspublishing.com

Mail: Mark Taber
            Associate Publisher
            Sams Publishing
            201 West 103rd Street
            Indianapolis, IN 46290 USA

Introduction

Upgrading is as American as apple pie and hot rods. In fact, the upgrade spirit we see today is most likely an offshoot of the hot rod craze that grew out of the 1950s. Back then, there was a seemingly never-ending contest to see who could make the hottest modifications to improve auto performance. A lot of this same enthusiasm can now be seen in a newer generation trying to squeeze all the megahertz, or now gigahertz, out of their PCs.

Despite the existence of a market seemingly flooded with commodity-priced PCs, there are still a large number of savvy PC users who like to tinker under the hood of their PCs and see what modifications they can make to improve computing performance.

Whether you place yourself within the ranks of the savvy PC user or the neophyte beginner, you don't have to sit on the sidelines any longer—nor do you have to wait to buy a new PC to see any type of performance gains.

Whether you merely want to add a bit more memory; want to make a wholesale upgrade of your motherboard, processor, and drive components; or want to build a PC from scratch, this book gives you the knowledge needed to feel comfortable tinkering under the hood of your PC.

It's time to roll up your sleeves and start getting dirty.

PART I

Diagnosing Problems and Planning an Upgrade

Hour

Hour 1

Making the Decision to Upgrade

It seems that a week hardly passes when news of a newer, faster, and more powerful PC isn't making headlines. Although most auto manufacturers have the luxury and breathing room of having to release new models only on a yearly basis, PC manufacturers sometimes appear to be releasing new models every quarter, if not more often. It's no wonder PC users are confused and more than a bit apprehensive each time they go shopping for a new PC. The intense competition of the hot PC market is both a blessing and a curse for users. If you've been watching PC prices nose-dive, you are already aware of the consumer blessing this competition has produced. Users appear to be cursed, however, by being forced to play the "wait-and-see" game: "If I wait just a little longer before I purchase, I can get a faster, more powerful PC and pay less for it."

You do have an alternative to the wait-and-see game. Despite the downward trend of PC prices and the seeming glut of below-$1,000 PCs hitting the market, many users are opting instead to upgrade portions of their existing

PC rather than purchase an entirely new PC. Although upgrading might not exactly match the performance of a new PC, as you will see over the next 24 hours, selective upgrading of certain key components in your PC can substantially improve performance in the areas that matter most to you, depending on how you use your PC.

During this hour, you will learn:

- When you should consider upgrading your PC and when you should forgo upgrading and purchase a new PC
- Which components in your PC can and should be upgraded and how to select the components to upgrade that will benefit you the most

When to Consider Upgrading Your PC

The first decision you are faced with is whether to upgrade or purchase a new PC. If you are still using a PC with a Pentium 100 processor (or heaven forbid, something older) the decision has already been made for you. Your old PC should be considered nothing more than an obsolete boat anchor or doorstop, and you should be concerned only with deciding how much you will spend on a new PC.

If you are still using a PC with a second-generation Pentium processor, the decision may not seem so clear-cut (even though it really is). The second-generation Pentium processors (that is, Pentiums with a clock speed of 300MHz or less) are at least six years old and are not really capable of running the current batch of software at an acceptable performance level. But if you are still running Windows 95 and are content to perform some light word processing and spreadsheet tasks, and you occasionally want to browse a few Web sites on the Internet or play a few (older!) games, you may be able to squeeze another year or two out of that creaking old dinosaur.

Consider the fact that you have to look not only at how you are currently using your PC, but how you are likely to use it in the foreseeable future.

If you have not moved up to a newer *32-bit* operating system such as Windows Me, Windows 2000, or Windows XP, you probably will in the next year because most major software manufacturers are now producing software optimized to run under these newer operating systems. Considering the speed of current processors, you should probably draw the line at a 500MHz Pentium II. If you are running anything slower, it's time to upgrade. If you insist on hanging on to that old PC, consider switching to a less-demanding operating system such as Linux (see Hour 23, "Upgrading to a New Operating System").

16-bit and *32-bit* are technical terms you will hear whenever the discussion turns to operating systems and programming, among other things. Quite simply, the terms refer to how computer instructions and data are processed by your computer, either in 16-bit units or in 32-bit units. Because a 32-bit unit is twice as large as a 16-bit unit, the assumption is that 32-bit programs and operating systems are twice as fast as their 16-bit counterparts. "Twice as fast" may be stretching it a bit, but the basic underlying assumption is generally true. Thirty-two-bit programs and operating systems are faster than their 16-bit counterparts.

What Components in My PC Are Upgradeable?

If you have browsed this book's Table of Contents (TOC), you already have an idea which components in your PC are upgradeable. If you haven't taken a quick look over the TOC, you may be surprised to learn that almost every component in your PC—including the processor, memory, video card, disk drives, and more—is a candidate to be upgraded.

Which components you decide to upgrade is often determined by how you use your PC, but not always. Some upgrades make sense simply because the price of the particular component is too good to pass up. In the last few years, the price of hard disk drives has dropped dramatically. You can regularly see 30–40GB hard disk drives advertised for under $200. Remember the old saying, "…you can never have too much money or too much hard disk space."

If you're wondering where to start with your upgrading plans, Table 1.1 can give you some ideas on how to deal with some problems or issues you might already be facing.

TABLE 1.1 Quick Troubleshooting Table

Problem	Possible Upgrade Solution	Hour
PC locks up or can't load more than a few programs simultaneously	Add more memory	6
Programs or files load very slowly from CD-ROM drive	Upgrade to faster CD-ROM drive	12
32-bit software won't install	Upgrade to 32-bit OS	23

TABLE 1.1   continued

Problem	Possible Upgrade Solution	Hour
Can't format larger hard disk drive	Upgrade your BIOS	7
Can't increase video resolution or number of colors displayed	Upgrade your video card	20
Repeatedly seeing "out of disk space" error message	Upgrade/add new hard disk drive	10
All PC operations run slower than expected	Upgrade your CPU	7
System clock losing correct time or has wrong time	Upgrade your BIOS	7

Upgrading Your Memory (RAM)

Your PC's memory typically is one of the easiest and least expensive components to upgrade (see Figure 1.1). Upgrading your PC's memory has the added advantage of improving its performance. Sometimes the improvement in performance is large and other times it is small, but there is always an increase of some type.

The terms *RAM* and *memory* are often used interchangeably. RAM is short for Random Access Memory and is the electronic memory (chips) that your computer uses for running programs and storing temporary data. RAM is not the permanent storage area for files.

Not all memory performance improvements are readily apparent. For example, if you boost the memory above 32MB in a PC still running Windows 95, the performance improvements may not be very noticeable because Windows 95 is optimized to its maximum performance level at around 32MB of memory. The extra memory won't necessarily be wasted, but the performance gains will be minimal.

Memory upgrades are covered and explained in detail in Hour 6, "Upgrading Your PC's Memory."

FIGURE 1.1

PC memory is probably the easiest of all upgrades you can make.

Upgrading Your Processor

Because your processor is largely responsible for how fast your PC and your programs run, upgrading your processor will generally make most things run faster. Bear in mind, if you replace the Pentium II 400MHz processor in your PC with a 500MHz Pentium II processor, your computer will not necessarily operate as fast as a PC built from the ground up, such as a 500MHz Pentium II computer. It is not just the processor that determines how fast your PC operates. Other technologies also come into play, and these differences contribute to the computer's speed and performance.

> *MHz* is the abbreviation for *megahertz* (millions of hertz per second) and is used as a measurement for the oscillating timing frequency used by processors. In simple terms, it is an indication of the relative speed of a processor.

Upgrading your processor generally yields some increase in performance. In Hour 7, "Upgrading Your CPU and BIOS," I explain how you can determine if and when it is advisable to upgrade and how to select an upgrade processor.

Upgrading Your Hard Disk Drive

Upgrading your PC's hard disk drive (see Figure 1.2) is probably the second most common upgrade behind memory upgrades, largely because of the dramatic drop in hard disk pricing and the increase in available hard disk sizes.

FIGURE 1.2

You can never have too much hard disk storage space.

Upgrading a hard disk is also relatively easy. Although adding a larger hard disk drive might not seem like a significant performance improvement, consider your own habits in file creation and how often you acquire new programs you would like to try—especially if you regularly download shareware programs from the Internet.

If you once had or currently have a small hard disk (small being defined as any hard disk 10GB or smaller), and you regularly find yourself deleting files to make room for new files or programs, you can appreciate the performance improvement offered by the addition of a larger hard disk.

Upgrading Your Video System

The majority of the time you choose to upgrade your video system, it will be for a specific application. For example, you might need a larger or higher resolution monitor (see Figure 1.3) to work with a specific application, such as graphic artistry or CAD (computer aided design). Many of the newer games also require better, faster video systems.

FIGURE 1.3
When purchasing a monitor, purchase one as large as you can afford.

Even if you are not a graphic artist or CAD engineer, there are still good reasons to upgrade your video system. In Hour 20, "Upgrading Your Video Card and Monitor," I explain what benefits you gain from these types of upgrades.

Upgrading Other PC Components

The few components mentioned in this hour are not the only items in your PC you can upgrade. In addition to memory, processors, hard disk drives, and video systems, you can also upgrade your floppy and CD-ROM drives, your PC's sound system, your modem (or whatever you use to communicate over the Internet), your computer's system board, chassis, power supply, and more.

In addition to upgrade information, I offer you some helpful hints on how to diagnose and repair problems involving your hardware components and a few tips for generally improving your PC's overall performance. I even show you where you can get testing and performance monitoring software (see Figure 1.4), which provides before and after ratings on your components so that you can actually see the improvements your upgrades are producing.

Lastly, I include an hour on upgrading your PC's operating system, if you haven't already done so, and why this can be one of the most important upgrades you can make. If you are not a fan of Windows in its various incarnations, Hour 23, "Upgrading to a New Operating System," will also show you Linux, an alternative to either Windows Me or XP.

FIGURE 1.4

FIGURE 1.4

The Benchmark component of Norton Utilities is one of several performance monitoring programs you'll be introduced to in this book.

Summary

In this hour, you learned what factors you need to consider when deciding whether to upgrade your PC. You also learned what components in your PC you can (or should) upgrade and the pros and cons of upgrading versus purchasing a new computer.

Q&A

Q With PC prices starting at the $400–$600 range, does it really make sense to upgrade a few components that can very quickly add up to $400?

A That depends on a number of factors: what kind of PC you're currently using, what you're using your computer for, how much money you have to spend, and how many computers you are thinking of upgrading. Keep in mind that PCs in the $400–$600 range are far from top-of-the-line computers with all the latest technology. At that price, you're generally looking at PCs that are eight months to a year old, if not older. That's not to say these PCs aren't a bargain. If you're currently using a Pentium II 300 with 32MB of RAM and a 4GB hard disk drive, spending $800 to get an Intel Celeron at 733MHz with 64MB of RAM and a 20GB hard disk drive is definitely a bargain.

Q I've peeked inside my PC and it looks like I would need a degree in electrical engineering to start removing and replacing the components. Can a novice with little or no technical experience really upgrade PC components?

A Absolutely. It may look complicated, but it really isn't. All you need is a minimum understanding of what each component does plus a little patience. In a lot of PCs, you don't even need a screwdriver because many manufacturers now include snap-in and snap-out components. All the components you will read about in this book are designed for end users to upgrade. You just have to know how to do it, which is explained in the next 23 hours.

HOUR **2**

Understanding the Components in Your PC

Before you can begin upgrading the various components in your PC, it may help you to be able to identify each component and have a basic understanding of how each component functions.

During this hour, you will learn:

- What precautions you must take before working on your PC
- How to identify the various components inside your PC
- A basic understanding of the function of each component in your PC

Eliminating Potential Hazards

Before you go tinkering around inside your PC, you must be aware of a few potential hazards that exist. Most of the potential problems you encounter can be far more damaging to your equipment than to you. Except for the power supply, the voltage inside your PC is far too low to be a serious hazard to you, but it can cause very serious damage to the sensitive electronic components.

This is one caution we cannot stress enough! The power supply in your PC is built using low release capacitors and contains more than enough wattage to kill you even after it is turned off and the plug is pulled. Absolutely, positively, *do not open* your power supply under any circumstances!

Although these precautions may seem obvious to anyone who works on any type of electrical equipment, they are nevertheless worth mentioning here:

- Unplug your PC before you begin any work on it that requires you to remove the cover. Too often, many users are content with merely pressing the on/off switch, but on/off switches have been known to malfunction or stick. To be absolutely certain that no power is running through your system, unplug the power cord either from the back of your PC or from the wall receptacle.

- Ground yourself to release any possible static electricity. This is especially important during the winter months when hot, dry air increases the potential for static electricity. All electronic components in your PC can be damaged or destroyed by one good jolt of static electricity. If you have a grounding wrist strap, attach it to your wrist. Otherwise, touch the metal case of your computer or the metal housing around the power supply to ground yourself. You can also touch a metal radiator pipe if you have one handy in your house or wherever you are working on your PC.

Static electricity is a bit hard to measure; however, to illustrate just how sensitive your PC's components are, the type of jolt you get from touching a doorknob after shuffling along a wool carpet in the winter is more than sufficient to destroy most components in your PC.

- Obviously, it should go without saying that you should not have water around, or any other liquids that can contribute to a possible electrical shock, when working with any type of electrical equipment.

- Be extremely cautious about working with any type of electrical equipment if you have a pacemaker or any type of heart condition.

- Make sure that you have an uncluttered workspace. A large kitchen table is an excellent place to work, and because many kitchens have tile or linoleum floors, you can also guard against static electricity at the same time. Consider spreading a large towel under or near your PC to catch any small screws that you might drop while working on your computer. White or light-colored towels make it easier to see small pieces.

Keep in mind, too, that some manufacturers will void your warranty if you open your case and go poking around inside your PC. Be sure that you check your warranty before you begin laying out your grand upgrade plans.

Differentiating Between Desktop and Tower PCs

PCs come in two standard configurations—desktop models and towers. Figure 2.1 shows a typical desktop model PC, and Figure 2.2 shows a basic tower configuration.

FIGURE 2.1

A typical desktop model PC.

Desktop models may come in several sizes, often with names such as full-size, baby-AT, or slim-sized to denote some difference in relative size, but they all follow the same basic design layout: a PC laid out horizontally or flat on the desktop.

Tower models also come in a variety of sizes with corresponding names such as mini-tower, midsize-tower, full tower, and so on. If you look closely, you can see that the design of a tower is basically just a desktop model turned vertically or on its side. Turning a desktop PC on its side to produce a tower model offers a few advantages. Towers generally take less real estate on your crowded desktop and larger tower models usually have additional space for more internal disk drives.

FIGURE 2.2

A typical tower model PC.

Even before tower models were developed, PC users got the idea that PCs can work just as well vertically as they do horizontally. Some innovative entrepreneurs even began marketing stands for PCs so that you could turn a desktop vertically. If you are still using a desktop model and you want to turn it on its side, go right ahead—just make sure that the PC is stable.

Regardless of whether you have a desktop or a tower PC, looking at it from the front you will likely notice several similarities. The first thing you will notice is one or more drives that use some type of removable media such as a floppy disk drive, a CD-ROM drive, a

DVD drive, or perhaps a removable media type hard disk drive. On the front of some PCs you may also find a reset button. A reset button generally is used to reboot your PC much the same as if you powered off and then powered on your PC—what's known as a cold boot.

You may have heard the terms *warm boot* and *cold boot*. The terms describe two methods of rebooting or restarting your PC. As the names imply, a *warm boot* is a reboot with the power on; a *cold boot* is a reboot with the power off. The difference between the two booting methods is more than just the presence of electrical power. A cold boot is a more thorough or complete boot-up process because it also releases any data that might still be in several system caches or memory holding areas. A cold boot runs a more thorough *POST*—Power On Self Test. A warm boot is less stressful on your electrical components.

2

Some PC manufacturers also place the on/off switch on the front of the PC to make access to it more convenient. Although this placement is just as common as placing the on/off switch on the back or the side of the PC, many experts consider it a mistake because it opens the PC to the risk of losing data if you accidentally hit the power switch and turn off your PC.

Identifying Your PC's External Connectors

Before you start poking around inside your PC, you should become familiar with the external connectors typically found on a PC. Most of these connectors are usually found on the back of your PC. (Figure 2.3 shows the typical array of external connectors.)

The following is a list of connectors you typically find on the back of a PC:

- **Serial port.** Used for connecting serial communication devices such as modems, printers, plotters, and so on. Serial ports can be either 9- or 25-pin D-shaped male connections. Typically you find two serial ports labeled 1 and 2 or A and B.

- **Parallel port.** Used for connecting parallel printers and some types of external removable media drives and scanners. Parallel ports are 25-pin D-shaped female connections.

Male and female connectors? For those of you who are not sure how to identify a male or a female connector, a male connector is one that protrudes and a female connector is one that surrounds or receives. If you are still not sure which is which, ask your mother.

- **VGA video port.** This connector is what you plug your monitor into. It is a 15-pin D-shaped female connector.

- **Keyboard port.** Your keyboard is connected to this port by one of two types of keyboard connectors—the larger AT-style connector or the smaller PS/2-style DIN connector.

- **USB (Universal Serial Bus) port.** A 12Mbit/sec interface that supports up to 127 devices.

- **Mouse port.** A standard port for plugging in a PS/2 mouse.

FIGURE 2.3

The rear view of a PC showing the external connectors typically found on a PC.

Mouse port

Serial ports | USB ports

Keyboard port | Parallel port

VGA video port

Identifying the Parts Inside Your PC

Before you begin working on your PC, it helps to be able to identify the basic components you might need or want to upgrade or repair. Think of it this way: Before you attempt to do any routine maintenance on your car, you should be able to identify items such as an oil filter, a spark plug, and a radiator. The same principle applies to your PC. Before you start pulling out your hard disk drives or your memory DIMMs, you have to be able to locate and identify them.

Identifying the Main System Board

After you remove the cover of your PC and look inside (remember to unplug your PC and ground yourself), you can see the main system board, also known as the *motherboard*—an affectionate term that supposedly originated in the days of Apple II computers (see Figure 2.4).

The terms *main system board* and *motherboard* are often used interchangeably and refer to the same component. Both are used in this book, so don't be confused.

2

FIGURE 2.4

A typical main system board.

The main system board is usually mounted on the bottom of your PC if you have a desktop model, or on one side of your PC if you have a tower model. The main system board can be thought of as a connection or communication terminal. Most of the other devices in your PC connect to it, either directly through one of the many connectors built in to the main system board or through an interface card that plugs into the main system board. (Main system boards come in a variety of sizes and shapes and are explained in greater detail in Hour 8, "Replacing Your Main System Board.")

Identifying the Microprocessor

The microprocessor, also referred to as the *CPU* or *chip*, is usually plugged into a socket or inserted into a slot on the main system board (see Figure 2.5) and is considered the brains of your PC. On some early model 486 computers, the CPU was soldered to the main system board, but CPUs haven't been soldered onto motherboards in more than a decade so don't worry that yours in permanently installed.

Figure 2.5

A microprocessor located on the main system board.

Most older microprocessors are roughly about 2 inches square, as you can see in Figure 2.5. Beginning with the Pentium II, Intel began housing their microprocessors in a container that is a little smaller than a VHS tape cassette (see Figure 2.6).

Figure 2.6

A Pentium III microprocessor.

Another difference you'll notice about the Pentium II and the Pentium III model CPUs is that the container that houses the CPU is not plugged into a socket as all previous models of microprocessors were. Pentium IIs and later microprocessors manufactured by Intel are plugged into the main system board using a slot designed especially for the Pentium II. (In case you're interested, the slot is called slot 1.)

The microprocessor executes the instructions written into the programs that you run on your PC. Some examples of microprocessors are Pentium, Pentium Pro, Pentium II, Celeron, Pentium III, and Pentium IV CPUs.

> Sometimes you can't see your microprocessor because it is covered by a heat sink. A *heat sink* is used to help dissipate heat generated by your microprocessor and often looks like a black (or blue or silver) square or rectangle with a lot of small projections protruding from it.

2

When you hear a reference to the speed of a particular PC, such as 500MHz, 600MHz, 733MHz, 766MHz, 1GHz, and so on, the speed reference is actually to the speed of the CPU.

Identifying Memory (RAM)

The memory in your computer (also called RAM, or Random Access Memory) is built in to modules called DIMMs (Double Inline Memory Modules). DIMMs are electronic modules that sit in slots, usually located on your main system board (see Figure 2.7).

FIGURE 2.7
DIMMs in slots located on your main system board.

Even though memory (RAM) and hard disk space are both measured in megabytes (MB), don't confuse the two. Memory is used by your PC to run programs, and disk space is used to store files.

Identifying Disk Drives

Typically, PCs come equipped with three types of disk drives—floppy disk drives, hard disk drives, and some type of optical drive such as a CD-ROM, CD-RW, or DVD drive. All have changed considerably over the past few years.

> To cover some general terminology and measurements, a *bit* is a plus or minus electrical charge (more commonly understood as 1 or 0). Eight bits equal one *byte*. A *kilobyte* (KB) is 1024 bytes (2^{10} bytes). A *megabyte* (MB) is one million bytes, and a *gigabyte* (GB) is a thousand megabytes or a billion bytes.

Originally, floppy disk drives were designed to accommodate 5 1/4-inch disks, and their capacity was only 160KB. Their capacity eventually grew to 1.2MB before they were gradually phased out and replaced by 3 1/2-inch drives. The 3 1/2-inch drive also went through its own evolutionary period, expanding from an original capacity of 720KB to its present storage capacity of 1.44MB.

Nowadays, virtually all PCs come equipped with a single 3 1/2-inch floppy disk drive (see Figure 2.8). However, a few manufacturers now offer you the option of including a Zip drive (see Hour 14, "Adding a Removable Media Drive") in addition to or even as a replacement for a 3 1/2-inch drive.

FIGURE 2.8
A 3 1/2-inch floppy drive in a PC.

PCs have had hard disk drives ever since IBM shipped its first PC/XT model back in 1984 with a 10MB hard disk drive. Since then, hard disk drives have become faster, and their capacities have expanded beyond what anyone could have imagined back in 1984. Now it is difficult to purchase a PC with a hard disk drive smaller than 16–20GB (gigabytes). Although floppy disk drives are easy to identify (just look for the device into which you insert a floppy disk), to the uninitiated, a hard disk may not have any identifying labels or obvious clues. Hard disk drives can be placed almost anywhere inside your PC. Typically they have a black or silver case, are usually less than 1 inch thick, and have a gray ribbon cable attached to one end. They may be mounted inside a chassis or cage and are not visible from the outside of the PC (see Figure 2.9).

FIGURE 2.9

A typical hard disk drive inside a PC.

Identifying Interface Cards

Interface cards are electronic circuit cards that enable your PC to connect to or interface with another device. There are dozens, if not actually hundreds, of different types of interface cards you can attach to your PC. To work with your PC, an interface card must be inserted into one of the slots located on your PC's main system board (see Figure 2.10).

Never remove or insert an interface card while the power to your PC is on. You can seriously damage both the card and your main system board.

FIGURE 2.10
*An interface card
inserted into one of
the slots on your main
system board.*

The most common type of interface card is a video display card, which enables a monitor
to work with your PC. If you follow the cord that runs from your monitor to your PC,
you see that it is plugged into a connector on an interface card. This is your video card.

On some PCs, the video card circuitry is built in to the main system board,
eliminating the need for a separate video interface card. You can, however,
upgrade these built-in cards by disabling them and then adding an actual
video card to your PC (see Hour 20, "Upgrading Your Video Card and
Monitor").

Here's a list of some other common types of interface cards you are likely to find inside
your PC:

- **Modem cards.** Used for communicating with other computers over telephone lines
- **SCSI (Small Computer System Interface) cards.** Used to attach SCSI devices
  such as scanners and external disk drives to your PC
- **Network interface cards.** Used to attach your PC to local area networks, or to
  cable modems or DSL modems (see Hour 16, "Adding a Cable or DSL Modem")

Identifying the PC Power Supply

The last device inside your PC that you have to be able to identify is your PC's power supply. As the name implies, the power supply provides electrical power to the devices inside your PC. *Transformer* might be a more appropriate name because the power supply actually converts or transforms AC power into DC power and steps down the voltage from 120 volts AC to 12.5 volts DC. The name *power supply* was tacked on originally, however, and has stuck through the years.

The power supply is easy to identify because the power cord plugs into the power supply from the outside of the PC. On the inside of the PC, you should be able to see numerous cables running from the power supply to many of the devices in your PC, such as the main system board and the disk drives.

Summary

In this hour, you learned about the major components found in most PCs and learned how to identify them in your own PC.

Q&A

Q Is it possible to install more than one video card in your PC so that you can use two monitors simultaneously?

A Adding a second video card is not a problem. The problem is getting your operating system to recognize the second card and to do something other than merely display the same video image on both cards and monitors. Starting with Windows 98 Second Edition, you can install two video cards and monitors and get them to display different images. You can also use Windows 2000 and Windows XP to produce a different image on each monitor. Refer to Hour 23, "Upgrading to a New Operating System," for information about upgrading your operating system.

Q Is there a limit to the number of disk drives you can attach to your PC? Can you mix IDE and SCSI drives?

A Most PCs can accommodate only two floppy disk drives because most PCs can only address floppy disk drives as either A or B. As for hard disk drives and removable media drives, you can theoretically attach up to 24 using SCSI—drives C through Z. However, you would probably encounter some practical obstacles such as available power and physical space, which would limit the number of physical drives to far fewer than 24. If you mix IDE and SCSI drives, you will have to boot your PC from one of the installed IDE drives. SCSI drives cannot be made bootable if an IDE drive is also installed in your PC.

Q Do any PCs contain more than one CPU?

A Yes. Recently, some manufacturers have released PCs or workstations with two or
four CPUs. These are usually positioned as high-end workstations and require an
operating system capable of supporting more than one microprocessor. Windows
NT 4.0, Windows 2000, Windows XP, and Linux all support multiple CPUs.

HOUR 3

Examining Your PC's System Configuration

In the last hour, you learned how to visually identify most if not all the major components inside your PC. During this hour, you will delve a bit deeper and learn how to examine the system configuration of your PC.

Learning about your PC's system configuration is important because when you upgrade a component, you usually want to make sure that the configuration settings are the same. Also, when you add a new component—such as a CD-ROM drive, a removable media drive, or a second hard disk drive—you often need to make configuration changes, and you want to be sure that you are not creating a conflict with an existing device.

Don't worry if some of the information mentioned in this hour seems a bit "techie," arcane, or unnecessary. Even if you don't need all the information for upgrading purposes, you might need it someday for troubleshooting.

During this hour, you will learn:

- How to check your PC's system configuration
- How to examine the configuration of some of the devices installed in your PC
- What interrupts are and how they are used by your PC and its devices

Obtaining a Systems Configuration Program

Most computers sold in the last few years come with some type of diagnostics and configuration checking program that is capable of providing you with the configuration information you want to examine in this chapter. If, however, your computer did not ship with a configuration/diagnostics program, you can download one of several from the Internet.

> *Configuration*, in the context used here, means how your PC is set up in terms of what communications ports it is using, what areas of memory are being used and how they are being used, what interrupts various devices are using, and so on. Basically, configuration means what devices are installed in your PC and how they are set up to work with each other.

One program you will likely want to keep a copy of is SysChk (http://www.syschk.com/) by Advanced Personal Systems (see Figure 3.1).

FIGURE 3.1

Advanced Personal Systems is the creator of the diagnostic program SysChk.

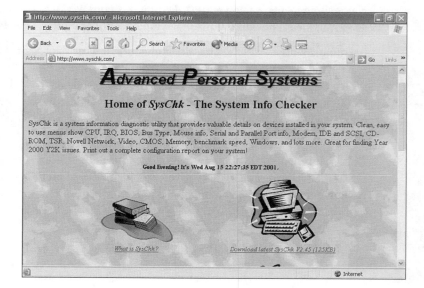

SysChk is an advanced analysis utility that enables you to examine the systems configuration of a PC. SysChk displays detailed information about the following components and systems:

- CPU and systems BIOS

> BIOS is the acronym for *Basic Input Output System* and is a set of instructions built in to your computer to control how information and data flow in and out of your computer.

- Input and Output (I/O) communications ports
- System interrupts and how they are used

3

> An *interrupt* is short for *Interrupt ReQuest* (IRQ). Most PCs built in the last 10 years or so have a total of 16 interrupts numbered 0 through 15. The original IBM PC had only eight. Interrupts are signals that various devices use to gain the attention of your CPU when they need processing time.

- Disk drives
- IDE/SCSI devices and configurations

> IDE and SCSI are interfaces for connecting disk drives and other devices of various types to your PC. IDE stands for *Integrated Drive Electronics* and is an interface that enables up to two devices to be attached to each port. Originally, IDE enabled data to pass to its connected devices at the rate of only 2Mbits/sec, but newer Enhanced IDE Ultra ATA/100 interfaces and devices can transfer data at the rate of 100Mbits/sec.
>
> SCSI (pronounced "scuzzy") stands for *Small Computer System Interface* and enables you to connect up to seven devices to the interface. Since the original SCSI standard was released, it has been updated several times and now includes SCSI-2 and SCSI-3, and can achieve data transfer speeds up to 80MB/sec.

- Video information
- Memory usage and configuration
- Network information (if one is present)
- CMOS information

CMOS stands for *Complementary Metal-Oxide Semiconductor*, which is a type of memory that can hold its contents using a very low electrical current. CMOS memory is used to store the configuration information of your computer; its electrical current is supplied by battery backup when your computer is turned off.

- Windows information (if a version is detected)

Task: Downloading and Installing SysChk

Before you can use SysChk, you must obtain a copy of the program. Follow these steps:

1. Log on to the Internet and start your Web browser.

2. Jump to the Advanced Personal Systems Web site at http://www.syschk.com.

   Select the link to download the latest version of SysChk. The program begins downloading to your PC (see Figure 3.2).

If you are running Windows 95/98/2000/Me/XP, you do not have to download a program such as SysChk. All of these versions of Windows come with utilities that analyze your PC's system configuration and produce a printout very similar to what you can get from SysChk. Later in this hour, I will show you how to obtain this information using the various versions of Windows.

If you do not have Internet access, you can still download the program. Most public libraries, colleges, and universities have Internet access PCs set up and available to the general public. You can use this publicly available Internet access to download the program. Bring your own floppy disks to transport the program back home with you.

3. The file you download, syschk45.zip, is in a compressed format and must be decompressed using a program that can decompress files in the ZIP file format.

If you do not already have a copy of WinZip or PkZip/PkUnzip for Windows, you can download a copy from either http://www.pkware.com (Pkzip for Windows) or http://www.winzip.com (WinZip). If you have to download a ZIP file decompression program, follow the instructions on installing the program.

FIGURE 3.2
Downloading the SysChk program.

Any time you encounter a file with the extension .zip, it means that the file is a compressed archive. The archive is compressed so that it takes up less storage space and downloads faster. To use the files stored in the archive, you need a program to decompress the archive. Pkzip for Windows (which also has a DOS-based version) and WinZip are Windows-based decompression programs.

3

4. Copy syschk45.zip into a temporary directory and then decompress the file. For the most effective use of SysChk, format a 3 1/2-inch floppy disk using the following command so that the disk will be bootable:

```
format a: /s
```

Then copy the files decompressed from syschk45.zip to the floppy disk.

Using SysChk on a bootable disk is necessary if you are running Windows NT 4.0, Windows 2000, Windows XP, or another operating system that prevents direct access to your PC's hardware. Regardless of which operating system you use, you get a truer reading—especially on memory usage—if you run SysChk from a bootable floppy disk as opposed to using a DOS/Command Prompt window in one of the many flavors of Windows.

Using SysChk to Examine Your PC

Now that you have your SysChk boot disk ready, you can begin to examine the configuration setup of your PC.

Task: Running SysChk

Follow these steps to run SysChk against your computer system:

1. Place the boot disk you just made into drive A.

▼   2. Reboot your PC either by pressing the **Ctrl+Alt+Del** keys or by turning the power
          off and then back on again. If you are running Windows 95/98/NT, make sure that
          you shut down your system properly first. If your PC prompts you to enter a date
          and time, press the Enter key at each prompt.

       3. To start SysChk, type **syschk** and press the Enter key. In a few seconds, the
▲   SysChk main screen appears displaying an overview of your system (see Figure 3.3).

FIGURE 3.3

*The opening screen of
SysChk displaying an
overview of your
system.*

As you can see on the Summary screen, SysChk displays a general overview of your
system, providing information on the following:

- CPU type and speed
- Total memory and memory usage
- Serial and parallel ports installed
- Video mode
- Disk drives installed

To obtain more detailed information, select one of the items listed in the window on the
left side of the screen. The detailed information about that component is then displayed
in the window on the right side of the screen.

Task: Examining Your Disk Drives

To show you how SysChk can display detailed information about the components and
systems in your PC, let's use it to examine your disk drives.

       1. Select option number 4, Disk Drives, from the left side of the screen using the up-
          arrow and down-arrow keys to highlight that selection. SysChk displays detailed
          information about the number and type of drives installed in your PC, beginning
          with the floppy disk drive (see Figure 3.4).

FIGURE 3.4

*SysChk displaying
information about the
floppy disk drive
installed in your PC.*

2. Use the left-arrow and right-arrow keys to select Disk 1 from the top of the right
   side of the screen; this is the first physical hard disk drive in your PC. SysChk
   displays information about that hard disk drive (see Figure 3.5). If you have more
   than one physical hard disk drive, SysChk displays a second selection called Disk
   2, and so on, for as many physical hard disk drives as are installed in your PC.

FIGURE 3.5

*SysChk displaying
information about
your first physical
hard disk drive.*

3. If your hard disk drive is partitioned into multiple logical drives, you can also
   display this information by selecting Logical from the top of the right side of the
   screen (see Figure 3.6).

FIGURE 3.6

SysChk displaying logical information about the selected hard drive.

4. If you want to find out whether your hard drive is using an IDE or SCSI interface, select option number 5, IDE/SCSI, from the left side of the screen. Next, select IDE 1 Info from the top of the right side of the screen; if your hard disk is IDE, SysChk displays IDE configuration information. If your hard disk is not IDE, SysChk does not display any information. If no information appears under IDE, select SCSI Info from the top of the right side of the screen and see whether SysChk displays configuration information about your hard drive interface (see Figure 3.7).

FIGURE 3.7

SysChk displaying information about your hard drive interface.

Using the up/down and left/right arrow keys, you can select all the components in your system and obtain detailed information about each one.

Task: Printing Your Configuration Information

To Do

In addition to displaying information about your PC, SysChk can also produce a printed copy of the information it obtains.

▼ 1. Select the P) Print option from the left side of the screen; SysChk displays its print menu (see Figure 3.8).

FIGURE 3.8

SysChk's print menu.

2. Select one of the available options depending on whether you want to send the
▲ output to a printer or to a file.

Make a hard copy printout of your system configuration and keep it in a safe place. This way you have a complete record of your PC's system information in the event that any or all of it has to be reentered into your PC.

Interrupt Conflicts

One of the most pressing problems you occasionally still encounter as you begin to upgrade different components in your PC is "interrupt conflicts." Most of the devices in your PC either directly or indirectly use an interrupt request, usually abbreviated IRQ, to communicate with the CPU. There are a total of 16 IRQs available in your PC (labeled 0 though 15); about half of them are already assigned to specific devices (for example, keyboard, floppy drive, printer, and so on). The number of free IRQs available for you to use varies according to what components are installed in your PC by the manufacturer.

If you use only Plug and Play components, interrupt conflict can be almost eliminated. Just remember, even though plug-and-play devices can resolve most interrupt conflicts, they can still occur. The basic rule is that each device must be assigned its own IRQ. When you have a conflict, you might get some type of error message from Windows or your software that a conflict exists, but there is no guarantee that any warning will be issued. In some cases, the device simply won't work and you won't discover the conflict until you go looking for it. Be sure to thoroughly check your component documentation for assigning or changing IRQs and what to do if a conflict occurs. Your documentation will also specify what IRQs you can assign to a particular device.

Alternatives to SysChk

SysChk is not the only utility available that can analyze your PC. Another program (a trial version) you can download over the Internet is a program called SiSoft Sandra from SiSoftware, located at `http://www.sisoftware.demon.co.uk/` (see Figure 3.9). This is an excellent utility that provides you with more information about your PC than you'll ever need.

FIGURE 3.9

You can download a copy of SiSoft Sandra from the SiSoftware Web site.

Another set of utility programs worth a preview are CheckIt and WinCheckIt by TouchStone Software at `http://www.touchstonesoftware.com/` (see Figure 3.10). WinCheckIt/CheckIt provides much of the same type of information as SysChk, but where SysChk runs in DOS, WinCheckIt/CheckIt runs in most versions of Windows.

FIGURE 3.10

Another choice of utility program you can use to check your PC's configuration is CheckIt or WinCheckIt.

You can also check a few other sites that offer PC systems utilities, such as CNET's Download.Com, located at `http://www.download.com` (see Figure 3.11), and Shareware.Com, located at `http://www.shareware.com` (see Figure 3.12). To locate diagnostic utilities, search each site using the keyword "diagnostic."

FIGURE 3.11

CNET's Download.Com Web site.

FIGURE 3.12
*CNET's
Shareware.Com Web
site.*

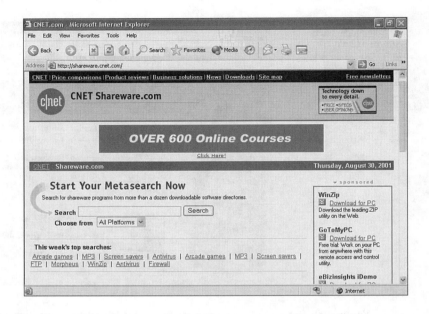

If you are running Windows 95/98/2000/Me/XP, you do not have to download a program such as SysChk, SiSoft Sandra, or WinCheckIt. These versions of Windows all come with utilities that analyze your PC's system configuration and produce a printout.

Task: Using the Windows Device Manager

Most recent versions of Windows 98/2000/ME/XP all shipped with a utility called the Device Manager, which produces almost the same amount of information as you have seen SysChk and WinCheckIt/CheckIt produce. Use the Device Manager in Windows XP by following these steps:

1. From the Start menu, select Control Panel to open the Windows XP Control Panel.

2. From the Pick a Category screen, select the Performance and Maintenance option.

3. From the Performance and Maintenance Screen, select System.

4. Select the Hardware tab and then select Device Manager to access the Windows Device Manager (see Figure 3.13).

5. To the left of each device category you see a plus sign (+). The plus sign indicates that additional devices exist or additional information is available about that device category. Click the plus sign to display a list of additional devices.

6. Highlight one of the devices listed and then right-click Properties to see information about the device (see Figure 3.14).

FIGURE 3.13

The Windows Device Manager.

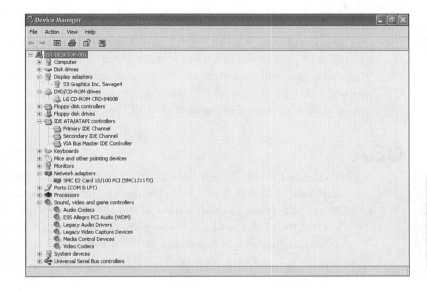

FIGURE 3.14

The Device Manager displaying information about one of the devices installed in your PC.

The Windows Device Manager can print the entire hardware configuration for you. On the main Device Manager screen, select the Computer option at the top of the device listing and then click the Print button.

3

Summary

In this hour, you learned how to use various utility programs to analyze the system configuration of your PC. You learned how to download from the Internet a general-purpose analysis tool and how to use the tools that ship with most recent versions of Windows to learn more about the devices and peripherals in your PC. The key benefit you will derive from these tools is that they can help you diagnose difficulties when an upgraded device causes a problem in your PC, such as a conflict with another device.

Q&A

Q You stated that there are only 16 IRQs (interrupts) available for use by devices installed in a PC. As I examine the information on IRQs in SysChk, however, it looks as though most of the IRQs are being used by the PC on devices that I did not install; there are not many IRQs left for me to use for additional devices. Is it possible or likely that I may run out of IRQs?

A It is not only possible, it has become a serious problem for a lot of users purchasing new PCs.

You're right when you noticed that most of the IRQs are being used by devices you did not install and that when you start adding devices, IRQs can appear to be in short supply. Many users are now discovering that by adding a SCSI card, a sound card, an internal modem, a network card, and so on, that they are running out of IRQs. There are ways to juggle IRQs—you can turn off devices not being used and you can sometimes enable two devices to share an IRQ, provided they are not used simultaneously. In later chapters, I'll give you some tips on how to make the best use of your scarce IRQ resources.

Q If most versions of Windows ship with utilities that can detect my PC's configuration, does that mean if I am running one of these operating systems that I do not need a utility such as SysChk?

A After you gain some experience in diagnosing and troubleshooting problems in your PC and become more familiar with hardware configuration issues, you can probably abandon (or at least put away on the shelf) a utility such as SysChk if you are running one of the most recent versions of Windows. When you are just starting out, however, I suggest that you use every systems analysis resource available. You may have noticed that the utilities in Windows aren't quite as thorough as SysChk or that the information is not presented in such a neat, easy-to-use package.

Hour **4**

PC Performance Monitoring and Diagnostic Tools

After you've made all of the changes and upgrades to your PC that you deem necessary, you might be curious to see how much improvement in performance your upgrades are making. To properly evaluate the upgrades you make, you need some type of hardware evaluation program, more commonly known as *performance monitoring* software.

Performance monitoring software enables you to take a set of base performance readings on your PC (before you begin making upgrades); as you make upgrades, you use the software to evaluate the (hopefully) improved performance in your PC.

This hour isn't just about testing your PC to see how much improvement you've gained from your upgrades. It also helps you locate a few tools that can help you diagnose any problems that might arise in your PC.

During this hour, you will learn how to:

- Locate a few performance monitoring tools you can use to gauge the performance gains resulting from your upgrades
- Identify several diagnostic utilities to help you identify any problems that might develop with your PC

Performance Monitoring Programs

In Hour 3, "Examining Your PC's System Configuration," you learned about using diagnostic utilities to analyze your PC to help you locate and solve potential problems such as conflicts between devices you install or upgrade. In this chapter, you are introduced to a few additional utilities you can use to analyze your PC, monitor your computer system's performance to see how much improvement in performance you're gaining from the devices you upgrade, and possibly also diagnose problems with your system.

Some of the utilities shown here are commercial products, whereas others are available free (or for a minimal shareware registration fee).

Ziff-Davis Media Benchmarks

For years, the gold standard for benchmark testing performance in PCs was the Ziff-Davis testing suites consisting of the WinBench and WinStone testing programs. Ziff-Davis has greatly expanded its suite of testing and benchmarking software to what is now called the Ziff-Davis Media Benchmarks. In addition to benchmarking overall PC performance and PCs running standard business-related software, Ziff-Davis now offers testing programs for 3D graphics, CD-ROM subsystems, audio subsystems, laptop batteries, Web clients, and networking performance.

The testing programs offer no diagnostic functions but are some of the best performance testing programs you can acquire.

The suite of programs stress-tests your PC by simulating a series of real-world computational tasks, such as calculating a long and complex spreadsheet, reformatting and repaginating a long Word document, querying a large database, and performing a series of graphic-intensive display operations. You can select to run any one or all of the tests in the suite (see Figure 4.1).

In its first few incarnations, the original WinBench and WinStone utilities were available for download. It wasn't long, though, before the programs were expanded and the total size of the two performance testing suites had evolved to well over 130MB; Ziff-Davis started distributing the two programs only on CD. The cost for the CD plus shipping and handling was $6.

Recently, Ziff-Davis began distributing a scaled-down version, which you can once again download from their site at `http://etestinglabs.com/benchmarks/winbench/winbench.asp`.

FIGURE **4.1**
*WinBench
performance-testing
a PC.*

FIGURE **4.1**
*WinBench
performance-testing
a PC.*

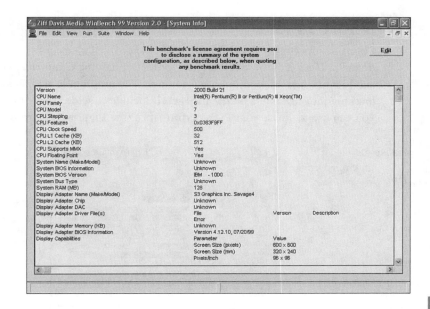

You can still order the complete set of testing suites from the site at `http://etestinglabs.com/benchmarks/reqfrm.asp` (see Figure 4.2).

FIGURE **4.2**
*You can order your
copy of the Ziff-Davis
Media Benchmark
testing suite from the
Ziff-Davis Web site.*

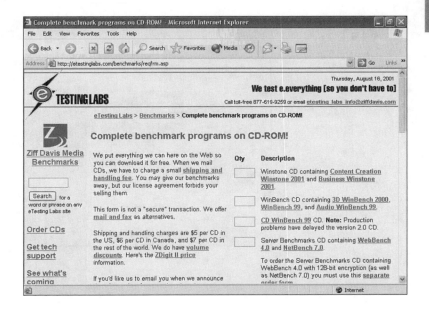

4

SiSoft Sandra

SiSoft Sandra (`http://www.sisoftware.demon.co.uk/sandra/index.htm`) was mentioned in Hour 3 as an excellent tool for identifying the components installed in your PC and identifying their configuration settings. The program is also one of the best benchmarking tools available on the Internet. It includes a wide array of benchmarking tools you can use to check your PC's performance (see Figures 4.3 through 4.6).

FIGURE 4.3

SiSoft Sandra reporting CPU benchmarks.

FIGURE 4.4

SiSoft Sandra reporting drive benchmarks.

FIGURE 4.5
SiSoft Sandra reporting CD-ROM/DVD benchmarks.

FIGURE 4.6
SiSoft Sandra reporting memory benchmarks.

Diagnostic Programs

Just as numerous performance and benchmarking utilities are available to give you an assessment of your PC's level of performance, you can also find an abundant supply of available diagnostic tools. Many diagnostic utilities are designed to inform you when a problem has developed, and there are also a few that periodically check your system for potential problems.

AMIDiag

If your computer is using AMI (American Megatrends, Inc.) BIOS (see Hour 7, "Upgrading Your CPU and BIOS"), you can download and run a diagnostic program to perform some rudimentary diagnostics tests (see Figure 4.7).

FIGURE 4.7

The main menu of the AMIDiag diagnostics utility.

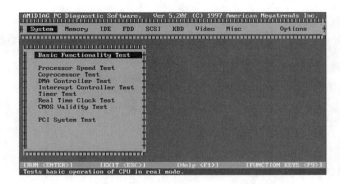

You can download a copy of AMIDiag at http://www.shareware.com (search for "diagnostics" or "amidiag"). If you want to purchase the full version, go to the AMI BIOS Web site at http://www.amibios.com.

The Norton Utilities

Besides including a performance monitor, the Norton Utilities also include a diagnostics application. Double-click the Norton System Doctor icon, and you will see an application screen similar to the one shown in Figure 4.8.

FIGURE 4.8

The diagnostics portion of the Norton Utilities, the Norton System Doctor.

The Norton System Doctor is a collection of monitoring utilities that you can set to monitor your PC's memory, disk drives, general systems operations, and Internet and network connections. For example, under the disk drive sensor section, you can set the System Doctor to monitor general disk integrity, disk fragmentation, the physical disk surface, or just the amount of free space available. Under the general system section, you can set System Doctor to monitor CPU utilization or check whether your anti-virus definitions are up-to-date. Under the memory section, you can set System Doctor to monitor memory usage and alert you when you're running low on system memory, swap file space, or Windows system resources.

As you can see, the Norton System Doctor can be set to monitor much more than just the physical components in your PC. The aim of this diagnostics program is not just to monitor the health of your physical PC, but also the health of your overall system.

Norton Utilities makes versions of its utility suite for all versions of Windows. Because of the differences in how Windows NT/2000/XP handle hardware access from the way Windows 95/98 work, it is very important that you install the correct version for your system. Do not attempt to use the version designed for Windows 95/98 on a computer running Windows NT/2000/XP.

More Diagnostics Programs You Can Purchase

In addition to the programs already mentioned, here are a few other diagnostic programs you might want to consider trying or purchasing to help keep your system operating at peak performance levels:

- **WinCheckIt/CheckIt**—You can get more information about WinCheckIt/CheckIt at `http://www.checkit.com/products/products.htm`.

- **PC Technician**—You can get more information about PC Technician at `http://www.windsortech.com`.

- **TuffTEST and TuffTEST-Pro**—This is another PC diagnostic test worth kicking the tires on at `http://www.tufftest.com/` (see Figure 4.9).

FIGURE 4.9
TuffTEST and TuffTEST-Pro are another set of PC diagnostic tools you might want to try.

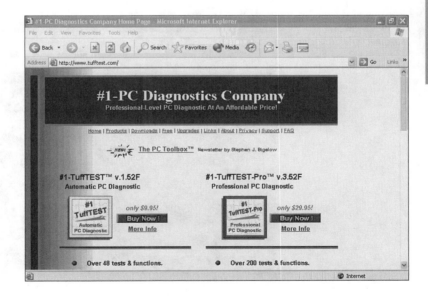

4

Hard Disk Diagnostics

One area of PC operations that many users seem to eventually have problems with is the PC's hard disk drive. Years ago, the saying was "…it's not *if* you will have hard disk problems, but *when*…." This seems almost passé now that hard disk technology has improved the reliability of hard disk drives to the point where most users never seem to experience a drive failure. Nevertheless, hard disk drives still do fail, and diagnostic programs are still designed to examine nothing but disk drives. One such program is Data Advisor from Ontrack Systems.

Ontrack Systems is primarily a data recovery company but produces Disk Advisor to help you avoid problems with your hard disk drive and hopefully avoid data loss. If you would like to download a copy of Data Advisor, go to the Ontrack Web site at `http://www.ontrack.com` (see Figure 4.10).

Remember, one of the best ways to avoid hard disk drive disaster is to perform regular backups.

> Not all problems are hardware related. There are viruses that can destroy your files and/or operating system and make it appear as though the hardware has developed a problem. Make sure that you are running a good anti-virus program in addition to periodically checking your hardware. Make sure that you also update the virus definition files regularly.

FIGURE 4.10

Ontrack offers a variety of hard disk services.

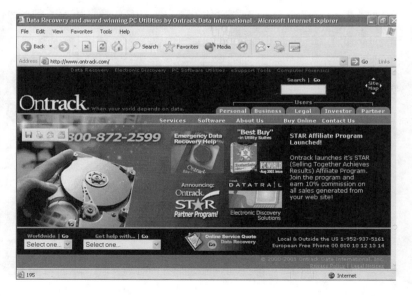

As you become more familiar with using diagnostic tools, you will also learn which problems require corrective action and which don't. Most of the programs mentioned in this chapter also usually explain these so-called "gray areas." This is to prevent you from needlessly spending time and money trying to correct a problem that is actually within the tolerances of normal operating parameters. If you are not in the habit of reading manuals, you should develop this habit when it comes to diagnostic utilities.

Summary

In this hour, you learned about a few programs you can use to help you assess the performance gains in your PC when you upgrade one or more components. You also learned about diagnostics tools you can use to help identify problems when they develop and a few diagnostic programs you can use to help spot small problems before they become more serious.

Q&A

Q What components in a PC are most likely to wear out?

A Two types of wear seem to occur most often in PCs: heat and mechanical. Parts that undergo extremes in temperature changes seem to show more signs of wear and often exhibit a higher failure rate. This is why all CPUs are equipped with some type of heat sink and occasionally fans. But heat is not as big a problem as mechanical wear. Components subject to mechanical wear, such as drives, still seem to exhibit the highest failure rates. Manufacturing improvements continue to increase the "mean time between failure rates" for drives, but any part in your PC that undergoes movement is subject to the fastest levels of wear and thus failure.

Q In the performance-testing programs you demonstrated, I could see how fast each component operated but how do I know what the speeds really mean?

A You have to remember that speed is relative.

Is 60mph fast? For a two- or a four-legged animal running on level ground, it is, but for a car at the Indianapolis 500, it isn't. You may have noticed that in many of the performance testing programs, the speed of your component being measured was often compared against other similar components. Comparisons like this help, but the final determination of speed is going to be very subjective. It's going to boil down to what you think is fast. If it happens faster than you expect, you will consider it fast. But if you have to wait for something to happen, chances are you are not going to think it is happening very fast.

Q Should I consider obtaining new diagnostic tools, or can I still use my old, trusty, reliable set that I have been happy with for the past few years?

A By all means get new diagnostic tools. Older tools may not be able to properly analyze and test newer components in your PC; newer testing programs will most likely contain more precise testing utilities. Older tools are like older parts—they need to be upgraded.

4

Hour 5

The Tools of the Trade

In this hour, you will learn what tools you need to upgrade and repair your PC. This section on tools is divided into two parts. The first part describes a simple set of hardware tools you will need to do most upgrades, and the second part lists a more advanced set of tools you should consider obtaining if you are inclined to pursue more complicated upgrades and repairs.

This hour also provides a more detailed list of precautions you should adhere to when working on your PC to make sure that you don't cause any damage to yourself or your PC.

During this hour, you will learn the following:

- What simple set of hardware tools you will need to perform simple upgrades and repairs
- What set of tools you will need to perform more advanced and complex upgrades and repairs
- What precautions you need to be aware of when you are working on your PC

A Simple Set of Tools

As you start to work on PCs, you'll quickly discover that you can perform about 90% of your upgrades and repairs with just a screwdriver. Make sure that you have both a medium-sized flat-head screwdriver and a Phillips screwdriver because some manufacturers favor one type of screw over the other. The exception here is Compaq. Since the first luggable Compaq was released in 1983, Compaq has used what are called Torx screws in all its systems (see Figure 5.1).

FIGURE 5.1

A Torx screwdriver—Compaq uses Torx screws in all its PCs.

A Torx screw has a six-pointed, diamond-shaped (or some might say, an asterisk-shaped) slot. Most of the screws in Compaq PCs can be removed with a T-15 size Torx screwdriver, but a few need a smaller size T-12 Torx screwdriver. You can pick up a set of Torx screwdrivers for a few dollars in most good hardware or home supply stores.

Jeweler Screwdrivers

Although many users get by for years with nothing more than a screwdriver for making simple repairs and upgrades, you may find that a few more tools make working on your PC a bit easier. Another inexpensive set of tools that you will sooner or later find almost indispensable is a set of jeweler screwdrivers (see Figure 5.2).

Jeweler screwdrivers are usually sold as a set of six miniature screwdrivers (three Phillips and three flat-blade). You will find these screwdrivers extremely useful if you think you might be doing a lot of work on your PC.

FIGURE 5.2

A set of jeweler screwdrivers.

Computer Toolkit

Many computer stores also sell small computer toolkits for $10–$20. These kits contain an assortment of PC-related tools (see Figure 5.3), some of which you may find useful and others of which you might not even be able to figure out what to use for.

FIGURE 5.3

A typical PC toolkit.

5

Three-Pronged Probe

One of the most useful tools you will run across in these types of toolkits is a device called a three-pronged probe (see Figure 5.4).

FIGURE 5.4

A three-pronged probe.

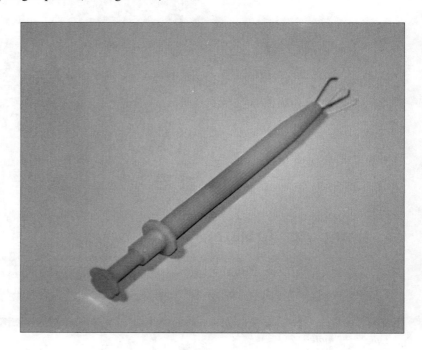

A three-pronged probe looks like a metal or plastic syringe with three moveable "fingers" where the syringe needle would normally be found. This is an invaluable tool for retrieving very small screws that you will invariably drop inside your PC. It's a lot easier and safer to retrieve the screw with a three-pronged probe than picking up your PC, turning it over, and shaking it until the lost screw comes tumbling out. A small pair of needle-nosed pliers or a small pair of surgical forceps, both sold in hobby and hardware stores, will work in place of the three-pronged probe, but you will likely find the probe easier to manipulate.

> Don't attempt to substitute a magnetic probe for a three-pronged probe. Magnetic probes can damage components inside your PC.

Pencil and Paper

Two other tools you should make sure that you have in your toolbox are a pencil and paper. Whenever you attempt to replace any component in your PC, you should always draw a diagram first, listing exactly where in your PC the component is being removed from and any cables or attachments connected to that component.

 Whenever you remove a cable from a component inside your PC, pay particular attention to the orientation of the cable. Several types of cables in your PC can be attached more than one way, which makes it extremely easy to accidentally install or replace a cable incorrectly.

While you have pencil and paper in hand, you should also get into the habit of keeping a log or journal of all the changes you make to your PC. This log should include all changes made to your system as well as components you add. Be sure to include the date the change was made plus any specifications on the component you add.

Labels

You will also find small self-sticking labels, such as Avery or Brady labels, extremely useful when working on your PC. You should attach a numbered label (numbered 1, 2, 3, and so on) to every wire or cable you remove, and mark on the diagram the corresponding numbered cable and its exact location inside your PC. This arrangement enables you to quickly and easily identify what each wire or cable is attached to.

Compressed Air

Finally, if you are like most PC users, you might open your PC once or twice a year, if that often. After 6–12 months or longer, you'll find a considerable amount of dust build-up in your system. A layer of dust in your PC causes more problems than merely one of aesthetics and a short bout of sneezing. A layer of dust can act as an unwanted layer of insulating material, trapping heat that otherwise would be dissipated through the normal fan-controlled air circulation system. In short, the more dust you let accumulate in your PC, the quicker it will overheat, and overheating damages the components in your PC and shortens their life spans.

One of the best solutions for preventing dust build-up is to periodically take the cover off your PC and "blow it out" using compressed air. Compressed air canisters (see Figure 5.5) can be purchased from virtually any office supply store for a few dollars and should be part of every PC user's repair and maintenance toolbox.

5

FIGURE 5.5

A compressed air canister, which you can purchase in most office supply stores.

If at all possible, take your PC outdoors before you "blow it out." Otherwise you'll end up making a bigger mess by merely shifting the dust from the inside of your PC to the outside of your PC and all over your desk and room. If you can't take your PC outside, at least move it off your desk and to a place where you can later vacuum the dust you blow out.

If you haven't already made your list of possible tools to purchase, here's a brief recap:

- PC toolkit (with Phillips, flat, and Torx screwdrivers)
- Jeweler screwdrivers (with mini-Phillips and flat screwdrivers)
- Three-pronged probe
- Pencil and paper
- Labels
- Compressed air

An Advanced Set of Tools

Unless you plan to become extremely involved in upgrading and repairing PCs, this section on advanced tools may seem overwhelming. But, read on. Although you may never get to apply this information to a hands-on situation, you may find it helpful the next time you have to take your PC in to a repair shop.

Soldering Iron

Very few computer experts recommend tinkering around inside your PC with a soldering iron—and with good reason. The individual components inside your PC, with very few exceptions, are meant to be replaced, not repaired. But keeping a soldering iron around in your toolbox can be quite handy if you know how and when to use it (see Figure 5.6).

FIGURE 5.6

A typical electrical soldering iron.

I keep a soldering iron in my toolkit, but I will admit that I haven't had too much use for it lately. In the past, I mostly used it to fix broken wires and create custom serial cables for an assortment of serial printers. Hour 22, "Selecting and Installing a Printer, Scanner, or Digital Camera," covers installing one or more printers to your PC. When you go shopping for a printer for your PC, one thing you will notice is that nearly 100% of the printers you see in computer stores come equipped with a parallel interface. Years ago, this was not the case. In fact, I can remember when it was next to impossible to get a laser printer with anything but a serial cable.

The problem was that there was nothing called a standard serial cable. Virtually every manufacturer had its own design for serial communications between a computer interface and a printer. This meant that if the printer manufacturer did not supply a cable for your particular computer, you were stuck with making your own. Making serial printer cables is not rocket science, but one tool you definitely need to accomplish the goal is a soldering iron.

Nowadays, I don't get too many calls to create custom serial cables for printers or too many other output devices. Most manufacturers wised up and realized that making serial cables was a dying art form and they stood a better chance of selling you a printer if you could also buy a standard cable and simply plug everything together yourself. I mostly use my soldering iron for repairing broken cables or cables chewed through by one of my cats.

Voltage Meter

Another somewhat uncommon tool I keep in my toolkit is a voltage meter (see Figure 5.7).

FIGURE 5.7

A voltage meter.

The primary functions of a voltage meter are measuring the flow of current and testing current continuity. Because most of the current you encounter inside your PC is DC (direct current), make sure that any voltage meter you pick up can measure both AC and DC voltage (most do). You'll use a voltage meter mainly to diagnose problems with your power supply. Each of the 4-pin connectors sprouting out of your power supply should deliver 5 volts of DC current. A voltage meter can help you quickly determine whether your power supply is failing or if one of the connectors has developed a short circuit.

Although the primary function of a voltage meter is to test voltage, if you buy one in the $30–$40 range, you'll wind up getting a few more useful functions that can be quite helpful in diagnosing and troubleshooting PC problems.

Another use for a voltage meter is as a continuity tester. When used as a continuity tester, you're more concerned with *whether or not* a current is passing through an electrical circuit than *how much* current is passing through the circuit. A good example here is in testing cables. Using the continuity tester, you attach one cable from your tester to each pin on your cable and test whether each pin (circuit) continues from one end of the cable to the other. It helps to know the configuration of the cable, but even if you don't you can still manage to test your cable using the trial-and-error method.

Safety Precautions When You Work on Your PC

Whenever you work on your PC, you must put a number of safety precautions into practice, not only to protect your PC from possible damage, but also to protect yourself from possible harm. Neither working on PCs nor PCs themselves is inherently dangerous, but you need to be aware of some hidden risks.

Unplugging Your PC

This is the number-one safety precaution you need to be aware of, and it cannot be repeated often enough. Either unplug your PC at the wall outlet or from the back of the PC. Don't merely rely on the on/off rocker switch because on/off rocker switches have been known to stick or malfunction. Besides risking a potentially lethal electrical shock, you can damage your PC and its internal components if you forget it is plugged in and try to remove an interface card or other electronic device while it is still receiving current. You could also accidentally drop a screwdriver or other metal tool on your main system board and cause a short, or worse.

> The only time you should ever work on your PC with the power on is when you are troubleshooting your power supply, and then be sure to exercise extreme caution.

Grounding Yourself to Prevent Static Electricity

5

Although not properly grounding yourself against static electricity is much more of a potential hazard to your PC than to yourself, don't underestimate this risk, especially during the cold winter months when circulating air in homes and offices tends to be drier than normal. Most of the sensitive electronic components in your PC (for example, microprocessors, memory DIMMs, interface cards, and so on) can be seriously damaged or even destroyed by a few stray jolts of static electricity. Make sure that you touch a metal object such as a desk, a chair, or a filing cabinet before you begin working on your PC. Better yet, use a grounding strap around one of your wrists (see Figure 5.8) and clipped to a metal part of your PC, and make sure that you unplug your PC.

Also, if possible, move your PC to a room that does not have a carpeted floor because most carpeting used in homes and offices contains synthetic fibers, which can increase the potential for static electric discharges.

In addition, you might also consider investing $30–$50 dollars in a small room humidifier. Besides being healthier for your PC, it makes the environment a bit healthier for you as well.

There is considerable debate on whether you should leave your PC plugged in or unplug it when you use a grounding strap to reduce the risk of a static electric discharge damaging your PC or peripherals. I consulted an expert, George Crawford, PhD. in Electrical Engineering at Penn State University, on the "leave it plugged in versus unplug it" debate. Dr. Crawford says you definitely want to make sure that the grounding strap is clipped to a metal component in your PC, such as the frame or chassis, and that the PC is unplugged so that you are at the same electrical potential as the device you are working on.

FIGURE 5.8
A wrist grounding strap used to prevent static electric discharges.

Keeping Magnets Away from PCs

Static electricity is not the only type of electrical charge you want to keep away from your PC. Magnetic charges can also damage some PC components such as disk drives and monitors. Make sure that any tools you use are not magnetized (for example, s crewdrivers and probes).

Summary

In this hour, you learned what tools you need to perform upgrades and repairs on your PC. You were given a list of simple tools you should include in your toolkit plus a few advanced tools you might want to consider including if you decide you want to do more complex diagnostics on your PC.

Q&A

Q Aren't some manufacturers producing PCs that you can take apart without the need for tools?

A Yes, sort of. Some manufacturers have been producing tool-less PCs that allow you to remove/replace most major components (disk drives, cards, and so on), but many of these components are merely attached to an easily removable chassis. Often you will find that you still need tools to remove the component from the chassis. For the most part, these PCs are easier to work on but I have yet to see one that requires absolutely no tools.

Q Is there ever a time that I *should* open my PC to work on it with the power turned on?

A Yes, but only when you are testing the power supply.

5

PART II

Upgrading the Main System Components

Hour

HOUR **6**

Upgrading Your PC's Memory

Upgrading the memory in your PC actually amounts to adding *more* memory to your PC. Unlike upgrading other components, such as your processor or CD-ROM drive, you rarely, if ever, remove the memory in your PC and replace it with better or faster memory unless all your memory slots are already filled. In fact, when you upgrade the memory in your PC, you have to be careful that you add memory that is identical to the memory already installed.

The only exception to this general premise is that you may opt to remove a memory module of one size and replace it with a memory module containing more memory. For example, if your PC contains three 32MB-memory modules, you may replace them with three 128MB-memory modules. Although this practice might at first seem wasteful, considering the rapidly southward direction of memory prices in the last few years and the performance gains from increasing the amount of memory in your PC, replacing smaller-sized memory modules with larger modules can actually make sound economic sense and at the same time increase the performance in your PC.

Upgrading your PC's memory probably gives you the most bang for your buck in terms of a how much a single upgrade can positively impact your PC's performance. Although upgrading the processor can affect the speed of most operations, upgrading the memory can extend the capability of your PC by enabling you to perform more tasks simultaneously, especially if you are running one of the more advanced operating systems such as Windows 2000, Me, or XP. Even if you are still running Windows 98 (please see Hour 23, "Upgrading to a New Operating System," if you are), a memory upgrade from 32MB to 128MB or more produces a dramatic boost in performance.

During this hour, you will learn the following:

- How memory works in your PC
- The different types of memory you can put in your PC and how to select the right type
- How to install memory in your PC

Memory Is Like Money—More Is Better

Gather 10 PC experts in a room, and you can probably get a consensus on the minimum amount of memory you should have for running various operating systems and environments. For Windows 98, most experts agree on at least 32MB; for Windows 2000 and XP, it's no less than 64MB. In each case, although these amounts enable you to operate adequately, adding more memory actually improves performance. Adding more memory enables you to run more programs faster, open more files, and perform more tasks simultaneously.

Your PC uses memory as a temporary storage area for your microprocessor to perform calculations, store data, and store programs you want to run. Anything stored in memory, or RAM as it is called, remains there only as long as the power to your PC remains on, which is why RAM is also referred to a volatile memory.

RAM, which is short for *Random Access Memory*, or simply called *memory*, is an electronic storage area used by your computer for data, information, and programs. RAM is where your computer moves information for rapid retrieval either before the information is saved to disk or as it retrieves previously saved information from disk. Your computer can access information in memory about 1,000 times faster than from disk. Even though memory and disk storage both use the same reference designators for size (for example, KB for kilobytes, MB for megabytes, and GB for gigabytes), when the term *memory* is used it always refers to the volatile electronic area where information is stored temporarily. It does not refer to your permanent disk storage area, which should correctly be called disk space, disk storage space, or hard disk space.

A lot of memory installed in PCs for about the last four years has been in the form of DIMMs (Dual Inline Memory Modules), shown in Figure 6.1. This is the type of memory module you should be looking at for your upgrades unless you failed to heed my earlier advice about dumping anything slower than a 500MHz PC.

FIGURE 6.1

A standard 168-pin DIMM.

A Timely Upgrade

While I was working on this book, one of my local computer stores ran a sale on memory. It was such a good sale that I decided it was time to follow some of my own advice. I decided to upgrade one of my older production PCs, an off-brand Pentium 450MHz with 64MB of RAM. I purchased two 64MB DIMMs. The PC had one 32MB DIMM, which gave me a grand total of 160MB RAM (32+64=96MB). This particular PC had Windows NT 4.0 installed, so in keeping with the philosophy of this book, I also upgraded the OS to Windows 2000.

The upgrade proceeded without a hitch, and when I booted up the PC, my PC's BIOS and Windows 2000 immediately recognized the total amount of RAM and continued right along without ever skipping a beat. The performance with the additional RAM even surprised me!

Literally everything seemed to run faster. Programs started much quicker. Files loaded faster. Even connecting to the Internet and running my Web browser seemed to take less time and run faster.

There's no guarantee that your upgrade will enhance your performance as much as mine did. However, if you are running a PC with a 32-bit operating system such as Windows 98/NT/2000/Me/XP that can make use of additional system RAM, going from 32MB of RAM to 160MB will produce a change you will definitely notice.

6

Different Types of Memory

Memory modules that physically appear to be the same can differ dramatically in the actual speed of the memory and the type of memory used in the module. This is why it is very important to install only the exact type of memory designed for your PC. You can consult your PC's manufacturer or your user guide to determine the exact type of memory you can use in your system especially if you are upgrading a slightly older PC. Most of the newer memory being sold is for PCs with newer Pentium III CPUs and with bus speeds of 133MHz. A lot of this memory won't work in older Pentium II PCs, which usually have a maximum bus speed of only 100MHz. Check your memory speeds carefully.

Here is a brief overview of some of the types of memory you may encounter, both in older style SIMMs and newer style DIMMs:

- **DRAM (Dynamic RAM).** The most common type of memory used in PCs. It is also the slowest and cheapest type of memory still used in memory modules.
- **FPM DRAM (Fast Page Mode DRAM).** Another type of DRAM, which is slightly faster than standard DRAM.
- **EDO DRAM (Extended Data Out RAM).** Another type of Dynamic RAM used in memory modules. It is faster and more expensive than standard DRAM.
- **ECC EDO RAM (Error Correcting Code EDO RAM).** A very reliable and more expensive type of EDO RAM. Used primarily on network file servers and high-end workstations.
- **SDRAM (Synchronous DRAM).** A faster and more expensive type of DRAM originally used in processor cache memory and also appearing in Pentium III–based and Pentium IV–based PCs.
- **DDR (Double Data Rate) SDRAM.** A newer designed SDRAM that allows RAM clock speeds up to (theoretically) 200MHz.
- **ESDRAM (Enhanced SDRAM).** Another type of SDRAM that can (theoretically) support bus speeds up to 200MHz.

It's hard to definitively explain how much faster one type of memory is than another. In some cases, it is next to impossible because manufacturers do not release the actual speeds of the types of memory they produce. You may see numbers such as 70ns or 60ns (ns=nanosecond=1/1000th of a second) used to represent SDRAM, DRAM, FPM DRAM, or EDO DRAM. After you start getting into DDR SDRAM and ESDRAM, however, you usually won't see speeds listed. Also, because memory technology is constantly changing and improving, all these values may be superceded by a newer, faster memory type. In case you're interested, in the previous listing the memory types are listed in the order of their relative speeds.

Another method you can use to check the type of RAM used in your PC is to check one of several Web sites specializing in selling memory. Two that immediately come to mind are Kingston (http://www.kingston.com/) and Crucial (http://www.crucial.com/).

Both of these well-known sites offer online databases you can access to find the exact type of memory used by your system (see Figure 6.2).

FIGURE 6.2

You can access the Kingston memory identification system to identify the type of memory for your PC.

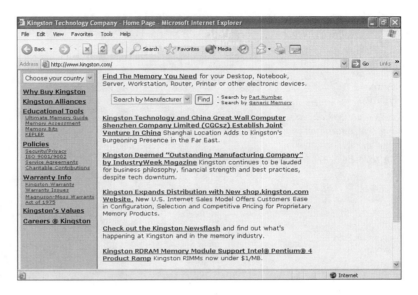

All you do is enter the manufacturer, system type, and model name, and the database will identify the exact type of memory installed in your PC by the manufacturer. It also will usually supply information on types of memory you can use for upgrading and the maximum amount of memory your PC can accommodate (see Figure 6.3).

If the PC you are currently using has standard DRAM installed, you might be tempted to spend a few extra dollars to upgrade to FPM or EDO DRAM. Don't waste your money. The slight difference in speed probably won't be significant without also upgrading your processor (see Hour 7, "Upgrading Your CPU and BIOS") and perhaps your main system board (see Hour 8, "Replacing Your Main System Board"). Although you won't see any significant performance boost in replacing standard DRAM with faster FPM DRAM or EDO DRAM, trying to cut costs and save a few dollars by replacing EDO DRAM with standard DRAM can have a dramatic effect on performance, albeit the wrong way. Using slower DRAM can noticeably degrade your PC's performance. This is a classic example of being penny-wise and pound-foolish.

Installing Memory in Your PC

Before you can finalize your memory upgrade plan, you first must determine how much memory is currently installed in your PC.

Back in the days when you used SIMMs (Single Inline Memory Modules) in your PC, you had to be concerned with matching the SIMMs and installing them in pairs. That nonsense ended when PCs moved up to DIMMs. As long as you use the same type of DIMM in your PC, you can place a 16MB DIMM in the first slot, a 32MB DIMM in the second slot, and a 64MB DIMM in the third slot, and never give it a second thought.

FIGURE 6.3

The Kingston memory type database displaying information on the type of memory used in an IBM PC.

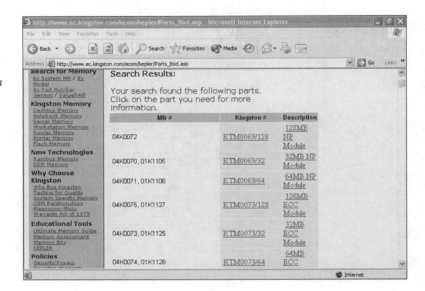

Installing DIMMs

Before you begin to install additional DIMMs in your PC, take a minute and look closely at how the existing DIMMs are installed in your computer. The first DIMM in your PC should be installed in the first slot (labeled slot 0). The next DIMM into slot 1, and so on. Most PC motherboards will have three or four slots for DIMMs.

Task: Installing DIMMs in Your PC

To install memory DIMMs in your computer, follow these steps:

1. Turn off the power to your PC and unplug the power cord. Remove the cover from the computer case.

Make absolutely certain that the power is turned off! If you attempt to install DIMMs in your PC with the power on, you are guaranteed to destroy the DIMMs and possibly also your motherboard! Also remember that all memory is susceptible to static electricity, so be sure to take proper precautions to reduce static.

▼   2. Insert the DIMM straight down into the slot (unlike the older SIMMs which
        installed at an angle). The clips for DIMMs fold inward when the DIMM is inserted
        and fold outward when the DIMM is removed (see Figure 6.4). The pressure of the
        DIMM forces the clips inward to hold the DIMM in place. To remove a DIMM, you
        simply press outward (and downward) on the clips and the DIMM pops up.

FIGURE 6.4
*A DIMM inserted into
a DIMM slot.*

DIMM socket latches   Insert DIMM   Close DIMM
                           into socket   socket latches

▲

Stretching Your Memory a Little Farther

Upgrading the memory in your PC is definitely one way to improve performance in your
PC, but you also want to make sure that you are using the memory you have wisely. Here
are a few tips you can put to good use to help stretch your memory as far as possible:

- If you are still running Windows 95/98, consider upgrading to Windows 2000, Me,
  or XP. If your PC has the horsepower to run these 32-bit operating systems, they
  do a much better job at managing memory than the Windows 95 or 98.

- Whatever version of Windows you are running, don't automatically start every
  program you think you might need. Even though Windows NT/2000/Me/XP do a
  much better job of managing memory than Windows 95/98, opening unnecessary
  programs wastes systems resources and degrades performance. If there are programs
  starting that you did not set to start, check your Startup folder to remove the
  programs. To remove programs from your Startup folder, simply drag the icon out
  and place it into another folder.

6

- If you are running Windows 95/98, make sure that you have the system set to enable Windows to manage your virtual memory settings (see Figure 6.5). Even if you are experienced in working with virtual memory or have received advice from your office guru on how to set virtual memory in Windows 95/98, leave this setting to the default value. You can find the Virtual Memory setting in Windows 98 by opening the Control Panel and then selecting System, Performance, and Virtual Memory.

FIGURE 6.5

The correct way to set virtual memory in Windows 95/98.

- If you are using any type of third-party disk compression software, turn it off. This software was advisable years ago before hard disk prices did a nosedive. Now these programs do little more than waste systems resources and degrade system performance. Windows 2000 and XP have built-in file and folder compression that you can turn on as you need or want it.

- If you are running Windows 2000 or XP, make the following change in virtual memory (RAM paging memory) to improve performance: Make the initial value and maximum value of your paging file the same (see Figure 6.6). If you make the maximum size larger than initial size, Windows 2000 and XP will waste resources adjusting the size up and down, and this continuous adjustment can affect performance. In XP, select System from the Control Panel and then select Advanced, Performance Settings, Advanced (again), and then Change.

Summary

In this hour, you learned about the various types of memory used in PCs, how to identify the memory installed in your PC, how to identify the type of memory needed for your upgrade, and how to upgrade the memory in or add memory to your PC. You also learned some tips on how to better manage your PC's memory depending on which operating system you are running on your PC.

FIGURE 6.6

Making your initial and maximum page file settings the same in Windows XP.

Q&A

Q Why do most PC manufacturers limit the number of DIMM slots on main system boards to three?

A Most likely because of space limitations. A main system board is only so big. As they got smaller, and with everything else they have to place on a board, the manufacturers decided to restrict the number of DIMM slots to (usually) three or four. You usually don't see those limitations on main system boards used in file servers because the memory requirements on file servers are considerably higher than on PCs.

Q Why is it so important to match your memory with your CPU and bus speed? You mentioned this several times.

A Memory that is faster than your CPU and bus speeds will slow down to accommodate your PC but you end up wasting money because you're paying more for faster memory that you are not using. Slower memory, on the other hand, will cause your CPU and everything else to slow down to wait for the memory to perform its operations.

6

HOUR 7

Upgrading Your CPU and BIOS

You learned in the last hour that upgrading your PC's memory is the first part of the performance upgrade equation. Upgrading your computer's CPU (central processing unit, also called the *processor* or *microprocessor*) is the other half of the coin if you want to beef up your PC's performance. The CPU is the brain inside your PC. The CPU processes the instructions in your programs and operating system and is the single most important factor in improving your PC's raw computing speed.

When a computer manufacturer designs a new model PC, 9 times out of 10 the design decision is influenced by the release of a new CPU. In the past few years, it seems that new CPUs are coming off the drawing board at a record pace, fueling what seems like a constant bombardment of new-model PCs.

Although this seemingly never-ending introduction of new-model PCs and new CPUs has produced a certain anxiety among computer buyers, it has also produced a cottage industry for upgrading PCs because one of the first components most users think of upgrading in their PC is the CPU.

And while most users who have given some thought to upgrading are keenly aware of the importance of upgrading their CPU, most still don't give a second thought (or even a first thought) about upgrading their BIOS (Basic Input/Output System).

In the past, upgrading your PC's BIOS ranked right up there in importance with getting your shoes resoled. But that all changed around the latter part of 1997. Word began to spread about something called the "millennium bug," and soon, just about everyone with a PC began scrambling to see whether his or her PC could tell the difference between the years 1900 and 2000. As we all know now, the so-called "millennium bug" was not really a bug; it was just another example of human shortsightedness.

Of course, the millennium bug was not the only reason you should have considered upgrading your BIOS. Some PCs need a BIOS upgrade if they are to accept an upgraded processor. And some PCs need a BIOS upgrade to work with a removable media drive or some other new technology that will soon be coming down the pike.

In this hour, you will learn the following:

- The basic differences between the various microprocessors available for your PC
- How to identify the type and speed of the CPU installed in your PC
- How to select and install a new CPU in your PC
- What your PC's BIOS is and what it does
- How to locate and install a BIOS upgrade for your PC

Understanding Processors

In the last few years, PCs have come to be identified by the type and speed of the CPU installed. For example, most of you have heard someone describe their PC by saying they have a "Pentium III 850," or a "Celeron 733." What they're referring to is the type of CPU installed in their PC and the *clock speed* of the CPU.

Clock speed is a measurement of how fast—its maximum speed—a particular CPU is set to operate. The speed is the measurement in megahertz (abbreviated MHz) of an oscillating timing crystal used to control how fast the CPU can perform internal operations. The term maximum used to imply that there was also a minimum speed, which is no longer the case. It was true with some early 286 and 386 processors that you could adjust the speed (although why anyone would ever want to use anything but the maximum speed is beyond me). Since the 486, however, the stated clock speed is the speed at which the CPU should be operating, according to the manufacturer. Later in this hour, you will see that is not always the case.

Intel Corporation (www.intel.com) makes most of the processors found in PCs today. The following sections discuss the processors Intel has made for PCs, starting with the Pentium.

The Pentium Series

Despite a succession of chips with numerical designations (for example, 186, 286, 386, 486), Intel chose not to call its next generation CPU the 586, but opted for the name Pentium because its legal department advised that numeric designations could not be copyrighted or trademarked. Intel released the first Pentium CPU in 1993. The original Pentium was developed to operate at a speed of 60MHz and delivered about twice the performance of a 486 operating at about the same speed (in megahertz).

The Pentium Pro Series

In 1995, Intel replaced the Pentium chip with the Pentium Pro, a processor optimized to run 32-bit applications. The Pentium Pro runs nearly twice as fast as the original Pentium when running 32-bit applications, but drops in performance when running 16-bit applications.

The Pentium Pro is physically larger than the original Pentium (see Figure 7.1), which necessitated that PC manufacturers redesign their main system boards to accommodate the larger sized chip. This change in size also means that an upgrade to a Pentium Pro from either a Pentium or a 486 requires a motherboard upgrade (see Hour 8, "Replacing Your Main System Board").

Figure 7.1

A Pentium and Pentium Pro, showing the difference in size.

The Pentium II Series

The Pentium II processor is essentially a Pentium Pro with MMX. Intel developed MMX (Multi-Media eXtensions) as a series of instructions built in to the processor to enhance audio and video functions. The original Pentium II was released in May of 1997 with a clock speed of 233MHz. Intel later released versions with clock speeds of 266MHz, 300MHz, and in 1998 speeds of 333MHz, 350MHz, 400MHz, and 450MHz.

7

Intel made another design change when it created the Pentium II processor. Intel designed the chip on a type of bus card that requires a special slot, termed *slot 1* on the main system board for the chip (see Figure 7.2).

FIGURE 7.2
A Pentium II CPU, which is inserted into slot 1 on a main system board.

Because of this design change, there is no upgrade path to the Pentium II chip from any other Intel-designed CPU. The only upgrade options are from a slower clock speed Pentium II to a faster clock speed Pentium II. Intel also made a Pentium II Xeon CPU, but this chip was directed at use in file servers. Even these types of upgrades are limited because of changes in the other supporting chips used in the main system board. In preliminary tests, the difference in performance between a 300MHz Pentium II and a 400MHz Pentium II was only 17 percent. The difference in performance between a 350MHz and 400MHz Pentium II was only 7 percent.

The Pentium III Series

In February 1999, Intel released the Pentium III processor running at a speed of 450MHz. Within a few months, Intel released Pentium IIIs running at speeds up to 650MHz and hinted that it probably would not stop until the Pentium III hit 1000MHz, which it eventually did.

As you might expect in the Pentium III line of processors, if you were to upgrade from a 450MHz to a 1000MHz Pentium III processor, you would see more than a 100% increase in CPU performance, but not necessarily a 100% increase in *PC* performance. Other factors at work in your PC—such as the speed of your memory, the speed of the bus, and the speed of other peripherals—affect and retard the overall performance. It is also doubtful that a motherboard originally equipped with a 450MHz CPU can handle the vast jump in speed to 1000MHz.

As with the Pentium II, the Pentium III was released in a Xeon version, which was designed for the increased demands of a file server. Even though Intel later released the Pentium 4 line of processors, it continues to produce Pentium III processors.

The Pentium 4 Series

In November 2000, Intel released the Pentium 4 processor running at speeds of 1.4GHz and 1.5GHz (gigahertz), and then unexpectedly backfilled with a 1.3GHz model. It didn't take long for PC manufacturers to release workstations built on these new chips, and the race was on again. Intel has already demonstrated a 2GHz chip that once again bumps up the upgrade bar. With the Pentium 4, Intel made another radical design change, abandoning the processor-slot design and returning to the processor-socket design: The Pentium 4 CPU needs a 423-pin socket on the motherboard. If you want to upgrade from a Pentium III to a Pentium 4, you'll need a new motherboard.

The AMD Series of CPUs

Although Intel still controls the lion's share of the PC processor market, it is not the only game in town. One serious competitor that many PC users have turned to for CPU upgrades is Advanced Micro Devices, Inc., more simply known as AMD. AMD can be found on the Web at http://www.amd.com.

AMD was founded in 1969, and today is the largest competitor producing Intel-compatible processors. AMD is especially popular among the upgrade crowd because its CPUs perform as well as Intel's.

AMD's K5 series of processors directly competes against Intel's Pentium and Pentium Pro series; its K6 and K7 series are competitive with Intel's Pentium II and Pentium III series. Most recently, AMD's Athlon series is running neck and neck with Intel's Pentium 4 series. Keep in mind that the two CPUs are not interchangeable. You must have a motherboard designed specifically for the chip you plan to use.

In addition to being cheaper than comparable Intel CPUs, another factor that makes AMD's earlier model CPUs attractive is that they are pin-for-pin compatible with most main system board sockets used by Intel's 486 and Pentium series processors. This means that if you currently have a 486 or low-end Pentium, and you want to upgrade to a Pentium Pro or Pentium II level processor, AMD's K5 and K6 chips will more than likely fit into your existing main system board CPU socket. However, AMD made a dramatic design change when it introduced its K7 series of processors and lost its pin-for-pin compatibility claim. Despite the motherboard redesign, AMD garners a sizeable market share because its prices are almost always cheaper than an Intel CPU of comparable speed.

7

Even though the K7 looks very similar to Intel's Pentium II and Pentium III series processors, the K7 will not fit into a slot 1 motherboard. The AMD K7 requires a motherboard with a proprietary slot designed to accommodate the K7.

The Cyrix Series of CPUs

Still another alternative to Intel is Cyrix Corporation, formerly a division of National Semiconductor. Cyrix was bought in 1999 by Via Technologies and has pretty much lost most of its separate identity. You can find Via/Cyrix on the Web at http:// www.via.com.tw/jsp/en/products/C3/c3.jsp.

Cyrix also makes socket-compatible processors that can replace or upgrade from Intel's Pentium and Pentium Pro series processors. Unfortunately, Cyrix has not kept pace in the neck-and-neck race between Intel and AMD; at last report, Cyrix produces processors with clock speeds only in the 500–700MHz range.

Identifying Your CPU

Before you can upgrade your CPU, you must correctly identify the CPU that is installed in your PC. In addition to identifying the CPU, you also have to know the clock speed of your CPU. After you identify the CPU in your PC, you can decide which CPUs lie along your upgrade path.

After you take the cover off your PC (make sure that you exercise all cautions mentioned in Hours 2, "Understanding the Components in Your PC," and 5, "The Tools of the Trade"), look for what is probably the largest chip in your computer. On many older computers, the processor is in a plastic holder called a *ZIF* socket (see Figure 7.3).

ZIF stands for *Zero Insertion Force*. One common problem in inserting chips is the possibility of bending or breaking the pins when you push (or jam) the pins of the chip into very tight socket holes. In a ZIF socket, you don't have to push the pins of the chip into a socket. Instead, you merely place the pins into oversized socket holes and move a lever that grabs and locks the pins and holds the chip in the socket.

If you discover that your CPU is soldered to your main system board and that your motherboard does not include an empty upgrade socket, replace the cover and forget about upgrading. If you want a faster PC, you have to purchase a newer PC or replace the main system board (see Hour 8).

FIGURE 7.3
An empty ZIF socket.

Don't be surprised if you remove the cover of your PC and don't see anything that looks like a CPU. On some smaller systems, it is common for disk drive housings to cover your CPU. If this is the case, you'll have to remove your disk drives to gain access to your CPU. Just pay careful attention to anything you remove (make a diagram if it helps you remember), and be sure to replace any components and cables exactly the same way you removed them.

After you've located your CPU, the first thing to look for is any writing on the CPU identifying what type it is. You are looking for information identifying the CPU as a Pentium, Pentium II, Pentium III, Pentium 4, or AMD (or Cyrix depending on the age) and information displaying its speed.

A heat sink and/or a fan covers many processors. A heat sink is nothing more than a metal attachment—often black, silver, or blue in color—that has several dozen fins or projectiles. Heat sinks are used to help dissipate the heat that processors give off. If you can't see anything identifying the processor type and speed, go back to Hour 3, "Examining Your PC's System Configuration," pull out SysChk (or one of the other utilities mentioned in that hour), and use it to identify your CPU.

7

You have to know exactly what type of processor is installed in your PC before you can purchase an upgrade. This information enables you to make sure that you purchase a faster upgrade processor as well as an upgrade CPU that is compatible with your computer system.

In choosing an upgrade processor, most experts recommend/suggest the 100 percent rule, which simply states that you should upgrade to a processor that is roughly 100 percent faster than what you currently own. For example, if you currently have a 300MHz Pentium, you should not consider upgrading to anything less than a 600MHz (or the next highest speed chip) processor. Obviously, you can upgrade higher up the scale if you are so inclined. The 100 percent rule should be your minimum upgrade.

In addition to speed, there are also slight voltage differences between some processors. If you know exactly what type of processor is currently installed in your PC, the company you purchased the upgrade from will be able to sell you an upgrade processor that is guaranteed to operate correctly in your PC. When ordering an upgrade processor, be sure to also get the make and model of the PC you are upgrading and the BIOS manufacturer and BIOS date. Note that you can obtain BIOS information using the SysChk utility.

In addition to power consumption differences, Intel has also made changes in the socket design and number of pins in its processor chips—even in chips within the same family. For example, the earliest model Pentiums (the 60MHz and 66MHz models) could not be upgraded to the faster Pentiums in the 75–200MHz range because the pin design was changed from 273 pins to 320 pins (and later to 321 pins).

PC Bottlenecks

Everyone knows what a bottleneck is. It is a narrowed portion of a bottle that restricts the flow of whatever is in the bottle. Well, PCs can also have bottlenecks. When you upgrade your CPU, the CPU may not provide as much performance improvement as you expect because of a bottleneck in your CPU.

Your PC was designed around the original CPU. When you upgrade the CPU, you may have a faster processor, but you still have all the remaining equipment, which was designed to work with the original, slower CPU. In other words, even though the upgrade processor processes data faster than the original CPU in your PC, the upgrade processor is slowed down by the speed of your other components, which do not operate at the same speed as your new CPU.

Does this mean that it is a waste of money to upgrade your CPU? No, because a faster CPU results in faster performance. But just keep in mind that the new CPU is still working through a bottleneck—your older system.

Virtually any device in your PC that operates at a certain speed can become a potential bottleneck when you start upgrading components such as memory (Hour 6, "Upgrading Your PC's Memory"), hard disks (Hour 10, "Replacing, Upgrading, or Adding a Hard Disk Drive"), CD-ROM drives (Hour 12, "Upgrading or Adding a CD-ROM/CD-RW Drive"), video cards (Hour 20, "Upgrading Your Video Card and Monitor"), and so on.

Removing and Installing a CPU

If your main system board (your motherboard) is equipped with a ZIF socket—and almost all socket 7 are so equipped motherboards (see Hour 8 for an explanation of socket 7 motherboards)—removing the current processor is a snap.

If you are replacing a CPU in a plug-in card, skip to "Task: Removing a CPU in a Plug-in Card from Slot 1."

Task: Removing a CPU from a ZIF Socket

To remove a processor from a ZIF socket, follow these steps:

1. Make sure that you are grounded before you remove the upgrade processor from its container. Swing the lever out slightly to unlock it, and then swing back the ZIF socket lever to release tension on the pins.

2. Gently lift out the processor.

If your motherboard does not have a ZIF socket, you can still remove your processor with a minimal amount of effort. Many companies that sell upgrade processors include a processor extraction tool with the upgrade. Several types of processor extraction tools are available. Figure 7.4 shows you two types.

Task: Removing a CPU Using a Processor Extraction Tool

To remove the processor using the extraction tool, follow these steps:

1. Follow the instructions that come with the processor extraction tool you purchase. If you purchase the large tweezer-like model, open its jaws wide enough to allow you to gently insert each of the two prongs under the sides of the CPU, and then gently squeeze the sides where the tool is its widest. This squeezing action gently lifts the CPU up and out of its socket. If you purchase the small pry-bar type of tool, gently insert it under each of the four sides of the processor and gently press down on the extraction tool. The tool is designed so that this downward pressure lifts up on the processor.

7

2. If your instructions call for you to repeat step 1, do so as many times as is necessary until you can gently lift the processor out of the socket. Remember to take your time so that you don't accidentally bend the pins. You don't have to hurry to remove a processor.

▲

FIGURE 7.4
Two types of processor extraction tools.

 If your upgrade processor is not shipped with an extraction tool, run down to the local computer store and purchase one. The tool costs only a dollar or two and is well worth the investment because it (almost) guarantees that you will safely remove the processor without damaging it or your system board.

As you remove your old processor, note that one corner of the processor is notched and/or has a marking dot (see Figure 7.5).

Note that the notched corner of the processor is lined up with a similarly notched corner of the socket. When you insert the upgrade processor, you must make sure that the notched corners (or the dot) line up exactly as they do with the old processor.

FIGURE 7.5
Each CPU has a notched corner to properly line up the CPU with the socket.

 If the notch on the upgrade processor is not lined up exactly with the notch on the socket, your PC will not operate correctly and you could damage the upgrade processor and possibly also your motherboard.

Task: Inserting the New Processor

To insert the upgrade processor in your PC, use these steps:

1. Make sure that you are grounded before you remove the upgrade processor from its container.

2. Locate the notch on your upgrade processor and on the processor socket.

3. Line up the notches and carefully insert the upgrade processor into the socket.

   If you have a ZIF socket, simply move the locking lever back to the lock position. If you do not have a ZIF socket, make sure that all the pins on the CPU are lined up with the holes in the socket, and then gently apply pressure to the center of the processor until it is firmly seated in the socket.

   Check to make sure that no pins are bent or sticking out the sides of the connectors. If you see any bent pins, use your processor extraction tool to remove the CPU. Then, using a pair of needle-nose pliers, very carefully straighten any bent pins and try again to insert the CPU into the socket.

Task: Removing a CPU in a Plug-in Card from Slot 1

If you are upgrading an Intel-based CPU installed in a plug-in card, the task is almost as easy as replacing a CPU into a ZIF socket.

To remove a CPU in a plug-in card, follow these steps:

7

1. Make sure that you are grounded before you remove the upgrade processor from its container. The CPU plug-in card is held in place by two clips on either side of the card in a cardholder. The holder supports the card vertically into slot 1. Flip the clips outward, releasing the card.

2. Gently lift the card up and out of the slot.

Task: Inserting a CPU Plug-in Card into Slot 1

To insert the replacement CPU card into slot 1, follow these steps:

1. Make sure that you are grounded before you remove the upgrade processor card from its container.

2. Read over the instructions accompanying your replacement CPU. The instructions will illustrate how to properly align the new CPU plug-in card into slot 1. Insert the CPU plug-in card into the holder and gently, but firmly, insert the plug-in card into the slot.

3. Flip the two clips on either side of the holder back to the upright position to hold the plug-in card securely in the slot.

If you are currently using a PC with an Intel CPU in a plug-in card and are considering upgrading to AMD's new Athlon CPUs, *don't*!

Although the Athlon CPU's plug-in card will fit into a motherboard designed with a slot-1 CPU slot, the Athlon CPU is electrically incompatible. The Athlon requires a different motherboard, which uses what is called a slot-A slot.

On many PCs, your new processor should be recognized and configured automatically to operate in your PC. If your PC displays an error message when you turn it back on, run your computer's hardware Setup program as you did in Hour 5 to configure the CMOS settings in your PC with your upgrade processor. Be sure to check your PC's instruction manual to see whether you need to set a jumper on the motherboard.

Overclocking Your CPU

In the last few years, some very industrious upgraders have discovered another way to get more bang for their bucks (or more precisely, more megahertz) out of their CPUs. The process is called overclocking.

Overclocking is simply running the CPU at a slightly faster speed than the speed certified by the manufacturer. When manufacturers test and certify their CPUs, many times they rate the CPU at a speed slower than the maximum the CPU is capable of running. In effect, they build in a little cushion to make sure that the CPU will perform at the stated speed. The key to overclocking is to adjust the CPU frequency/bus frequency ratio on your motherboard to a higher setting than is specified for your particular CPU. The CPU frequency/bus frequency ratio is often expressed as a timing setting such as 2x, 2.5x, 3x, 3.5x, 4x, and so on. To overclock your CPU, simply set the ratio to the next higher setting, if your CPU is not currently using the top setting.

Overclock at your own risk!!! Even though many overclockers swear that this practice is perfectly safe, overclocking is not supported by any CPU manufacturer, and there is a potential for damaging or destroying your CPU and motherboard by overclocking. If you are curious about overclocking your CPU, check out one of several Web sites that explain this practice in more detail, such as http://www.sysopt.com/overfaq.html.

Understanding What Your BIOS Is and What It Does

The next time you turn on your PC, pay close attention to the information displayed onscreen. The BIOS, which stands for Basic Input Output System, is software, or more correctly called *firmware*. It enables your computer to boot and your processor to access the hardware devices such as the hard disk drive, video card, system clock, and other peripherals. The BIOS also controls the POST (the Power On Self-Test), the diagnostic and initialization program that runs every time you turn on your computer.

Firmware is essentially software that has been embedded into certain chips in your computer and that runs automatically without intervention on your part. The distinction is usually made between programs that you can easily change, erase, and delete—software—and programs that you cannot easily alter—firmware.

7

Every BIOS is specific to a certain type of motherboard, so even if you notice that the BIOS in your computer is made by the same company that manufactures the BIOS in your neighbor's computer, it doesn't necessarily mean that the BIOS in one is identical to the other. If the two of you have different makes of PC, you can almost guarantee that the BIOSes are different in each.

The BIOS in various computers varies in size and functionality somewhat, but a core portion is about 64KB in size in every computer that claims to be IBM PC compatible.

Why You Need to Upgrade Your BIOS

Your BIOS was made about the same time as your computer, and although it may have served you well so far, many things have undoubtedly changed since your computer was manufactured. New types of peripherals have been invented, disk drives have gotten larger, and new types of video cards with higher resolutions have been created, among other things. In short, the BIOS in your computer has remained static while the rest of the computer industry has continued at its usual hectic, dynamic pace. For example, the BIOS in some early model 486 computers was designed while most hard disk drives were still around 200–400MB in size. When users of these computers attempted to install larger hard disk drives—in the 2–4GB range—they discovered that their computers could not recognize more than the first 528MB of their new multi-gigabyte hard disk drives.

The reason behind this problem was that the BIOS in their computers was not able to understand *Logical Block Addressing* (LBA). In simpler terms, it means the BIOS cannot address all the storage space on the hard disk drive beyond the first 528MB because that is as high as it can count. The answer to this problem is simply to upgrade the BIOS. If you find that no BIOS upgrade is available for your PC (another hint that it's time to purchase a new PC instead of upgrading your current model), sometimes you can solve problems similar to the LBA problem by applying a software patch.

How Do I Upgrade My BIOS?

Early 486 model computers had chips on the motherboard that stored the BIOS routines and that had to be physically replaced in order to upgrade the BIOS (see Figure 7.6).

Later model 486 computers and all computers since the first Pentium models have what is called *flash BIOS*, which means that you can run a program on a floppy disk to upgrade your BIOS, which is then stored in *EEPROM* chips. No physical replacement of chips is necessary.

> *EEPROM* stands for *Electrically Erasable Programmable Read Only Memory* and is a special type of chip used to store your BIOS programs. Under normal circumstances, the programs stored in EEPROM chips are stored permanently. You can, however, use special programs to update and replace the programs stored in EEPROMs. This is what happens when you upgrade flash BIOS.

Figure 7.6
BIOS chips on an older 486 mother-board.

Don't attempt a BIOS upgrade just for the heck of it. BIOS upgrades are serious undertakings; you should perform a BIOS upgrade only when you are absolutely certain that you need the upgrade. In most cases, you can consult with the computer's manufacturer to determine whether you need to upgrade your computer's BIOS.

Determining Whether You Need to Upgrade Your BIOS

If you install a new peripheral and it doesn't work and you have checked every part of the installation procedure and everything checks out okay, chances are you need to upgrade your BIOS. In most cases, this problem surfaces when you attempt to install not just a new peripheral but a new type of peripheral (for example, installing not just another hard drive but your first network card).

Also, if you receive notice from your computer dealer or from your PC's manufacturer that there is a defect in your current BIOS and they recommend that you upgrade, it is time to upgrade.

Establishing the Type of BIOS You Have

If you have a Pentium or later processor in your computer, you can rest assured that you have a flash BIOS. If you have a 486 processor, your chances are 50–50 that you have a flash BIOS (if you are still using a 486-based PC, forget the BIOS upgrade and just purchase a new PC; you're way overdue for one).

7

If you still have your original documentation, which lists the type of BIOS in your PC, the documentation also likely indicates whom to contact about upgrading your BIOS.

If you don't still have the original documentation that came with your PC, there is another method to determine the type of BIOS in your PC. Turn on your PC and write down all the BIOS information displayed when your computer boots. The BIOS information is usually displayed in the upper-left corner of your screen just after the PC completes the POST (Power On Self-Test). Look for the name of a company and a number that looks like some sort of serial number or version number. That number is the BIOS version (see Figure 7.7).

FIGURE 7.7
The BIOS version appears onscreen after the POST.

```
GPCI 4.03.09

CPU=486DX  66 MHZ
0000640k System RAM Passed
0015360k Extended RAM Passed
System BIOS shadowed
Video BIOS shadowed
Mouse initialized

Intel Plug and Play BIOS Extensions Version 2.07
Copyright © 1993 Intel Corporation All Rights Reserved
```

You can also check your CMOS settings using one of the system-checking utilities mentioned in Hour 3, "Examining Your PC's System Configuration," for BIOS information (see Figure 7.8).

After you have the BIOS information about your PC, you can contact your PC's manufacturer to find out what type of BIOS you have. Be sure to also have the model of your computer when you contact the manufacturer or check the manufacturer's Web site.

Different Methods for Upgrading Your BIOS

If you do not have flash BIOS, and you insist on retaining and upgrading your old 486 (so you can experiment with Linux), you can contact your PC's manufacturer about ordering a new set of BIOS chips (good luck!). You can also contact one of two BIOS upgrade companies, Micro Firmware, Inc. and Microid Research (Unicore Software). Micro Firmware can be reached at 800-767-5465 or 405-321-8333. You can also contact Micro Firmware at http://www.firmware.com. Microid Research can be reached at 800-800-BIOS and 508-686-6468. Microid's Web site is located at http://www.unicore.com; the company's MR. BIOS site is at http://www.mrbios.com, or you can try http://www.sysopt.com/bios.html.

FIGURE 7.8
The SiSoft Sandra utility displaying BIOS information.

If you do have flash BIOS in your PC, and you have Internet access, you can most likely download the program to update your PC from a variety of sources. Look at the Web site run by your PC's manufacturer. Most computer manufacturers run a Web site and provide BIOS and other upgrades and updates for their customers. If your PC's manufacturer does not maintain a Web site, you can look on the Web sites run by several of the leading BIOS manufacturers. The following is a short list:

- **Phoenix/Award**—http://www.ptltd.com
- **American Megatrends, Inc. (AMI)**— http://www.megatrends.com

You can also check the company from whom you purchased your PC if you did not purchase directly from the manufacturer.

Installing Upgrade BIOS Chips

If you order BIOS upgrade chips for a computer that does not have flash BIOS (in my opinion, throwing good money after bad, but that's another story), it's very easy to install the chips yourself.

7

Task: Installing BIOS Upgrade Chips

To install BIOS upgrade chips onto your PC's motherboard, follow these steps:

1. Turn off and unplug your PC.

2. Discharge any static electricity by first touching the exterior of the PC's metal case, and then remove the cover from your PC.

3. Examine the new BIOS upgrade chips you ordered. Notice the size of the chips, their markings or labels, and most importantly, look for a notch or dot in one end of the chips (see Figure 7.9).

4. Now look on your motherboard and find chips that look similar to the chips you ordered. If you're not sure, check your PC's documentation for the exact location of your computer's BIOS chips. Record which direction the orientation notch is positioned.

5. Before you remove a chip, check your instructions for the order in which you must replace the chips. You want to make sure that you install the replacement chips (if there is more than one chip) in the correct socket.

6. The chips you ordered should have been shipped with a tool resembling a large set of tweezers with the tips turned inward. This tool is similar to the processor extraction tool shown in Figure 7.4, earlier in this hour. You also should have received instructions on how to use the chip extractor to remove your old BIOS chips. If the instructions are not included, simply place each of the turned-in tips under the long edges of the chips and gently lift upward, rocking back and forth, until the chip lifts out of its socket. Repeat this procedure for all your old BIOS chips. If a chip extractor did not come with your new BIOS chips, a trip to your local computer store can usually remedy this oversight.

> If you don't have a chip extractor, you can remove your chips by gently prying them out using a small flat-blade screwdriver. Just make sure that you pry one side and then the other, a little at a time, until each chip is loosened enough to remove. Keep in mind, however, that a chip extractor is the safest and preferred method for removing chips.

7. As per your instructions, replace your old chips with the new chips you ordered. Make sure that you insert the new chips with the orientation notch facing in the same direction as the chips you just removed. Be very careful not to accidentally bend any

▼ of the pins on the chips as you insert them into their sockets. If the pins are spread too far apart, place the chip on its side on a hard surface such as a tabletop and gently roll the pins until they are a little closer together. By placing the chip on its side and rolling it, you make sure that you bend all the pins together.

8. Double-check your work to make sure that the new chips are properly installed in the socket, that they are oriented properly, and that no pins are bent. When everything looks okay, turn on your PC. If the new BIOS chips are properly installed, your PC

▲ should boot as before.

FIGURE 7.9

A notch on one end of the BIOS chip indicates the chip's proper orientation.

Upgrading Flash BIOS

Upgrading a PC with flash BIOS is a snap. If you ordered the BIOS upgrade program from the manufacturer or your dealer, the program should come on a bootable disk. If you downloaded the BIOS upgrade program from the manufacturer's bulletin board or Web site, follow the instructions that came with the download to create a bootable upgrade disk.

Task: Upgrading Flash BIOS

To upgrade your flash BIOS with a bootable upgrade disk, follow these steps:

1. Turn off your PC.
2. Place your BIOS upgrade disk into your floppy disk drive and turn on your PC.

7

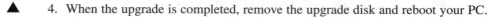

3. The bootable disk should automatically start the upgrade program and upgrade your flash BIOS. Watch your screen for any prompts asking you to enter any information about your PC. The entire upgrade procedure should take about 1–3 minutes.

▲ 4. When the upgrade is completed, remove the upgrade disk and reboot your PC.

> Make sure that you do not reboot or turn off your PC while you are upgrading your flash BIOS. You can permanently damage the BIOS—and your computer—if you do.

Summary

In this hour, you learned the evolutionary history of the Intel line of processors beginning with the Pentium. You learned what upgrade paths exist for the various processors and that you do not have to stick solely with CPUs made by Intel.

You also learned about some of the functions of your computer's BIOS, and some of the operations that can go wrong when your BIOS does not function with your computer or its devices. You learned what you have to do to identify the type of BIOS installed in your computer, and what you have to do to upgrade your PC's BIOS.

Q&A

Q What are the advantages and disadvantages of upgrading with an AMD processor as opposed to an Intel processor?

A The major advantages are cost and a longer upgrade path. AMD processors are a lot less expensive than Intel processors and still use the same socket as the original Pentium processor, which enables you to upgrade to a Pentium Pro or Pentium II level (equivalent) CPU without having to also upgrade your motherboard. The major disadvantage is that it is not always possible to directly compare the performance of AMD processors to Intel processors. One method of determining computing performance is by comparing the speed of the CPU, but part of performance is affected by the speed and efficiency of the motherboard housing the CPU. Because an Intel Pentium II level CPU is using a totally different type of motherboard than an AMD Pentium II level processor, it's hard to make a direct comparison between the CPUs, even when they are rated at the same speed.

Q Why did manufacturers switch from BIOS on chips to flash BIOS?

A To make it easier to issue upgrades. Although it is a lot safer to embed the BIOS on chips you cannot erase or accidentally delete, it is also considerably more expensive both for the manufacturer and for you, the user, to upgrade the BIOS.

Flash BIOS is a good compromise between ease of use and safety. As you've seen in this hour, it's fairly easy to locate a flash BIOS upgrade and use it to upgrade your BIOS. Despite how easy it is to upgrade flash BIOS, you can't easily delete the BIOS using a flash BIOS upgrade.

Q Can my BIOS be infected by a virus?

A Because BIOSes can be flashed, yes. It is most likely to occur when you are booting your PC with an infected floppy disk, so make sure that you scan any suspect floppy disks before you boot your PC with the floppy disk.

7

Hour 8

Replacing Your Main System Board

Many computer experts believe that main system boards are better candidates for being replaced than upgraded. The reason for this belief is that any time you upgrade your main system board significantly, you most likely need to upgrade several other components in your PC as well. The CPU, memory, and possibly several of the interface cards in your PC will probably have to be upgraded to match the performance gains offered by the new system board. Rather than replace this much of your PC, it might be cheaper to forgo the main system board upgrade and just purchase a new PC.

For most users, the only financially justifiable reason for replacing a main system board is if the one currently in your PC is damaged. In that case, you'll replace the board with one identical or similar to your current board. You might also upgrade your motherboard if you are considering upgrading your CPU to the Athlon series in the AMD CPU line. These chips require a motherboard with a special slot/socket to accommodate them. Regardless of your reason for replacing your main system board, in this hour you will learn all you need to know to accomplish this sometimes tricky procedure.

During this hour, you will learn the following:

- How to identify the type and size of your current system board
- How to choose a replacement system board
- How to remove your current system board and replace it with a new board

Are You Upgrading or Replacing?

As I said earlier, most experts believe that if you upgrade your main system board to a model that is a significant advancement over the one currently installed in your PC, it is likely that you will have to replace other components as well, such as the CPU, memory, and one or more interface cards (usually your video card at the very least).

Depending on how old your current PC is and what a new system board and components will cost, upgrading may or may not be a bargain.

 Main system boards are also referred to by the somewhat less technical name "motherboard." The two terms are used interchangeably in this chapter.

Although the price of a new system board may only set you back $150–$250, after you add in the cost of the CPU, memory, and a new video card, your upgrade could be done for less than $400:

System board with 750MHz AMD series CPU	$220.00
128MB SDRAM	50.00
Video Card w/ 128MB VRAM	95.00
TOTAL	365.00

Check the advertising supplements in your Sunday newspaper and you'll see several companies willing to sell you a complete, new PC for around $800–$1000, and they'll probably toss in several hundred dollars worth of bundled software to sweeten the deal. Current system and peripheral prices make the upgrade fairly practical, or they will at least give you something to think about.

Another reason to upgrade your system board and CPU is if you decide to build your own custom-designed PC. If a custom-built PC is in your future, the information in this hour will be instrumental in helping you do that.

How System Boards Have Changed

8

Main system boards have undergone dramatic changes since IBM released its first PC back in 1981. Most of the major changes and advances seen in system board design have resulted from changes or advancements in bus design, chipsets, and processors. Here is a brief overview of the six major bus designs that have been incorporated into PCs since 1981:

- **8-bit (or "original IBM PC") bus.** The original 8-bit bus design used in IBM PCs, XTs, and early PC-compatible computers.

- **16-bit ISA bus.** The first 16-bit bus was essentially a 16-bit upgrade of the original IBM PC bus; the ISA (Industry Standard Architecture) bus was used originally in the IBM AT computer and AT-compatible computers.

- **Micro Channel Architecture bus.** IBM's proprietary 32-bit bus; used in its PS/2 computer line. No manufacturer other than IBM ever used this bus design because other manufacturers did not want to pay license fees to IBM.

- **EISA bus.** The computer industry's response to IBM's proprietary MCA bus; used mainly in network file servers manufactured by Compaq; EISA stands for Extended Industry Standard Architecture. In addition to the EISA bus cards, you can also use ISA bus cards.

- **VESA local bus.** The first 32-bit bus design used in 486 computers that was fast enough to support graphical environments.

- **PCI bus.** Designed to overcome many of the speed limitations of the VESA local bus to support the higher bus speeds required by the Pentium processor line.

The 486-based PCs used both VESA local bus and PCI bus system boards. The first 486-based PCs were created using the VESA local bus design, but later were switched to the more advanced PCI bus. Pentium-based PCs have mainly used system boards with a PCI bus.

Bus design changes are not the only factors that have affected system board design changes. Main system boards have also undergone changes in their physical size and shape. Since the first 486-based PC rolled down the assembly line, system boards have come in one of seven basic sizes: standard AT, baby AT, LPX, ATX, and NLX are the older designs. In the last 2–3 years, some manufacturers have started shipping what is called a "baby ATX" motherboard and more recently a "micro ATX" motherboard. These diminutive ATX form-factor boards are scaled-down versions of the original ATX system board and usually have fewer PCI or memory slots.

Before you can select a replacement system board, you first must correctly identify the board currently installed in your PC. Because computer cases are often designed to accommodate a particular form-factor system board, if you purchase the wrong board, it may not fit your case.

The Standard AT System Board

This type of motherboard is so called because it roughly matches the size of the mother-board used in the original IBM AT computer—12 inches wide by 13.8 inches in depth. By today's standards, this is a very large board and fits only into full-sized desktop and tower computer cases (see Hour 9, "Upgrading Your PC's Case and Power Supply"). Most system board manufacturers have all but abandoned this size motherboard in favor of the smaller designs.

The Baby AT System Board

The baby AT system board, as you might guess, is a scaled-down version of the standard AT-sized motherboard. The miniaturization is caused by advancements in technology that enable many of the components on motherboards to be reduced in size. Figure 8.1 shows the basic layout of the baby AT motherboard.

FIGURE 8.1
Baby AT form-factor motherboard.

Figure 8.2 shows you the difference in size between the standard AT-sized motherboard on the left and the baby AT-sized motherboard on the right.

FIGURE 8.2
*Standard AT mother-
board and baby AT
motherboard showing
the difference in size.*

8

The LPX Motherboard

TheLPX (and also the "mini-LPX") motherboard is easily identified by a unique design element not present in any other motherboard design. The LPX motherboard (see Figure 8.3) has a riser card inserted into a slot on the main portion of the board. The riser card contains slots into which your interface cards are inserted. The LPX design was developed by Western Digital and is still used in PCs manufactured by IBM, Compaq, and Gateway.

FIGURE 8.3
*The LPX and
mini-LPX motherboard
form factors.*

You may encounter two problems with an LPX motherboard: Because of the use of the riser card, these boards generally have less potential for expandability because they have fewer expansion slots. The other problem is that you may have difficulty finding a replacement motherboard except from the manufacturers who generally charge more for replacement boards than a third-party vendor.

The ATX Motherboards

The ATX motherboard, designed by Intel in 1995, is sort of a hybrid baby AT and LPX model, which at first appears to be turned sideways. This is the design used in many of the PCs manufactured in the last few years and is considered by some to be the de facto standard design. The design of the ATX enables PC manufacturers to produce fewer crowded and congested hardware configurations, making it easier to access components you might want to upgrade. Figure 8.4 shows the basic design of the ATX motherboard.

FIGURE 8.4
The ATX motherboard layout showing the location of PC features.

Because of the layout and positioning of components on the ATX motherboard—such as the location of the power connectors, mouse connectors, and keyboard—the ATX motherboard will not fit in cases designed for either the standard AT or baby AT motherboards.

The baby ATX and micro ATX motherboards are simply scaled-down versions of the standard ATX motherboard designed to fit into a case with a smaller footprint (see Hour 9).

The NLX Motherboard

The NLX motherboard was designed specifically for computers using the Pentium II processor. The NLX design contains many of the best features of both the ATX and LPX boards (see Figure 8.5).

FIGURE 8.5

The basic layout of the NLX motherboard.

Installing a New System Board

Regardless of which motherboard size or style you purchase, replacing your existing system board requires careful planning. Although replacing a motherboard may at first appear to be a major technological undertaking, in reality all you need is a little bit of planning and a bit more patience (and of course a screwdriver or two) to accomplish the job successfully.

Remember to unplug your PC and ground yourself before you remove the PC's cover. Make sure that you carefully remove each component from your existing motherboard and make sure that you place all the components on a safe surface, such as an uncluttered tabletop, where they cannot be damaged physically or by static electricity.

Task: Removing Your Old Motherboard

▼ To Do

Follow these steps to remove your old motherboard:

1. The very first task you must perform is to make a diagram of all the connections (ribbon cables, jumpers, thin-wire cables, interface cards, and so on). Pay particular attention to the orientation of each connector, especially those connectors that can be attached more than one way, as can ribbon cables. Notice that most ribbon cables have a red strip on one edge of the cable. This red strip is used to orient the first pin—called pin 1—to its correct position with the connecting plug. Be sure to label or identify each connecting device attached to your motherboard.

▼

2. Read and reread any and all instructions that come with your new motherboard. There might be steps you need to take either before or after you install the new motherboard, such as moving jumpers.

3. Examine your existing motherboard in its case to see exactly how it is attached to the case. Notice the number and position of screws and nonmetallic connectors and supports.

4. Remove all interface cards from your motherboard by first removing the retaining screw and then gently lifting the card out of its slot. Sometimes, you may have to gently rock the cards to get them out. If any cables are attached to any of the interface cards, carefully remove and label each of the cables.

5. Carefully remove the memory DIMMs and the processor installed in your computer. If it is awkward to remove these now, you can wait until you have removed the motherboard from the case to remove the processor and memory DIMMs.

6. Remove any cables attached to your motherboard and label them one at a time. Note the orientation of the power cables connected to your motherboard. The power cables are the two multi-wire, multi-colored cables running from the power supply to the motherboard.

One way to easily remember how to reattach the power cables from your motherboard (on all but ATX motherboards) to the power supply is that the black wires are always on the inside edges of the two connectors next to each other.

7. When all components and connectors have been removed from your motherboard, remove the screws and standoff connectors (the small plastic supports) holding your motherboard in the case. Carefully remove the motherboard from the case. Note the orientation of your motherboard to its case. If you still have to remove the CPU and memory, do so and carefully put these chips in a safe place.

Now that you have your old motherboard out of the PC's case, half of your job is done. To install your replacement motherboard, you merely have to follow the same steps you took to remove your old motherboard, only in reverse order.

Task: Replacing the Motherboard in Your PC

Here's what you have to do to replace the motherboard in your PC:

1. You might find it easier if you insert the CPU and memory into the new motherboard before you place the board back into your PC's case. If necessary, review Hours 6, "Upgrading Your PC's Memory," and 7, "Upgrading Your CPU and BIOS," on how to insert DIMMs and CPUs.

8

▼ 2. Place the new motherboard in your case, paying attention to any possible changes in the standoff connectors and connecting screws. Be sure to use all your screws to allow for proper grounding. Also, be careful not to damage the underside of the motherboard.

3. Replace the power connectors according to the diagram you made when you removed your old motherboard.

4. Replace your interface cards. On some older motherboards, users occasionally had problems with interface cards being placed over processors, but new motherboard designs, such as the ATX motherboard, rearranged the placement of CPUs and cards to avoid this problem. The biggest problem you can encounter with replacing all your cards is making sure that the new motherboard has the same number of expansion slots as your old motherboard. Be sure to reconnect any cables that were attached to the cards.

5. Perform any setup operations dictated by the instructions included with your new
▲   motherboard such as setting CPU speed and voltage.

When you have reattached everything to your new motherboard that was removed from your old motherboard, you are ready to turn on your PC and test your handiwork. If your PC fails to start or displays any errors, note the error and check the instructions that came with your new motherboard. Recheck your work. When you have corrected the problem causing the error, retest your PC.

More Info on System Boards

If you're interested in getting more specific information on system boards, here are a few companies and Web sites you can check:

- **Abit**—http://www.abit.com/
- **ASUS**—http://www.asus.com/
- **DFI**—http://www.dfi.com/
- **EliteGroup**—http://www.ecs.com.tw/
- **FIC**—http://www.fic.com.tw/
- **Gigabyte**—http://www.gigabyte.de/
- **Intel**—http://www.intel.com/intel/product/components.htm
- **Iwil**—http://www.iwill.net/home/home.asp
- **Micro-Star**—http://www.msi.com.tw/about/main.htm
- **Soyo**—http://www.soyo.com.tw/
- **Supermicro**—http://www.supermicro.com/product.htm
- **Tyan**—http://www.tyan.com/products/html/systemboards.html

After you get all the information you're looking for on various system boards, you might want to check Tom's Hardware Guide (http://www.tomshardware.com/) for technical performance comparisons on various boards.

Summary

In the past hour, you learned about the various types of main system boards used in PCs, how to identify the various types of system boards, what criteria you use in deciding whether you want to upgrade your system board, and how to remove and install a system board.

Q&A

Q Where did the term "motherboard" originate?

A The term actually predates the original IBM PC and goes back to the Apple II computer. As the story is told, when the Apple II came out, it had more of a home/hobbyist image as opposed to a corporate/business image. Someone decided that the term "main system board" seemed rather harsh and cold and did not keep with the "softer, gentler" image Apple was trying to project. So, in an attempt to soften the terminology, someone started calling the system board a "motherboard" and the term has just held on.

Q All the motherboards mentioned are one-piece boards. Did manufacturers ever make multi-piece motherboards?

A Yes, but they mainly consisted of proprietary designs and were never standardized. Occasionally you will still see these multi-piece designs, but they are rare.

HOUR 9

Upgrading Your PC's Case and Power Supply

Upgrading your PC's case and power supply may seem like a fairly inconsequential upgrade, but believe me, there is a method to this madness. As you begin to upgrade or, more specifically, add components to your PC such as additional hard disk drives, CD-RW or DVD drives, removable media drives, and so on, you are adding components that require both space and electrical power. Look ahead to the many chapters on adding some type of disk drive and you will see how often I mention that *if you have an empty drive bay*...yada yada yada.... Well, not too many PCs leave the factory with four or five empty drive bays. And if you have been giving some thought to adding a CD-RW drive, a Zip drive, and a second hard disk drive, you might be stopped dead in your tracks when you discover that you have only one empty drive bay left in your PC (if that).

As for electrical power, too many PC users have learned the hard way that as you continue to add components, you cannot just keep adding Y-connectors (see Hour 10, "Replacing, Upgrading, or Adding a Hard Disk Drive") and expect everything to function properly.

Upgrading your PC's case and power supply may seem like major surgery, but it is something the average PC user can easily accomplish with just a screwdriver, a little time, and a little patience.

During this hour, you will learn the following:

- What features to look for in selecting a new case or power supply
- The different types of PC cases available
- What steps you must follow to transfer your motherboard and peripherals from your existing case into a new case

Deciding to Upgrade Your Case and Power Supply

When you purchased your current PC, you probably thought it came in a perfectly adequate case. Everything was neatly arranged; the drives, motherboard, interface cards, and so on all fit together in a nice, neat, orderly package. So, why would you want to pull everything out and stuff all your components into a new box? Well stop for a moment, remove your PC's cover, and take a long, hard look inside your PC and see how much room there is for adding any extra drives or other components. Can you add one or two more hard disk drives? Can you add an internal Zip or Jaz drive? Can you add a CD-RW drive? Can you add a DVD drive? Can you add a tape drive?

For whatever reason (most often to keep costs down), some manufacturers use a fairly small case when they design and manufacture their PCs. Whether the reason is to keep the package you place on your desk as small as possible or to keep the manufacturer's costs down by keeping their package (and packaging) smaller, the end result is that you have a PC that may not be as expandable as you'd like.

Although most PCs can very easily be upgraded into a new case, some PCs, because of their proprietary design, cannot be upgraded simply because their manufacturers used a nonstandard motherboard and case design. If you open your PC and see a motherboard that does not seem to fit the designs mentioned in this chapter (or in Hour 8, "Replacing Your Main System Board"), the chances are good that your system cannot easily be upgraded, and you should not even attempt to upgrade to a new case unless you also consider upgrading your motherboard as well.

The obvious answer to the need for more room is simply to swap your existing case for a new one. If you read Hour 8, you're already aware of what it takes to replace the motherboard in your PC; to replace the case, you follow the same procedure, but reverse the process: Instead of placing a new motherboard in your existing case, you are placing your existing motherboard in a new case. To save yourself some time, remember that you probably don't have to remove the processor and memory DIMMs from your motherboard when removing it from one case and placing it in another.

Don't try to cut corners by leaving your interface cards in their slots when you move the motherboard from one case to another. Although it is not impossible to move a system board with all the peripherals in place, it's generally not a good idea because of the risk of accidentally damaging your interface cards.

What to Look for When Shopping for a New Case

Although the process is not exactly like buying a new car, when shopping for a new computer case, you want to look for certain features. Here are some of the features in a new case that definitely make your life easier and your upgrades smoother:

- **Multiple drive bays.** The main reason you are purchasing a new case is probably to add additional drives (hard disk drives, CD-RW drives, DVD drives, removable media drives, and so on), so make sure that your new case has more drive bays than you currently need so that you have room to expand (see Figure 9.1). Most cases have a mixture of 3 1/2-inch and 5 1/4-inch drive bays. The 3 1/2-inch drive bays are used to add additional hard disk drives (possibly also a second 3 1/2-inch floppy drive), and the 5 1/4-inch bays are used for CD-RW and removable media drives. If you run out of 3 1/2-inch bays with the proper mounting hardware, you can place a hard disk drive into a 5 1/2-inch drive bay. Keep in mind that some replacement cases may come with only one or two 3 1/2-inch drive bays.

If you have SCSI hard disks, CD-RW drives, or removable media drives in your PC, it is possible to purchase a separate case that only houses your SCSI drives. These SCSI cases include their own power supply and fans and are a good way to remove some of the devices responsible for the heat buildup inside your PC. You will have to purchase a new cable for your SCSI chain because the cable you have now only works inside your PC. If you do decide to pursue this option, and you plan to retain some devices inside your PC as well, make sure that your SCSI card supports both external and internal devices simultaneously. Some SCSI cards don't.

FIGURE **9.1**

A computer case with extra drive bays.

Extra drive bays

- **Multiple fans.** Keep in mind that as you add additional drives and other components into your PC, you also add more devices that produce heat. Look for cases with at least two fans to help disperse the extra heat buildup—in addition to the fan on the power supply. If possible, try to find a case with large fans or check the documentation to see whether you can add an extra fan.

- **Large power supply.** In this case, "large" means wattage, not physical girth. Try to get a power supply in the range of 250–400 watts. Keep in mind that those additional drives you plan to add all require extra power to operate.

- **Extra power connectors.** Although extra power connectors are not essential, having a few extra saves you a trip to the local computer store to purchase Y-connectors (see Figure 9.2).

- **Sturdy construction.** If you purchase locally, rather than through the mail, examine the case before you buy it (be sure to examine the actual case you purchase, not just a display model). Try to get a case that seems like it is constructed with heavier gauge steel rather than a flimsy type of sheet metal. Look to see whether the seams are even and that all seams meet with no gaps. Check to see that the cover or door fits securely and is easy to open or remove. If you purchase your case by mail order, try talking to several computer consultants in your area to see whether they can recommend one or more brands for you to purchase.

FIGURE 9.2

You can supplement extra power connectors with a few Y-connectors.

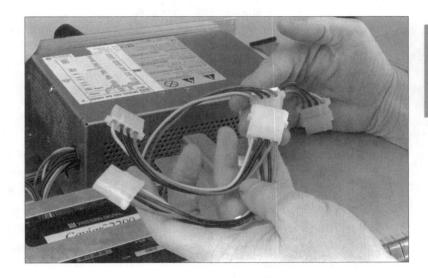

- **Front panel indicators and controls.** Many cases come equipped with several front panel indicators and controls. Although not all are essential, some can come in handy. The essential controls include a reset button, an on/off switch (which prevents you from having to reach around back to turn on your PC), and a drive activity indicator light. Make sure that instructions are included with your case to let you know how to connect the front panel controls and indicators to your motherboard. If your existing case has front panel indicators and controls, make note of how and where these controls are connected to your motherboard.

- **Removable mounting plate and drive bays.** A removable mounting plate (see Figure 9.3) makes it easier to install and access your motherboard. Removable drive bays, both internal and external, make it easier to install and access any drives that you install in your PC.

External drive bays hold drives that are physically accessible to you, such as floppy disk and CD-RW or DVD drives. Internal drive bays are bays holding drives that you don't need to physically access, such as hard disk drives.

FIGURE 9.3
A removable mounting plate makes it easy to access your motherboard.

- **Color Choices.** While hardly essential to upgrading, a lot of manufacturers have caught on to the fact that many PC users are tired of staring at beige or dull gray cases and have started offering cases in virtually every color of the light spectrum, including clear or transparent.

Cases (which are also referred to as "chassis"), just like PCs, can be purchased as either desktop or tower models and come in a variety of sizes. Desktop case sizes are usually referred to as standard, baby AT, slimline, and micro. Desktop cases usually don't offer you as much expansion space as do tower cases. Just make sure that the case you purchase is designed for your type of motherboard (see Hour 8).

Tower cases usually have a larger variety of available sizes, such as mini-tower, medium, large tower, server-size, super-sized, and mega-sized. Usually the difference in sizes is caused by the number of drive bays and the size (wattage) of the power supply.

Desktop units have the advantage of occupying a smaller piece of your office real estate and are generally less expensive than tower cases. Tower cases, on the other hand, offer more room for expansion and can be placed on the floor next to your desk so that they don't take up any valuable desktop space. When you place a tower on the floor next to your desk, you likely have to purchase expansion cables (that is, longer cables) for your monitor and keyboard.

Another option you might want to consider are rack-mount cases (see Figure 9.4).

Years ago, rack-mount cases were used only in large network server rooms, but with the proliferation of home networks and more users setting up their own Web servers, it's not impractical to think of upgrading to a rack-mount case.

FIGURE 9.4

A rack-mount case fits into a standard 19-inch relay rack.

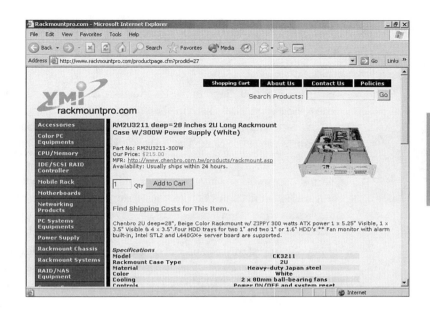

Rack-mount cases fit only into a standard 19-inch electrical relay rack (which you can purchase from over the Internet from companies such as Black Box or RP Electronics, or from your local electrical supply store), not something you typically find in the average home or basement office unless you have an extensive home network to go with it. The advantages of using rack-mounted cases is that they are typically a lot larger and offer a lot more expansion potential than most other larger cases. The downside however is the expense. Do a search on rack-mount cases and you'll see what I mean.

Upgrading Your Case

There are no hard and fast rules for upgrading your PC's case except that you should be patient, methodical, and make note of anything you remove or disconnect. However, here are a few suggestions you might want to follow after you unplug the power cord, ground yourself, and remove the cover from your existing PC case.

Grounding yourself is extremely important to prevent damage from static electricity, but be sure to exercise the same caution with each component that you remove from your PC. Make sure to place your drives, system boards, DIMMs, and your CPU someplace where they are not subject to damage by static electricity.

▼ To Do

Task: Upgrading Your PC's Case

The following is one method you can use to replace your existing case with a newer model:

1. Make sure that you diagram the location of every component before you move or remove anything. This diagram should include drives, cables, power connectors, and any miscellaneous items installed in your PC. Note also how any mounting hardware is installed. Make sure that you know how each component will fit into the new case.

2. Carefully remove your interface cards first. If cables are attached to any of the cards, remove the cables before you attempt to remove the cards. One card at a time, remove the screw securing the card in place and lift the card out of its slot. Place each card in a safe location so that it is not damaged.

3. Remove your disk drives and ribbon cables. Again, note how they are connected and which cables are connected to each drive. Also remove any mounting hardware used to support your disk drives. Carefully note how the mounting hardware is installed and where all mounting screws are installed.

4. Remove your memory SIMMs (or DIMMs) and CPU. When removing the SIMMs/DIMMs, be careful not to damage the SIMMs, DIMMs, or the clips holding them into each slot (see Figures 9.5 and 9.6). If your CPU is inserted into a ZIF socket (see Figure 9.7), remove the fan and/or heat sink if there is one, unclip the latch, lift it up to release tension on the pins of the CPU, and lift your CPU out of the socket. This step is often done by users as a means of making sure that the CPU and memory SIMMs are not accidentally damaged. If you feel comfortable leaving the CPU and SIMMs/DIMMs in place, do so.

FIGURE 9.5

Clips used to secure SIMMs in their slots.

▼

FIGURE 9.6

Clips used to secure DIMMs in their slots.

Clips

FIGURE 9.7

A ZIF socket securing a CPU on a mother-board.

5. After every component has been removed from your case and motherboard, stop for a minute and note the remaining cables attached to your motherboard. Note in particular how the two power cables are attached to your motherboard's power connectors. In most cases, the two black wires on each power connector (if you have an AT-style motherboard) are next to each other (see Figure 9.8). Check to see whether your PC follows this convention. If it does not, make note of how the

power cables are attached to the motherboard. Also note whether your disk drive ribbon cables are attached to connectors on your motherboard. If they are, note the direction and position of the red edge of the ribbon cable. Note, too, whether a series of smaller cables and wires are attached to your motherboard from your case's front panel. These are for your front panel indicator connections and controls. Finally, note the placement of screws and standouts (plastic supports) for your motherboard. Remove all screws, making sure not to accidentally damage your motherboard with the tip of the screwdriver, and then remove your motherboard and put it in a safe place.

Figure 9.8

The two black wires on the power supply connectors (on an AT-style motherboard) are usually next to each other, as shown here.

You don't normally remove the power supply because almost all new cases come with power supplies already installed.

To install your motherboard and components into the new case, simply follow the previous five steps in reverse order, making sure that you pay close attention to your diagrams and notes. Just be patient, take your time, and you should have no trouble installing the motherboard and components into your new case.

When you have double-checked every connection and diagram you've made, plug in your PC and hit the power switch. Your PC should boot up just like before. If your PC does not boot, unplug the electrical cable. First check the power connectors to your motherboard to make sure that they are properly positioned. Then check to make sure that the SIMMs (or DIMMs), CPU, and the peripheral cards—especially the video card—are all properly seated. In most PCs, these are usually the components that, if not properly installed, keep your PC from booting.

Where You Can Purchase a New Case

Here are a few sites where you can purchase PC cases online:

- **Case Outlet**—http://www.caseoutlet.com/
- **Hansan Systems**—http://www.hansansystems.com/
- **Fum Da Electronics**—http://www.fumda.de/no_frames/pc_case.htm
- **Oak Computers**—http://www.oakcomputers.com/cases.html
- **Acme Technology**—http://www.acme-technology.co.uk/pc_cases.htm
- **Color Cases**—http://www.colorcases.com/

Power Supplies

When you purchase a new case, it usually comes equipped with a power supply, but you can also purchase power supplies separately. The two main reasons for purchasing a separate power supply are as follows:

- Your existing power supply fails.
- You want to add additional devices to your PC, and your existing power supply does not output sufficient wattage. Older PCs with only a few internal devices have been shipped with smaller wattage power supplies. If your power supply is in the 75–125W range, you should consider replacing it for this reason.

The most important factor to consider when purchasing a new power supply is whether it fits in your existing case. If you do not purchase a new power supply from the same company that supplied your original power supply, it probably is a good idea to remove the power supply you are replacing and take it with you to your local computer store. This way you can compare the new power supply to the old one, check for size, and make sure that the power connection cables, mounting screws, and off/on switch are all in the same relative positions.

One caution that cannot be repeated too often is the importance of making sure that you reconnect the power supply cables to your motherboard properly. Make sure that you note how the power supply cables (on an AT-style motherboard) are connected before you remove them. In most cases, the two black cables (on an AT-style motherboard) are next to each other when the two connectors are plugged into the motherboard. If you accidentally reverse these connectors, you can fry your motherboard. On an ATX-style motherboard, there is only one connector, which can fit only one way.

You can easily remove your existing power supply with just a screwdriver and a little patience. Remember to label each cable you remove and, most importantly, make sure that you unplug the power supply before you begin removing it from your case. Be careful that you remove only the screws holding the power supply in the case and do not accidentally remove the screws from the power supply itself.

> Don't even think about trying to open a failed power supply to attempt repairing it. First, they usually aren't worth repairing; a new power supply can be purchased for around $20–$30. Second, power supplies are all manufactured with slow discharge capacitors, which can carry a considerable (and dangerous) charge even after they are unplugged.

Summary

In this hour, you learned about upgrading your PC's case and power supply. You learned what criteria are important in selecting a new case and received a few tips on how and where to purchase one. You also learned step-by-step how to remove the components in your existing PC and how to reinstall them into your new case.

Q&A

Q **Is heat buildup really a problem with PCs nowadays? I thought all the solid state electronics and miniaturization eliminated most of the previous heat buildup problems.**

A You're right when you say that solid state electronics and miniaturization have reduced a lot of the heat buildup problems, but when you start adding multiple hard disk drives, tape drives, Zip drives, and so on, you are also adding more heat sources in your PC. Take a look at the insides of your PC; if you have almost anything newer than a 486/33, chances are you see a heat sink glued to the top of the CPU. Heat dissipation has been a major concern for all processor manufacturers because, as they keep adding transistors to CPUs (1–5 million or more depending on the type you have), CPUs keep getting hotter. Compare the heat sink on the top of a 800MHz Pentium III to the heat sink on the top of a 486/66. The Pentium III heat sink isn't larger just so that it fits the CPU. You may also have noticed that some PC manufacturers place an auxiliary fan on the CPU in addition to the heat sink. Heat buildup is still a problem, which is why it pays to make sure that any new case you purchase has a minimum of two large fans. One of the often unmentioned advantages of the SCSI interface is that it enables you to remove some of these heat-producing components (hard disk drives, CD-ROM/RW drives, Zip and Jaz drives, and so on) outside of your PC into one or more separate cases.

Q **The fan in my case seems adequate for removing any heat buildup. Do I really also need a fan mounted on my CPU as well?**

A Yes! Definitely! As CPUs get faster, they get hotter as well. Not only do you need a fan on your CPU, you should also make sure that your CPU has a heat sink installed. The fan/heat sink on the CPU will help dissipate any heat buildup and the fan, or fans, inside your case will help dissipate any heat buildup in your case, which could damage components other than your CPU.

Q **Does it make a difference whether you operate your PC with the top off? I've seen some PCs with warning labels saying not to, but the PC seems to operate just the same with the top on or off.**

A Operating your PC with the top or cover on or off gets back to the problem of heat dissipation. Your PC case is designed with a certain airflow pattern in mind, and when you remove the top or cover, you disrupt its airflow. It's okay to operate your PC for a few minutes with the cover removed, but you should not make a habit of operating your PC for any length of time with the cover off.

9

PART III
Upgrading Your Drives

Hour

HOUR 10

Replacing, Upgrading, or Adding a Hard Disk Drive

Just as we've seen memory prices nose dive over the past few years, prices on hard disk drives have also dropped. In 1984, a Seagate 30MB hard disk drive cost around $350. Now you can easily pay less money for a drive 2000 times larger and considerably faster.

As an added bonus, although hard disk prices have been dropping steadily, the storage capacities on hard disk drives have been steadily inching upward. Now, it's fairly common to see new PCs advertised with hard disk storage capacities in the 40–60 *gigabyte* range.

A *gigabyte* is a thousand megabytes, and a megabyte is one million bytes, so a gigabyte is one billion bytes. Gigabyte is commonly abbreviated GB. To give you a real-world example of how big a gigabyte is, the text in this chapter is approximately 70K. On a 1 gigabyte hard disk drive, I could store more than 14,000 copies of this chapter.

If the PC you are currently using has less than 10GB of disk storage, you are long overdue for an upgrade. You will find that installing a hard disk drive in your PC is extremely easy.

During this hour, you will learn the following:

- The differences between an IDE and a SCSI interface and hard disk drive, and how to decide which is better for your PC
- How to install a hard disk drive as either an addition or a replacement for the drive you currently have installed
- Whether you should consider one of the newer FireWire hard disk drives

Is Your Upgrade an Addition or a Replacement?

Like memory, when you upgrade your hard disk drive, in most cases you are actually adding a second disk drive to your system rather than replacing a smaller, slower hard disk with a larger, faster drive. In most PCs, accommodating a second hard disk drive is no problem. There are very few reasons why you should ever be forced to remove your existing hard disk and replace it with a new one. The following are the exceptions:

- Your PC physically does not have room (that is, there is no empty drive bay) for a second hard disk drive.
- You are switching from IDE drives to SCSI drives.
- Your hard disk drive fails and has to be replaced.

IDE Versus SCSI

The first major decision you have to make in upgrading your hard disk is choosing between the two types of drives[md]IDE and SCSI. In most cases, the decision is made for you by the type of disk controller installed in your PC. For the last five years, most PCs have been manufactured with an IDE controller built in to the system, but in the last year or two, some PC manufacturers have offered customers a choice between *IDE* and *SCSI*.

 IDE stands for Integrated Drive Electronics, and *SCSI* (pronounced "scuzzy") stands for Small Computer System Interface. You might also see IDE listed as EIDE, for Enhanced Integrated Drive Electronics, which was a faster enhancement on the original IDE specification.

SysChk, the systems diagnostic/configuration program you ran in Hour 3, "Examining Your PC's System Configuration," should have identified the type of *disk controller* and drive you have installed in your PC.

A *disk controller* is the interface that connects your disk drives to your motherboard. The controller can either be built in to the motherboard, as are most IDE controllers in most PCs built in the last few years, or they can come in the form of an interface card that is installed into one of the slots on your motherboard.

IDE is currently the more popular and widely used of the two disk types, primarily because IDE devices are cheaper to manufacture than SCSI devices. IDE also seems to have a slight edge in disk performance. Depending on how you have your PC configured and what operating system you are planning to use, a SCSI controller can actually give you better overall system performance. This is particularly true if you install two or more hard disk drives in your PC and use a true 32-bit operating system, such as Windows 2000, Me, or XP.

Even though IDE drives are slightly faster than SCSI drives, SCSI drives do offer some significant advantages over IDE drives:

- SCSI drives put far less strain on your CPU than IDE drives. This can result in overall higher levels of system performance and reliability.

- SCSI drives perform better in 32-bit multitasking operating systems, such as Windows NT 4.0, 2000, or XP because SCSI controllers and drives can perform disk reading and writing tasks while other operations and programs are running.

- You can attach up to 15 SCSI drives or devices to a single SCSI controller; IDE drives are beginning to narrow the gap here, but using an IDE RAID controller you can attach at most only 6 IDE drives.

- A slower SCSI device, such as a CD-ROM drive, does not degrade the performance of a faster SCSI device (a hard disk, for example) if both are connected to the same controller. On older IDE controllers, a slower CD-ROM drive degrades the performance of a hard disk if both are on the same controller. That is why most PCs in the past were shipped with two IDE controllers on the motherboard—one for the hard disk drives and one for your CD-ROM drive. On newer systems with EIDE (Enhanced IDE drives), each device can operate at its optimal level of performance.

10

- A SCSI cable can be up to 10 feet long, enabling you to install multiple external (outside of your PC) SCSI devices; IDE cable can usually be no longer than about 15 inches, which limits most IDE devices to being installed inside your PC.

Although SCSI controllers and drives can be configured to produce a higher level of performance, SCSI drives are still mainly used in high-end workstations and network file servers rather than in standard desktop PCs.

Perhaps the biggest incentive for using IDE drives is their cost. A comparable IDE drive can easily cost half the price of a SCSI drive.

Also, because SCSI controllers are rarely built in to motherboards, you also need to purchase a SCSI controller (minimum of about $100) to install SCSI drives and devices.

Installing an IDE Drive in Your PC

As mentioned earlier, you can install only two IDE drives or devices on a single IDE controller. Most manufacturers now build two IDE controller connectors on their motherboards so that you can install two hard disk drives on one controller and a CD-ROM drive on the second controller. IDE controller connectors are easy to spot on your motherboard. Just look for two 40-pin connectors side-by-side (see Figure 10.1). On newer systems that support the UltraATA/66 or UltraATA/100 specifications, these connectors will have 80 pins.

FIGURE 10.1

IDE controller connectors on a motherboard.

> *UltraATA/66* and *UltraATA/100* are both IDE specifications that provide faster disk performance than the older UltraATA/33 or EIDE specifications.

> Before you purchase a new IDE drive, make sure that your system can support the UltraATA/66 or UltraATA/100 specification (most new drives are made for these specifications). If your system cannot support these newer specifications, don't despair; you can simply purchase an IDE interface card that does support the newer specs.

10

IDE drives use a series of jumpers on the drives to designate whether a single drive is installed on one controller or whether multiple drives are installed on the same controller. The jumpers are installed on a 3×2 matrix of pins often found on the end of the drive near the power connector, but can also be found on the hard disk drive circuit card. When you purchase a hard disk drive, the instructions indicate where the jumper pins are located and how you are to designate the drives.

When multiple drives are installed on the same controller, one drive is designated the primary or "master," and the other drive is designated the secondary or "slave."

If two drives are installed on one controller, you must install the jumpers on one drive as you see in Figure 10.2 to designate it as the primary or master. You need to install the jumpers on the second drive to designate it as the secondary or slave (see Figure 10.3). If a single drive is installed on a controller, no jumpers are usually installed.

Replacing an Existing Hard Disk Drive

The easiest way to install a hard disk drive is by replacing an existing drive with a new drive because you can use the existing drive as your model for installing the new drive. All the mounting screws and connecting cables should be the same, eliminating any guesswork on your part.

> When replacing an existing drive with a new drive, one of the first considerations is to determine how you are going to back up or transfer the files from the old drive to the new drive. If you have some sort of backup device (for example, a tape drive or a removable media drive, such as a CD-RW or a Zip drive), this greatly simplifies the file transfer process. If you do not have a backup device, your only option is to back up your data files onto floppy

disks and reinstall your operating system and programs onto the new drive after it is installed.

A number of disk image copying programs are available on the market— such as Norton Ghost and Drive Image—that can simplify this task, but these programs usually require some sort of large storage or backup device to temporarily store the disk image. If you have access to a network file server, these disk image copying programs can be a godsend.

FIGURE 10.2

Jumpers designating one drive as the primary or master.

FIGURE 10.3

Jumpers designating one drive as the secondary or slave.

A disk image program reads your hard disk drive and makes an exact copy of the drive contents sector-by-sector regardless of what you have stored. The program then makes an exact copy of your drive byte-for-byte and notes where on your hard disk each byte or sector is stored.

Task: Replacing an Existing IDE Drive

To replace an existing drive with a new drive, follow these steps:

1. Unplug your PC and exercise all the safety precautions described in Hour 5, "The Tools of the Trade," such as grounding yourself to prevent static electric discharges.

2. Locate the existing drive in your PC. Diagram how each cable is connected to the drive and how the drive is mounted in your PC. Note all connecting screws and mounting hardware and how the drive is physically installed in your PC.

3. Disconnect the 4-wire power cord from the hard disk drive.

4. Disconnect the ribbon cable from the hard disk drive. Note how the ribbon cable is attached to the drive (that is, the position and orientation of the red stripe, if there is one, on the ribbon cable).

5. Remove any screws used to mount the hard disk drive to your PC. Some PC manufacturers place the hard disk into a mounting bracket, and some manufacturers mount guide rails onto the sides of the drive. Most manufacturers try to install two mounting screws on each side of the drive for a total of four mounting screws to hold the drive securely in place.

6. Check to see whether any jumpers are installed on the existing drive. Follow the guidelines mentioned earlier for correctly installing jumpers on the new drive. Use the existing drive as your model, and make sure that you place the jumper (if there is one installed) on the new drive the same as the jumper is installed on the existing drive.

7. Attach the new drive to any mounting hardware or bracket, if one is used in your PC, and reinstall the drive into a drive bay or mounting position in your PC.

8. Reattach the ribbon cable and the 4-wire power cord to the drive.

▲ To Do

10

Although it is impossible to incorrectly reattach the power cord, it is possible to misalign the ribbon cable as it is reattached. Put it on, and if it doesn't work, reverse it. You have a 50/50 chance of getting it right (or getting it wrong).

When you turn on your PC for the first time, you will probably have to re-run your CMOS hardware Setup program to configure the new drive. This procedure varies from PC to PC—some newer PCs considerably automate this process, whereas some older PCs may require you to enter hardware values for the new drive, such as the number of drive heads, tracks, and sectors. This information is supplied with the drive, so make sure to hold onto your documentation. The only thing left to do is to format the drive (as explained in your documentation) and restore your files from whatever backup medium you used. Again, the documentation that came with your backup device will explain what you have to do.

If your computer does not recognize your hard disk drive or reports a storage capacity far smaller than the reported size of the drive, it is possible you have an older BIOS in your PC that does not recognize large (larger than 550MB) drives. See Hour 7, "Upgrading Your CPU and BIOS," for more information on replacing your existing BIOS.

Adding a Second Hard Disk Drive

Adding a second drive is usually just as easy as replacing an existing drive provided that you have an empty drive bay available. Again, you can use the existing drive as a template for how the second drive will be installed. When adding a second IDE drive, remember that one drive has to be designated the primary or master, and the other drive has to be designated the secondary or slave. In most cases, the existing drive is designated the master, and the drive you are adding is designated the slave. By designating the new drive as the secondary or slave, you do not have to concern yourself with backing up the files on the existing drive or installing an operating system on the new drive. The new drive (after it is formatted) will simply appear as the next drive letter after your existing drive (usually drive D:).

If you have a CD-ROM drive installed in your PC and you are adding another hard disk drive, your CD-ROM drive will be bumped down a drive letter. For example, if your CD-ROM drive is designated drive D:, after you add another hard disk drive, the new hard disk drive becomes drive D: and your CD-ROM drive becomes drive E:. Usually this is not a problem except when the software you install from a CD-ROM requires you to leave the CD-ROM in the drive while the program is running (as many games do). In this scenario, your program is looking for your CD-ROM files on drive D: instead of drive E:. If this happens to you, see whether there is a way to reconfigure your program to look on drive E: from the CD-ROM. If you can't reconfigure the software, you will have to reinstall it. If you do want to reorganize your drive designations, go into the Computer Management section of the Control Panel. But before you do that, make sure that you none of your software expects to see programs or CDs on a specific drive.

10

You also must note how the ribbon cable is attached to the existing drive and attach the ribbon cable in the same position to the new drive you are adding. Note, too, that there are two connectors on the ribbon cable for attaching IDE devices. Because you are designating one drive the master and one drive the slave, it does not matter which connector you attach the new drive to (see Figure 10.4).

Before you begin, make sure that your PC has sufficient physical room for a second drive (that is, that you have an empty drive bay), and make sure that you have all the mounting hardware (for example, support frame, guide rails, and so on). Many hard disk drive kits now come with several sets of mounting hardware to cover all contingencies, but it never hurts to tell the sales representative what type of computer you have to ensure that the drive kit you purchase will work with your system. Most computer stores that sell hard disk drives also sell mounting kits (if the hard disk drive you purchase does not come with a mounting kit), and the kits usually identify most of the computers they are designed to work with.

Also, if you find that you are missing a 4-wire power cable, you can pick up a Y-connector (see Figure 10.5) at almost any computer store for around $5.

FIGURE 10.4

This figure shows two IDE drives and the positioning of jumpers and the ribbon cable.

FIGURE 10.5

A Y-connector used to attach two devices to a single power connector.

Installing a SCSI Drive in Your PC

Installing SCSI hard disk drives and devices is quite different from installing IDE drives. When you install SCSI hard disk drives and devices in your PC, you are creating what is called a "SCSI chain." The SCSI chain consists of a SCSI controller card, a SCSI cable, one or more SCSI devices, and a SCSI *terminator* at each end of the chain. It is important to remember that the terminators are always at both ends of the SCSI chain. I mention this because the end of a SCSI chain can be any of the following:

- A SCSI controller card with a built-in terminator
- A SCSI device, such as a hard disk drive, a CD-ROM drive, a tape backup drive, a scanner, and so on, also with a built-in terminator
- A physical SCSI terminator

Most newer SCSI controller cards are designed with both an internal and external connector for attaching SCSI devices (see Figure 10.6). Because of this design, a SCSI controller card can be in the middle of your SCSI chain or at either end, depending on whether you have internal or external SCSI devices or both. Most newer SCSI controller cards can also be self-terminating if they are at the end of the SCSI chain.

 When we say you need a *terminator*, we do not mean that you need the big guy with the Austrian accent from the movies by the same name. You need an electronic component that signals the end (both ends) of the SCSI chain. Terminators come in various shapes and sizes, but usually connect to the end of your SCSI chain using the same type of connectors as your other SCSI devices.

10

Internal Connector

FIGURE 10.6

A typical SCSI controller card showing both internal and external connectors.

External Connector

Another important difference in installing SCSI disk drives and devices is that every device on a SCSI chain has to have a unique ID number. SCSI ID numbers are simply a way of identifying one device from another on the SCSI chain. SCSI ID numbers are similar to designating one IDE drive the master and one the slave. For example, if you have three cats, you would not name them all "Max" because they would get confused when you called them. The same applies to SCSI devices. Unless they have unique ID numbers, confusion can occur when you have to access a particular drive or device.

In most instances, the SCSI controller is given the SCSI ID number 7, which means that you can use ID numbers 0–6 for your SCSI drives and devices; on newer SCSI controllers, you also can use the ID numbers 8–15. For hard disk drives, SCSI ID numbers are usually set using a series of jumpers, much the same way you use jumpers to designate IDE drives connected to the same controller. The instructions accompanying the drive explain how to install the jumpers for a specific ID number. You do not designate a SCSI drive as master or slave as you do with IDE drives. If you plan to boot your PC from the SCSI drive, its ID number must usually be 0. If you have both IDE and SCSI drives in your PC, you must boot your PC from the IDE drive, in which case the SCSI drive ID can be any number from 0–6.

Physically installing the SCSI drive into your PC is about the same as installing an IDE drive in regards to physical location and mounting hardware. You may have a bit more latitude and room to work because SCSI cables can be a lot longer than IDE cables.

Task: Installing a SCSI Disk Drive

To install an internal SCSI hard disk, follow these steps:

1. Unplug your PC and exercise all the safety precautions described in Hour 5, such as grounding yourself to prevent static electric discharges.

2. Install the SCSI controller card in an empty slot in the PC.

3. Set the SCSI ID on the drive according to how you plan to use it (that is, will you boot from the SCSI drive, will the SCSI drive exist in the PC with an IDE drive, and so on). In most cases, the ID number for the drive is set using jumpers.

4. Install the SCSI drive using the mounting hardware you have.

5. Attach the power cable to the SCSI drive.

6. Attach the SCSI cable to the drive. In every case I have seen, SCSI cables are notched or in some way designed so that the cable can be attached to the drive in only one way (see Figure 10.7).

7. If the internal SCSI drive is the only SCSI device you are installing, make sure that the SCSI cable (that is, the SCSI chain) is terminated after the drive. Make sure that the other end of the SCSI chain, which should be the SCSI controller, is also

▼ terminated. Many newer SCSI controllers will self-terminate if they detect that they are at the end of the SCSI chain.

FIGURE 10.7

A notched SCSI connector on a SCSI cable.

10

▲

If you install an external SCSI device such as a scanner, termination is no longer at the controller card but at (or after) the last external device. Likewise, if you install an additional internal SCSI device such as a SCSI CD-ROM drive after the hard disk on the SCSI chain, the termination now falls after the last device on the chain. Just remember to terminate *both* ends of the SCSI chain. Be sure to remove any other terminators so that there are only two on the chain.

If the SCSI drive is the only drive in your PC, you do not have to make any changes in your CMOS settings unless you are removing an IDE drive and replacing it with a SCSI drive. In this case, you have to turn off or disable all *IDE parameters* (settings) in your CMOS hardware settings. You will have to run your hardware Setup (CMOS) program and in most cases set your IDE drive settings to "unused" or "disabled."

IDE parameters are the settings you make in your hardware Setup (CMOS) program to identify the characteristics of your drive. These settings include the number of read/write heads on your drive, the number of physical

platters (the metal disks that actually make up your hard disk), and the
number of tracks and sectors defined on each platter surface. The surface of
each hard disk platter is divided into a number of concentric rings called
tracks. Each track in turn is divided into a number of wedge-shaped units
called sectors.

Adding a Second SCSI Drive

If you ever decide to add a second SCSI drive, you need only to set the SCSI ID number
to a number not being used before installing the drive into an empty drive bay. For example, if the first SCSI drive has the SCSI ID number 0, set the SCSI ID number of the second drive to 1. The next time you start up your PC, your SCSI controller will
automatically detect the new SCSI device inserted in the SCSI chain.

Preparing Your Drives for Software

Before you can install files and software onto your new drive, you must create one or
more disk partitions using FDISK or a similar utility and format the drive. A partition is
nothing more than a defined area on your hard disk that you use to store files.

Using FDISK to Create a Disk Partition

If you use FDISK (which is stored on your DOS disk), you simply start up your computer using your DOS disk, and then start FDISK by typing **FDISK** at the DOS prompt.

You have to set one, and only one, partition to be the active partition. The
active partition is on the drive to which your computer boots. If you are
adding a second drive, do not accidentally reset the active partition to the
second hard disk drive, or your computer will not start.

Task: Using FDISK to Create a Partition

To create a partition using FDISK, follow these steps:

1. Insert the DOS disk into the floppy drive and start up your computer. Start FDISK
   by typing **FDISK** at the DOS prompt.

2. From the menu of FDISK options shown in Figure 10.8, select option 1, Create
   DOS Partition. In most cases, you create a single partition on your entire hard disk
   drive.

FIGURE 10.8

The main menu in FDISK.

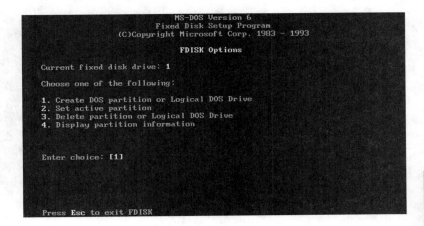

```
                    MS-DOS Version 6
                 Fixed Disk Setup Program
          (C)Copyright Microsoft Corp. 1983 - 1993

                      FDISK Options

Current fixed disk drive: 1

Choose one of the following:

1. Create DOS partition or Logical DOS Drive
2. Set active partition
3. Delete partition or Logical DOS Drive
4. Display partition information


Enter choice: [1]



Press Esc to exit FDISK
```

10

If you want to divide your hard disk into two or more logical drives, FDISK enables you to create more than one partition on a new hard disk drive that you install. (You might want to create totally separate (logical) disks (partitions) to store data on or to somehow separate other types of files. Creating logical drives is a matter of personal preference.) If you decide to create multiple partitions on a single physical drive, the usual configuration is to divide the drive 50/50—make 50% of the drive into the first partition and 50% of the drive into the second partition. But you can divide the drive in any configuration you want. Remember, too, that each partition you create exists as a drive with a separate drive letter (for example, C:, D:, and so on) on your PC.

3. Make one partition the active partition. This will be the partition (drive) to which you will start up your PC (see Figure 10.9).

4. Press Esc twice to exit FDISK and restart your PC.

Using Partition Magic to Create Your Partitions

One problem with using FDISK to create your partitions is that FDISK is typically a DOS-based utility and limits your partition sizes to 2GB. If you are using Windows 98, you can create large partitions (larger than 2GB), but you must create them as *FAT32* partitions. If you are using Windows NT 4.0, 2000, or XP, you can also create partitions as *NTFS* partitions.

FIGURE 10.9

FDISK showing one partition set as the active partition.

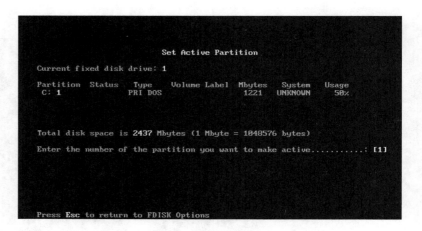

```
                              Set Active Partition
Current fixed disk drive: 1

Partition  Status    Type      Volume Label  Mbytes   System    Usage
   C: 1              PRI DOS                   1221    UNKNOWN    50%




Total disk space is 2437 Mbytes (1 Mbyte = 1048576 bytes)

Enter the number of the partition you want to make active..........: [1]






Press Esc to return to FDISK Options
```

> *FAT32* is a partition type used in Windows 98, 2000, Me, and XP for supporting larger partitions and for more efficient file storage on large hard disk drives. *NTFS* is a secure partition type originally created under Windows NT 4.0, but now also available under Windows 2000 and XP.

Partition Magic is a disk partition creation utility that not only allows you to create partitions larger than 2GB, but also allows you to resize your partitions (make them larger or smaller) regardless of whether you are running Windows 95/98 or Windows NT 4.0/2000/XP (see Figure 10.10).

Formatting Your Drive

After you create your partition(s), you must format your hard disk. Formatting prepares the hard disk to accept and store files. Regardless of which operating system you eventually plan to install on your PC, you can first perform a simple DOS format, but only create a FAT16 disk partition up to 2GB. Then, if you need to change the formatting to a larger partition or to format the partition as FAT32 or NTFS, you can safely reformat the drive.

> On IDE drives, make sure that you don't perform what is called a "low-level" format. This is a procedure that is done at the factory and should not be performed by an end-user because you can ruin the drive if you do. You need a special utility to do a low-level format; typing **FORMAT** as instructed to do in the following task performs a high-level format.

FIGURE 10.10

Partition Magic's main interface showing one partition.

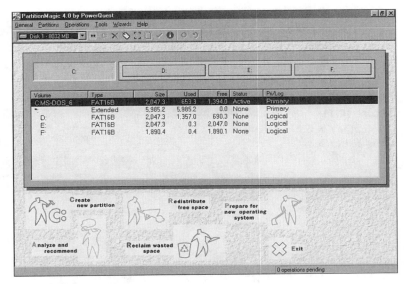

Task: Formatting Your Hard Disk Drive

To format your hard disk, follow these steps:

1. Start your PC with your DOS disk.

2. If you are formatting the hard disk as your startup drive, type this command to format the drive and install DOS system files to make the drive bootable:

   ```
   format c: /s
   ```

3. If you are formatting a drive that will not be a bootable drive, type this command, where *x*: is the drive letter of the drive you are formatting. Make sure that you format each partition you create.

   ```
   format x:
   ```

Installing an Operating System on Your PC

After your hard disk drive is formatted, you can decide what operating system you want to install on your PC (see Hour 23, "Upgrading to a New Operating System"). Follow the instructions accompanying the operating system you plan to use to determine whether any additional preparation is necessary before you install the operating system.

Alternative to IDE and SCSI Drives

It used to be that your only choices for upgrading or adding a hard disk were IDE or SCSI devices. Now there is a third choice: FireWire. LaCie (at www.lacie.com)

manufactures an external FireWire hard disk drive that is said to perform as well as most IDE and SCSI drives. The LaCie FireWire hard disk drive (see Figure 10.11) is sold as an external drive, which means that all you do to install it is plug in the cable from the hard disk to the FireWire card in your PC, the same way you would plug in an external SCSI drive to your PC.

FIGURE 10.11

The LaCie FireWire hard disk drive.

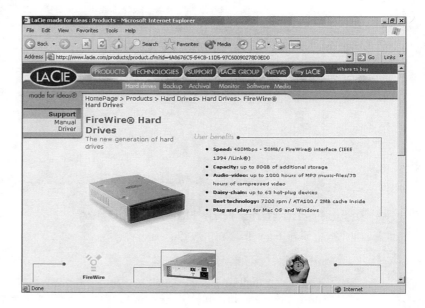

Although performance of the FireWire hard disk is said to be up to par with comparable-sized IDE and SCSI drives, the big drawback to FireWire hard disk drives is price. Early FireWire drives are roughly twice the price of their IDE cousins, and this does not include the cost of the FireWire interface card if your PC doesn't already have one. But like all innovations, as time goes on, expect the price to drop. Currently, there's no indication that a FireWire drive might fit a particular application better than either an IDE or SCSI hard disk drive (SCSI drives, for example, work better in file servers than do IDE drives).

Tips on Improving Your Hard Disk Performance

After you finish installing a hard disk drive in your PC and install the operating system, there are still a few things you can do to keep your drive operating in peak form.

Defrag Your Hard Disk Regularly

As you use your computer, you are continually creating and deleting files[md]even if you are not aware of it. Many software programs create temporary files that are deleted when you exit the program. When you format your hard disk, you are actually dividing it into small areas called sectors. Without going into a lot of technical detail, every time you create a file, your operating system saves a set number of bytes into every sector. When a sector is filled, your operating system uses the next available sector to save more of the file, and so on, until all the file is saved into however many sectors it needs. The sectors do not have to be next to each other to store parts of the same file. The operating system keeps track of which sectors are storing which files. So in a relatively short period of time, it's not only possible, but very likely, that your files are scattered all over your hard disk.

Although your operating system does a good job of keeping track of your files and finding all the sectors where a file is stored, locating files scattered all over your hard disk can take time and slow your PC's performance. To solve this problem and literally put your files back together (or at least move the files into adjacent sectors), you can use programs called hard disk defrag (defrag being short for defragmentation) utilities.

You should regularly defrag your hard disk to keep the performance at peak levels. Figures 10.12 and 10.13 show before and after defrag shots of hard disk drive partitions. "Regularly" can vary depending on how you use your PC, but you should make a habit of checking your drives for fragmentations at least once a week.

10

FIGURE 10.12

A hard disk drive before it is defragged.

FIGURE 10.13

A hard disk drive after it is defragged.

Never use a defrag utility unless it is specifically made for your operating system and its file storage system. Many users who used a defrag utility designed for DOS on their PC with Windows 95 discovered after it was too late that the DOS defrag utility damaged most of the files on the PC. Also, if you are using Windows 98 and have your hard drive formatted for FAT32 (a file storage system used in Windows 98/2000/Me/XP), make sure that your defrag utility can work with FAT32.

Delete Unneeded Files

As I said earlier, many programs create temporary files on your hard disk and are supposed to delete these files when you exit the program. But sometimes, for various reasons, these temporary files remain on your hard disk. Unneeded files take up valuable space on your hard disk and slow its performance.

All versions of Windows include a service or a utility you can use to locate and remove these unneeded files. Most of the time these files have the extension .TMP or .BAK.

One way to locate and remove these unneeded files is by using File Manager, which is included in every version of Windows.

Task: Removing Unneeded Files

To remove all files with the extension .TMP or .BAK, follow these steps:

1. Start the Windows Search utility. Select Start, Search, All Files and Folders to open the utility.

2. Choose the drive you want to check by selecting the drive letter icon in the Look In drop-down box.

3. Type *.TMP (or *.BAK) in the All or Part of the File Name text box and click Search. The Search utility performs a thorough search of the drive you select and locates every file with the extension .TMP or .BAK (see Figure 10.14).

FIGURE 10.14
The Windows Search utility locates all files with the extension .TMP.

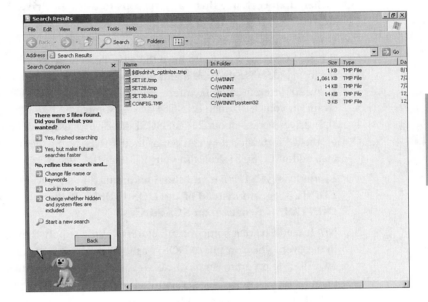

4. Highlight the files with the extension .TMP and press the Delete key to delete these unneeded files.

Some temporary files in Windows are files that Windows is using. While Windows is using these files, you cannot delete them.

Summary

In this hour, you learned how to install a hard disk drive into your PC regardless of whether you are replacing your existing drive with a new, larger drive, or merely adding a second drive to your system. You learned the differences between IDE and SCSI hard disks, and hopefully learned enough to decide which one to purchase. You also learned about the newer FireWire drives that one day might seriously compete with IDE and

SCSI drives in the PC marketplace. You also learned a few tips on what you can do to keep your hard disk drives operating at peak levels of performance.

Q&A

Q Other than cost, are there any reasons to use IDE drives instead of SCSI drives?

A Cost is still the big reason why the majority of PCs are manufactured with IDE drives. SCSI drives seem to have the advantage in every other category. Performance-wise they are about the same, with only some minor discrepancies between different manufacturers, but remember that IDE drives place a greater strain on your CPU than do SCSI drives, something like 60% of CPU resources for IDE drives versus about 2% for SCSI drives. For users concerned about squeezing all the performance they can out of their CPUs, SCSI seems the way to go. You can also add more SCSI drives in your PC than IDE drives.

Q I bought a SCSI drive and the documentation says to use the manufacturer's FDISK program instead of the DOS FDISK. Is there a problem with using the DOS FDISK program on SCSI drives?

A No. It could be that some manufacturers simply supply their own FDISK program in the event you don't have DOS, or they have built extra functionality into their own FDISK program. In most cases, you can safely use either program unless the manufacturer specifically says not to use the DOS FDISK program. The DOS FDISK program will also only allow you to create partitions with a maximum size of 2048MB (2 gigabytes), which is the maximum size that DOS can address.

HOUR 11

Replacing Your Floppy Disk Drive

In this hour, the focus is on replacing rather than upgrading your floppy disk drive because floppy disk drives have not seen much in the way of advancements in about the last 8–10 years. Perhaps the last change in floppy disk drives occurred several years ago when most manufacturers standardized on the installation of a single 3 1/2-inch floppy disk drive, removing the 5 1/4-inch drive as a standard feature. If you haven't noticed, software is no longer shipped on 5 1/4-inch disks, and that disk size seems to have gone the way of the dinosaurs. It may not be long before the 3 1/2-inch floppy disk drive is also relegated to being a museum piece because most software these days is shipped on CDs.

Although there was a brief flirtation by some manufacturers with the 2.88MB floppy disk drive, this device never really caught on and the standard is still the 1.44MB 3 1/2-inch floppy disk drive.

Whereas upgrading your floppy drive is not an issue, periodically these workhorses do go bad and you find yourself having to tear out the old one and replace it with another 3 1/2-inch drive. Many of you may do this simply for nostalgia reasons because the average PC will continue to work without a functioning floppy disk drive and there isn't much use these days for floppy disks.

This chapter teaches you all you need to know to accomplish this minor repair. Of course, many of you may have a bad floppy disk drive and not know it because there is so little use now for floppy disk drives.

During this hour, you will learn the following:

- What changes have occurred in floppy disk drives since the days of the original 5 1/4-inch 160K models
- How to safely remove a floppy disk drive and replace it with a new unit

A Brief History of Floppy Disk Drives

Since the original IBM PC was released in 1981, floppy disk drives have evolved considerably. The first PCs were equipped with single-sided drives with a capacity of only 160K. When IBM released DOS 2.0 to support the IBM PC/XT and its hard disk drive, it also slightly upped the ante on floppy disk drives with a slight change in its disk formatting layout from eight sectors per track to nine, which also effectively increased storage capacities on both single-sided and double-sided drives. Shortly thereafter, single-sided drives began to be phased out and the standard was double-sided drives. If you're a student of PC hardware history, you may also know that floppy disk drives then were full-sized drives instead of the half-height drives that later appeared.

During the next few years, PC floppy disk drives evolved remarkably, as shown in Table 11.1.

TABLE 11.1 Evolution of the Floppy Disk Drive

Type	Capacity	Size
Single-sided, single density (8 sectors/track, 40 tracks)	160K	5-1/4"
Single-sided, single density (9 sectors/track, 40 tracks)	180k	5-1/4"
Double-sided, single density (8 sectors/track, 40 tracks, 2 sided)	320K	5-1/4"
Double-sided, single density (9 sectors/track, 40 tracks, 2 sided)	360K	5-1/4"
Double-sided, double density (15 sectors/track, 80 tracks, 2 sided)	1.2M	5-1/4"

TABLE 11.1 continued

Type	Capacity	Size
Double-sided, high density (9 sectors/track, 80 tracks, 2 sided)	720K	3-1/2"
Double-sided, double density (18 sectors/track, 80 tracks, 2 sided)	1.44M	3-1/2"

Replacing Not Repairing

In the past few years, many books on upgrading PCs have included chapters on repairing floppy disk drives. But floppy disk drives have been reduced to inexpensive commodity status and can be readily purchased at most weekend computer fairs for as little as $10–$15, so it makes little sense to worry about repairing what has literally become a "throw-away" computer component. There's also no concern with compatibility issues because all 3 1/2-inch floppy drives are virtually the same, nor do you have to be concerned with whether you have the correct mounting hardware because all the mounting hardware is already in place inside your PC.

> Even though floppy disk drives are not as essential to day-to-day computer operations as they once were, at roughly $10–$15 a pop, it makes good sense to keep a spare on hand as an emergency repair unit.

Diagnosing a Broken Floppy Disk Drive

Diagnosing a problem with a floppy disk drive is usually pretty simple and straightforward. In most cases, you discover the problem when you boot your PC (most POST operations will mention a non-functioning floppy disk) or when you attempt to use the drive, such as reading from or writing to a floppy disk (assuming that you even still have and use floppy disks). Following is a short list of symptoms that can appear when your floppy disk drive is malfunctioning. Check the drive using multiple disks to make sure that your problem is drive related and not disk related:

- Disk activity light does not come on when attempting to use the drive
- Cannot read a disk in the drive
- Cannot write to a disk in the drive
- Programs fail to recognize that a disk is in the drive
- Cannot format a disk in the drive

Keep in mind that any or all of these symptoms can also occur if the ribbon cable or power cord attached to the drive is loose or removed (see Figure 11.1).

FIGURE 11.1

Loose cables can cause your floppy disk drive to appear to be malfunctioning.

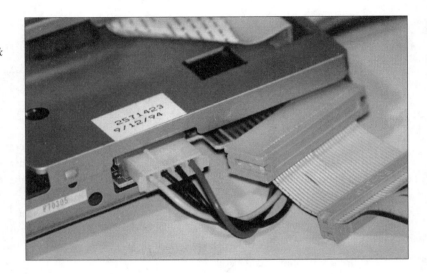

So before you break out your toolkit and swap out the drive with your spare, make sure that you check the cables. You'd be surprised how easily and frequently cables come loose.

If you check the cables and they are securely in place, be sure to also check your CMOS settings (see Hour 3, "Examining Your PC's System Configuration"). Make sure that they show a 3 1/2-inch, 1.44MB floppy disk drive as your A: drive. Also check to make sure that no other device you have installed is trying to use the same interrupt request (IRQ) setting that your floppy disk drive is using.

If your cables are secure and your CMOS and IRQ settings are correct and your drive still is not functioning correctly, it's a safe bet your disk drive is malfunctioning and you need to replace it.

Replacing a Broken Floppy Disk Drive

Replacing a broken floppy disk drive is as easy, if not easier, than installing a hard disk drive (see Hour 10, "Replacing, Upgrading, or Adding a Hard Disk Drive").

Task: Replacing a Floppy Disk Drive

To replace a floppy disk drive, follow these steps:

1. Unplug your PC and ground yourself before removing the cover.

2. Examine your PC to see how the floppy disk drive is installed in your computer's case. Note how many screws are holding the drive in place and the locations of the cables attached to the drive. You may have to remove the front bezel (face plate) to slide the drive out.

3. Identify (and label, if necessary) where and how the cables are attached to the drive before you remove the cables. If you have to remove any other cables or chassis parts to gain access to your floppy disk drive, make note of these also. Notice that the power connector for a 3 1/2-inch drive is smaller than the standard power connector (see Figure 11.2).

FIGURE 11.2

The power connector for a 3 1/2-inch floppy disk drive.

4. Remove all the screws holding the drive in place (see Figure 11.3), and carefully remove the drive from the drive bay.

5. Insert the new drive into the drive bay.

6. Replace all hardware mounting screws.

7. Reconnect the ribbon cable to the drive, making sure that you reattach the cable the same way it was attached to the original drive. Your ribbon cable might have two different connector types (see Figure 11.4). The second connector on the ribbon cable was previously used to connect drive B:, which on earlier model PCs was a 5 1/4-inch floppy disk drive (another carryover for PC nostalgia).

8. Reconnect the smaller power cord to the new drive.

11

FIGURE 11.3
Removing the floppy disk drive mounting screws.

FIGURE 11.4
The ribbon cable attached to your floppy disk drive.

When everything has been reattached and reconnected, turn on your PC to test your work. Notice whether the light on the drive comes on when you start up your PC. If the light comes on and stays on, it means that you have the ribbon cable on backward (reverse the cable). Place a floppy disk into the new drive and perform a few routine tests on the drive. Try issuing the DIR A: command to see whether you can read the contents of the disk. If there's no light, which usually indicates a setup problem, try DIR B:. If you are using Windows 95, 98, NT, or 2000, you can use Windows Explorer to test your drive instead of DIR A:. Try formatting a disk in the drive and copying a few files to the disk. If all these tests work s atisfactorily, you can be fairly certain that the disk drive you just installed is working okay.

Alternatives to a Standard 1.44MB Floppy Disk Drive

If your floppy disk drive goes belly up, there are alternatives when selecting a replacement drive. You might want to consider one of several high capacity removable media drives (see Hour 14, "Adding a Removable Media Drive") that will also read and write standard 3 1/2-inch, 1.44MB floppy disks. Most of these drives plug into one of your two IDE ports—the same connectors to which you connect your hard disk drives. Although these high capacity drives will read, write, and boot from standard 3 1/2-inch disks, they will set you back a few more bucks than a standard 3 1/2-inch drive. If you choose to use the high capacity media they are designed for, expect to also pay a bit more than you will for formatted 3 1/2-inch high-density floppy disks.

Summary

In this hour, you learned about the evolution of floppy disk drives, how to diagnose some problems that can occur with them, and how to replace a malfunctioning floppy disk drive.

Q&A

Q Why did manufacturers abandon the 5 1/4-inch floppy disk drive?

A It's only speculation, but it appears there are probably several reasons. PC users have always looked for better methods of storing more data. The 3 1/2-inch 1.44MB floppy disk is smaller and more convenient than the 5 1/4-inch 1.2MB floppy disk and stores (slightly) more data. The 3 1/2-inch drive is also a better storage medium than the 5 1/4-inch because it is more rigid and less susceptible to physical damage.

Q Do you think it is likely that the 3 1/2-inch floppy will be replaced by another storage medium?

A History at one time might have indicated yes, but it's probably safe to say no. Software manufacturers have for years used the medium of choice as a means for distributing software. In the last few years, most software has been distributed on CD-ROMs, which unfortunately are read-only, making them unsuitable as a replacement for the current 3 1/2-inch floppy disk and drive. Bootable and read-writeable CD-ROM drives appear to be the most likely candidate for the medium that will be replacing the 3 1/2-inch drive, especially because the costs for CD-RW drives have now dropped below $100. Some manufacturers have been giving buyers the option to replace their 3 1/2-inch drive with a 100MB Zip drive (see Hour 14).

11

The price of Zip drives has been dropping steadily and they appear to be gaining a certain amount of acceptance, but it is probably still too soon to tell if the 100MB Zip disk and drive will replace the 3 1/2-inch floppy disk and drive. Some manufacturers have also developed high-capacity drives that will read and write to standard 3 1/2-inch, 1.44MB disks, but no PC manufacturer has standardized on this type of hardware.

Hour **12**

Upgrading or Adding a CD-ROM/CD-RW Drive

A few years ago, a CD-ROM drive was something of a luxury item, and a CD-RW (CD Re-Writable) drive was something many computer users still considered the ultimate extravagance. Nowadays, a CD-ROM drive is standard equipment in a PC, and some PC manufacturers have already started replacing them with CD-RW drives as standard equipment.

The main factor that has helped to push CD-ROM/CD-RW drives into the mainstream are their continuing drop in price. A top-of-the-line 56x (56-speed) CD-ROM drive is in the $40–$50 price range, and average CD-RW drives can now be had for less than $100.

Whether you're looking to upgrade the old CD-ROM drive you have in your PC to a more advanced and functional model or to add a new CD-RW drive to your system, you need to know the ins and outs of installation.

During this hour, you will learn the following:

- How to select a CD-ROM/CD-RW drive
- Whether to choose an IDE drive or a SCSI drive
- How to install both internal and external CD-ROM/CD-RW drives

Selecting a CD-ROM/CD-RW Drive

Despite all the hoopla you've read and heard about *DVD* drives replacing CD-ROM drives and making them obsolete, it hasn't happened yet. Considering the rate at which manufacturers are still cranking out new models of CD-ROM and CD-RW drives, this switch to DVD technology doesn't appear to be happening anytime soon.

> *DVD* stands for *Digital Video Disc* and is a rather new digital technology very similar to CD-ROM technology. DVDs differ from CD-ROMs in that DVDs can store several times the capacity of CD-ROM discs (CD-ROMs can store approximately 650MB).

The first thing you must understand about selecting a CD-ROM or CD-RW drive is its speed terminology. The first CD-ROM drives transferred data at a rate of 150Kbps (kilobytes per second). This initial speed came to be known as "single-speed" and was written as "1x." As CD-ROM drives progressively got faster, their speeds were measured in comparison to the initial single-speed drives. For example, a double-speed (2x) drive transferred data at a rate of 300Kbps (150Kbps×2=300Kbps). A quad-speed (4x) drive transferred data at a rate of 600Kbps (150Kbps×4=600Kbps). A six-speed (6x) drive transferred data at a rate of 900Kbps, and so on.

At last report (or the last time I bothered to check the computer shop ads in the Sunday newspaper), several manufacturers had released 56-speed (56x) drives, and if history is any indicator, the advancement in CD-ROM technology won't stop there.

In selecting a drive, the data transfer speed is likely to be the first factor you consider, but it should not be the only factor. How fast a CD-ROM drive can transfer data is important, but how fast your CD-ROM drive can locate data (a parameter called its *seek time*) is also important.

Just as is true with your hard disk drive, the structure on a CD-ROM drive is composed of sectors and tracks. Seek time is defined as how fast the magnetic head (or in the case of a CD-ROM drive, the laser read head) that reads data can move from one track to another. Although CD-ROM drives cannot approach the seek time speeds of hard disk drives, around 8–10ms (milliseconds), a CD-ROM drive seek time of around 110ms is considered excellent.

Another factor to consider is the cache size on your CD-ROM. A *cache* is a holding area of memory built in to the drive to temporarily store data as it is being processed. Most drives have a cache of around 1–4MB; anything larger is a premium.

When you're considering a CD-RW drive, there are some additional factors you should consider. When you are describing the speed of CD-RW drives, you generally see three numbers written AA*x*/BB*x*/CC*x* where:

AA*x* is the speed when recording to standard blank recordable CDs

BB*x* is the speed when recording to re-writeable CDs

CC*x* is the speed when reading CDs

For example, if you have a CD-RW drive advertised as 6x/4x/24x, this means that it is a 6x-speed drive when recording standard blank CDs; it is a 4x-speed drive when writing to rewritable CDs; and it is a 24x-speed drive when reading CDs.

Earlier recordable CD drives were designated CD-R; if you're wondering what the difference is between a CD-R drive and a CD-RW drive, both can record to blank CDs but only the CD-RW can record on rewritable (that is, reusable) CDs. Most CD-R drives have been replaced by CD-RW drives—another reason why CD-RW drives are slowly replacing other types of data backup devices. So if you drop by your local weekend computer fair and see an unbelievable bargain on CD-R drives, now you know why. Pass on that puppy.

12

Also, in case you're wondering about CD-RW media prices, just recently I saw ads for a package of 25 blank CD-RW discs priced between $20–30. It's a safe bet that prices will continue heading south.

Don't let speed be the absolute deciding factor in deciding on a CD-ROM or CD-RW drive. Just as you do with any other peripheral, you should check product reviews periodically in PC magazines and journals and on Web sites that specialize in reviewing new PC products, such as CNET's Computers.com at `http://computers.cnet.com/ hardware/0-1091.html` (see Figure 12.1).

FIGURE 12.1
*CNET's
Computers.com Web
site, one of the pre-
miere product review
sites.*

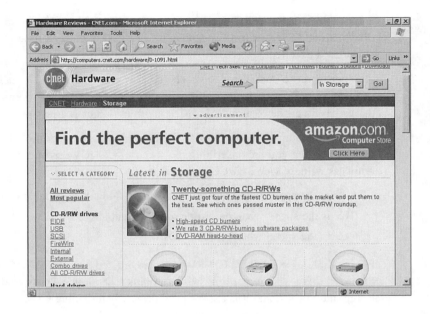

However, if speed is your number one hang-up, don't despair. Go to the
`www.cdspeed2000.com` site, download the CD-ROM speed comparison utility, take it in
with you when you visit your local computer store, and test to your heart's content (see
Figures 12.2 and 12.3), or use it to verify the speeds of the CD-RW you eventually
purchase.

SCSI Versus IDE

Just as you had to decide between IDE and SCSI when you were selecting a hard disk
drive in Hour 10, "Replacing, Upgrading, or Adding a Hard Disk Drive," you also have
to decide between IDE and SCSI when selecting a CD-ROM or CD-RW drive. The same
factors concerning performance and cost apply when selecting a CD-ROM/RW type.

If you already have a SCSI controller installed in your PC, you are way ahead in terms of
performance if you select a SCSI CD-ROM/RW drive. SCSI CD-ROM/RW drives, like
SCSI hard disk drives, do not place as much strain on your CPU. If you already have a
SCSI controller in your PC for your SCSI hard disk(s), you will most likely want to
select a SCSI CD-ROM/RW drive. If your hard disk drive is IDE, you will most likely
select an IDE CD-RW drive for your PC.

FIGURE 12.2

The CD Speed 2000 site for testing CD-ROM, CD-RW, and DVD drive speeds.

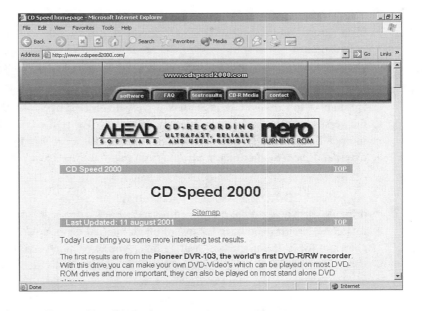

FIGURE 12.3

Running the CD Speed 2000 CD-ROM speed test.

12

Installing the Drive in Your PC—Internal Versus External

As far as the physical installation is concerned, a CD-ROM drive is no different than a CD-RW drive. The difference between the two installations appears when you install the software for the drive. As you will see later this hour, after you perform the physical installation, you must install the hardware driver for your drive. With a CD-RW drive, you also must install some type of CD recording software. Once again, don't worry about which software product to buy; all CD-RW manufacturers include some type of recording software with the drives they sell.

If you plan to install a CD-ROM/RW drive with an IDE interface, the decision on internal versus external has already been made for you. All IDE CD-ROM/RW drives are internal because the IDE interface does not allow for a cable long enough to connect an external drive. Another major advantage an internal drive has over an external drive is its lower cost.

An internal CD-ROM/RW drive is generally about $40–$50 cheaper than an external drive because an external drive requires a case and a separate power supply. The only real consideration you have for installing an internal drive is whether your PC has physical room for it. If you are out of drive bays, you have no choice but to install an external drive. Internal CD-ROM/RW drives are all a "standard" size and occupy what is called a "full-sized" drive bay slot (see Figure 12.4).

FIGURE 12.4
An internal CD-ROM drive in a drive bay slot.

Task: Installing an Internal IDE CD-RW Drive

▼ To Do

Installing an internal CD-RW drive is no more difficult than installing a hard disk drive.

> Just as you were instructed to do in Hour 5, "The Tools of the Trade," when handling any delicate electrical components inside your PC, make sure that you properly ground yourself to protect against static electricity and also make sure that you unplug your PC before working on it.

To install an internal drive, follow these steps:

1. Select a drive bay in your PC that you can use to install the drive. Make sure that you also remove the front panel on the case covering the empty bay. Make sure that you have an unused power connector you can plug in to the drive. If you don't have an unused power connector, go to your local computer store and pick up a Y-connector. Unplug one of your power connectors from another device and attach the Y-connector.

2. On most PCs built in the last three or four years, you find two IDE interfaces, usually labeled "primary" and "secondary" (see Figure 12.5). Your hard disk drive (if you have an IDE hard disk installed in your PC) should be attached by a cable to the interface labeled "primary." Make sure that you have a cable that will reach from the secondary interface to the bay where you are installing your new drive.

FIGURE 12.5
Primary and secondary IDE interfaces on the motherboard.

Primary IDE interface

Secondary IDE interface

12

▼ 3. If you have to install any guide rails on the sides of your drive, install them according to the instructions accompanying the drive (see Figure 12.6). If drive rails are
not included, but needed, be sure to pick up a set from your local computer store.

*Guide rails of various
sizes used for
installing CD-RW
drives and other
peripheral devices.*

4. Insert the drive into the drive bay and attach the ribbon cable from the secondary
(slave) IDE interface to the 40-pin IDE interface on the rear of the drive (see
Figure 12.7).

Even though IDE interfaces can accommodate two IDE devices, do not connect the CD-RW drive to the same interface you connect your IDE hard disk
drive to. The CD-RW drive, which is a much slower device than a hard disk
drive, will degrade the performance of the hard disk drive if they're on the
same interface.

If your PC has only one IDE interface connector, don't panic. Instead, just
make a quick trip to your local computer store and purchase an IDE interface card. Such a card usually runs in the vicinity of $25–$30. Don't worry
about it conflicting with any of your existing IRQs or memory addresses.
Most manufacturers realize that the IDE interface card is added as a secondary interface and usually assign it IRQs and addresses that are the same
as a secondary interface. Just remember, when in doubt, ask the salesperson
or the store's in-house technical guru.

▼

FIGURE 12.7
The rear of a typical IDE CD-RW drive showing interface, power, and sound connections.

Sound card connection

40-pin IDE interface connection

4-pin power connection

5. If you also have a sound card in your PC (see Hour 21, "Upgrading or Adding a Sound System to Your PC"), you can connect the audio cable to the audio connector on the rear of the CD-RW drive. Without the audio cable, you will not be able to play audio CDs through your sound system.

6. After everything is connected to your drive, adjust the drive so that it is even with the front opening of the drive bay. Tighten the screws to secure your drive in place.

7. Just as you did when you installed your hard disk drive, you will probably have to run your computer's hardware Setup program to complete the hardware installation. Also, you should have some type of software installation disk that you will need to run to install the appropriate driver, depending on the operating system you are running. If you are running Windows 95/98/2000/Me/XP, when you restart your PC, Windows should automatically detect your newly installed CD-RW drive and install the proper driver (a feature known as "Plug and Play").

In addition to a hardware driver for your drive, the disk that comes with your CD-RW drive also includes a number of utilities for your drive. One of the most enjoyable utilities is one that enables you to play music CDs on your new CD-RW drive. If you don't have a sound card in your PC, you can simply plug a set of headphones into the connector on the front of the drive next to the volume control.

Installing an Internal SCSI Drive

Installing an internal SCSI CD-ROM/RW drive is almost exactly the same as installing an internal IDE drive. The cable is a bit different, and just like with installing a SCSI hard disk drive, you have to set the SCSI ID on the CD-ROM/RW drive according to the instructions that came with your drive. Remember, too, that the SCSI ID number (0–6) you assign to the drive has to be unique.

All SCSI devices, such as hard disk drives and CD-RW drives, leave the factory with a preset SCSI ID, which in most cases you can leave as is. Just be sure to check that the ID set on the device isn't an ID you are already using on your SCSI chain. Two devices on a SCSI chain with the same ID will not operate.

Remember to check the termination on your SCSI chain. Some SCSI CD-ROM/RW drives come with a factory-installed terminator. If your CD-ROM/RW drive is not placed at the end of your SCSI chain, you have to remove the factory-installed terminator, or the devices on the chain after the CD-ROM/RW drive will not operate. Check your CD-ROM/RW documentation on how to remove the terminator. In many cases, you simply have to remove a jumper.

Installing an External Drive

Installing an external CD-ROM/RW drive is even easier than installing an internal drive. External CD-ROM drives used to be available only as SCSI drives, but now you can also find a few manufacturers producing external drives using either USB or Firewire interfaces. Regardless of which type you select, the manufacturer will almost always ship the drive with the appropriate cable needed to connect your drive to your interface.

If you are trying to decide between SCSI, USB, and Firewire, consider this: SCSI will be the fastest but most expensive; Firewire should rank second in both speed and cost, and USB will be the slowest and least expensive.

Many external SCSI CD-ROM/RW drives also ship with a SCSI interface card, which saves you the trouble and expense of having to purchase a SCSI card separately. If you find that you do have to purchase a SCSI interface card, check with the manufacturer of the drive to see whether any types of SCSI cards are recommended or whether any types of SCSI cards may not work with your CD-ROM/RW drive.

After you have the drive, cable, and interface card, literally all you have to do is plug them together. Insert the card into an empty slot (most likely SCSI, but also USB or Firewire if your PC doesn't already have one) in your PC (see Figure 12.8). Next, connect one end of the cable to the connector on the end of the card (the connector protruding out of the back of your PC) and the other end of the cable to the connector on the drive (see Figure 12.9).

FIGURE 12.8

Inserting the SCSI interface card into an empty slot in your PC.

12

With some SCSI CD-ROM/RW drives, you receive a SCSI terminator. The terminator looks like the plug on the end of the SCSI cable without the cable attached (see Figure 12.10). If you are installing a USB or Firewire drive, don't worry that you can't find a terminator—there isn't one.

There are two SCSI connectors on the back of your SCSI CD-ROM/RW drive. If you have to use the terminator to terminate your SCSI chain, plug the terminator into one connector and plug the SCSI cable into the other connector.

FIGURE 12.9
Plugging the SCSI cable into the interface card and into the CD-RW drive.

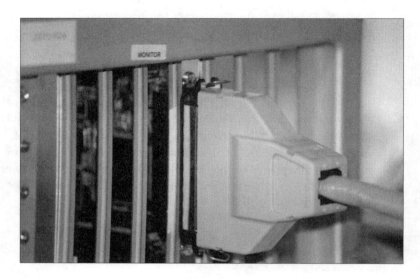

FIGURE 12.10
A typical SCSI terminator.

Remember that only the device at the end of the SCSI chain should be terminated. If the CD-ROM/RW drive is not at the end of the SCSI chain, you do not have to terminate the chain at the CD-ROM/RW drive.

> Don't panic if one or both of the SCSI connectors on the back of your CD-ROM/RW drive looks different than the typical 50-pin Centronics connector commonly found on many SCSI devices. Four types of SCSI connectors are used on SCSI devices: the 50-pin Centronics connector, the 25-pin D-connector, the 50-pin mini-SCSI connector, and the 63-pin SCSI connector.

Now, just plug in the electrical cord supplying power to the external drive, run the Setup program for your PC, install the driver for the CD-ROM/RW drive from the disk included with your drive, and you're done.

If you are running Windows 95/98/2000/Me/XP, your newly installed CD-ROM/RW drive should be detected when you restart your PC, and Windows will attempt to automatically install the appropriate driver. Make sure that you have your Windows disks handy. If you are using Windows NT 4.0 or another operating system, check your CD-ROM/RW documentation on how to load the appropriate driver for your OS.

What About DVD?

Undoubtedly, you've heard or read a lot of the recent press that DVD has been receiving and may be wondering whether you want to upgrade to a DVD drive instead of a CD-RW drive. If you do, consider the following:

- DVD drives (at least the second-generation DVD-2 drives) are compatible with commercial CD-ROM discs and CD-R (CD-Recordable) and CD-RW (CD-Writable) discs. The first generation of DVD drives did not read CD-R and CD-W discs. Make sure that you read the fine print and get a second-generation DVD-2 drive or upgrade kit.

- DVD drives are going through many of the same growing pains that early CD-ROM drives went through—namely, speed and cost. DVD drives read CD-ROM discs at 12x speeds.

- Upgrade kits for DVD drives can be a bit confusing and problematic for some users to install, especially because the upgrade kits include a "decoder" interface card that must be compatible with your existing video card. It is also possible to encounter IRQ conflicts when installing this new card in your PC.

- DVD upgrade kits are currently running in the neighborhood of $200–$300. But just like the initial price of CD-ROM drives, DVD prices are expected to drop as they become more plentiful.

12

- Recordable DVD drives currently are available in three competing and incompatible formats, DVD-RAM, DVD-R, and DVD-RW. It is definitely worth waiting until this market has a shakeout and one format quashes the other (remember the competing Beta and VHS video formats?).

On the plus side, however, reports say that nothing currently on the market can match the quality of audio and video delivered by DVD. DVD was originally designed as a new distribution medium for home movies to compete with (or replace) analog VHS. The main requirement for the original DVD specification was the capability to store a typical two-hour movie on a single side of the discs. DVD discs currently store about 4.7GB of data (compared to only 650MB for CD-ROM discs) and include multiple audio tracks or vastly improved digital audio.

Many DVD upgrade kits include adapters for connecting the output from your PC to your TV to enable you to watch DVD movies either on your PC monitor or on your living room TV. Acceptance among the major Hollywood studios has been exceptionally good, and by early 2001, there were more than 10,000 titles released in the new DVD movie format. Software manufacturers have not responded quite as fast. Early 2001 saw barely more than a handful of software titles, but vendors are still promising that titles will be forthcoming.

If you do find that you want to purchase and install a DVD drive in your PC, head straight for Hour 13, "Adding a DVD Drive."

Summary

In this hour, you learned about CD-ROM/CD-RW drives and how to select a drive as either an upgrade or a new component in your PC. You also learned about the differences between IDE and SCSI CD-ROM/RW drives and how to install each type. You learned about DVD drives as well and some of the information to help you decide whether you want to upgrade to a DVD drive.

Q&A

Q Are CD-ROM discs like phonograph records? In other words, is there something written on both sides of the discs?

A No, CD-ROM discs contain information on only one side—the side opposite the label, regardless of whether it is a software or music CD-ROM. Some DVD discs, however, have information on both sides. The tip-off is if you see a label: If you see a label on one side of the disc, it's a safe bet there is information on only the other side.

Q   Because CD-ROM/RW drives and DVD drives both read discs using reflected light from a laser rather than a needle in a groove like a phonograph record, does this mean that CD-ROM/RW and DVD discs are immune to scratches?

A   No, not at all. Although there is no physical contact between the device and the medium, CD-ROM/RW and DVD discs can be damaged if scratched. Scratches on CD-ROM/RW and DVD discs can interfere with the capability of lasers to properly read the data stored on the discs. You should exercise the same level of caution with your CD-ROM/RW and DVD discs that you did years ago with your phonograph records. Even though there are so-called "scratch repair" kits on the market, don't rely on these to bail you out for careless handling.

12

HOUR 13

Adding a DVD Drive to Your PC

Even though they've been around for about four years, many PC users still think of DVD drives as the newest, hottest technology, especially because so few PCs currently have them.

PC software vendors haven't embraced DVD technology as rapidly as the movie industry, but you can find a few software titles currently available on DVD, especially those that would still require a stack of CDs, such as the first 110 years of the National Geographic (see http://www.nationalgeographic.com/cdrom/). The CD edition of this title comes on 31 CDs!

Regardless of your reasons for wanting to acquire a DVD drive, during this hour you will learn:

- What DVD is and how it differs from CDs
- What to look for in a DVD installation kit
- How to install a DVD drive in your PC
- Why it is still too early to consider writable DVDs

What Is a DVD?

DVDs look a lot like CDs, but there is a world of difference between the two media. Both are 120mm in diameter, but whereas CDs store a maximum of about 650MB of data, DVDs currently top out at around 4.75GB of data—about seven and a half times larger.

DVD originally stood for Digital Video Disc because the intended used for DVDs was as a new storage medium for full-length movies. But as the new storage medium began seeing usage as a repository for software and other mega-storage items, the name was officially switched to Digital Versatile Disc. Almost no one calls them by their official name, so just refer to them as DVDs.

Like CDs, DVDs store data as a series of pits etched on a reflective substrate layer of plastic, which is read by a laser. DVDs achieve their gargantuan storage capabilities by reducing the size of the data pit from 0.83 microns to 0.40 microns (a micron is 1,000th of a millimeter) and by placing the ridges of the one concentric groove closer together— from 1.6 microns to just 0.74 microns. With a smaller target, you also need a tighter laser beam. Whereas the laser in CD-ROM drives uses a 780-nanometer wavelength, the laser beam in DVD drives uses only a 640-nanometer wavelength.

Enough with the rocket science. Just think of it as smaller data bits packed a lot closer together.

What You Will Find in a Standard DVD Upgrade Kit

When you purchase a CD-ROM drive, you get a drive and maybe a ribbon cable to attach the drive to your IDE or SCSI port. In a DVD upgrade kit, you will find a little bit more than just the DVD drive and a ribbon cable. In addition to the DVD drive, you will (should) also find what's called an *MPEG-2* decoder card.

 MPEG-2 is an international graphics standard established by the Motion Picture Entertainment Group (MPEG) for audio and video compression and playback.

The decoder card (see Figure 13.1) is attached to your existing video card to allow DVD playback through your PC's video system.

FIGURE 13.1

A typical DVD decoder card that you will find in most DVD upgrade kits.

When you purchase a DVD kit, make sure that you choose one that includes an MPEG-2 decoder (hardware) card and not one that uses software for MPEG-2 playback. The hardware option is far superior to software emulations. Also, make sure that your decoder card supports resolutions at least up to 1,280×1,024.

For an internal drive you should also find an IDE ribbon cable in your upgrade kit. Most internal DVD drives for PCs are IDE (or more precisely, EIDE—Enhanced IDE). Most of the SCSI DVD drives you find are DVD-RAM drives (more about this later in this hour).

 DVD-RAM drives are one of two competing writable DVD drive formats and most are SCSI instead of IDE (or EIDE).

You will also find a video cable for connecting your decoder card to your existing video card, and a cable to connect to your sound card.

Installing a DVD Drive in Your PC

Installing a DVD upgrade kit is no more difficult than installing a CD-ROM drive (see Hour 12, "Upgrading or Adding a CD-ROM/CD-RW Drive") and a video card (see Hour 20, "Upgrading Your Video Card and Monitor"). Basically, what you will be doing is installing another device about the same size as a CD-ROM drive and another card similar to your video card.

13

Task: Installing Your New DVD Kit

> As you learned in Hour 5, "The Tools of the Trade," whenever you handle any sensitive electrical components inside your PC, make sure that you have unplugged your PC power supply and grounded yourself to prevent static electric discharges.

To install your DVD upgrade kit, follow these steps:

1. Make sure that you have an empty 5 1/4-inch drive bay in your PC and an empty slot on your motherboard. Also make sure that you have removed the front panel on the case covering the empty bay. Make sure that you have an unused power connector you can plug in to the drive. If you don't have an unused power connector, go to your local computer store and pick up a Y-connector. Unplug one of your power connectors from another device and attach the Y-connector. Make sure that the empty slot matches the type of decoder card in your kit (ISA versus PCI).

2. You should find two IDE interfaces, usually labeled "primary" and "secondary," on your motherboard. Your hard disk drive (if you have an IDE hard disk installed in your PC) should be attached with a cable to the interface labeled "primary." Make sure that you have a cable that will reach from the secondary interface to the bay where you are installing your new DVD drive. If you already have a CD-ROM drive attached to the secondary IDE port, you can attach the DVD drive to this same cable. Just make sure that the cable will reach the connectors on both the CD-ROM and DVD drives. The easiest way to ensure an easy fit is to install one drive (CD-ROM or DVD) on top of the other in your drive bays (see Figure 13.2).

> If you decide to install your DVD drive in a PC that already has a CD-ROM drive, make sure that you designate one of the devices the "master" and the other device the "slave." Your documentation will illustrate how you need to set the jumpers to make these configuration settings. You make the master/slave distinction only if you are placing two IDE devices on the same IDE port. If each device is connected to its own IDE port, you should be able to connect the device using the default setting configured by the manufacturer.

3. If you have to install any guide rails on the sides of your drive, install them according to the instructions accompanying the drive. If drive rails are not included, but needed, be sure to pick up a set from your local computer store.

FIGURE 13.2
A DVD drive and a CD-ROM drive installed together.

4. Insert the drive into the drive bay (see Figure 13.3) and attach the ribbon cable from the secondary IDE interface to the 40-pin IDE interface on the rear of the DVD drive (see Figure 13.4).

FIGURE 13.3
Insert your DVD drive into an empty drive bay.

13

5. Connect the audio cable to the audio connector on the rear of the DVD drive and connect the other end of the cable to your sound card, following the instructions

▼ that accompanied your upgrade kit. Without the audio cable, you will not be able to hear audio when you watch DVD movies.

FIGURE **13.4**
Attach the IDE ribbon cable to the DVD drive.

6. Attach the power cable to the power connector on the back of your DVD drive.

7. Insert the decoder card into the appropriate type of slot (ISA or PCI) on your motherboard (see Figure 13.5). Remove the cable connecting your monitor to your video card. Connect the video loopback cable in your upgrade kit from the decoder card to your video card as shown in the instructions included in your upgrade kit (see Figure 13.6). Then connect the cable from your monitor to the video connector on your decoder card. You also must connect an audio cable (supplied with your kit) from your existing audio card to the decoder card if you want to hear audio from your DVD games and movies.

8. After you have everything connected to your DVD drive, adjust the drive even with the front opening of the drive bay and tighten the screws, securing your drive in place.

9. You should have some type of software installation disk or CD/DVD that you have to run to install the appropriate drivers, depending on the operating system you are running. If you are running Windows 95/98/2000/Me/XP, when you restart your PC, Windows should automatically detect your newly installed DVD drive and
▼ install the proper drivers (a feature known as "Plug and Play"). If you are running

Windows NT, check the documentation accompanying the drive for instructions on installing the proper driver and software.

10. Replace your PC's cover. Plug in the PC and turn it on. If your kit comes with sample DVDs, pop one in and see how it looks. If your kit doesn't include one or more sample DVDs, it's time to make a trip to your local video rental store.

FIGURE 13.5

Insert the decoder card into an empty slot on your motherboard.

FIGURE 13.6

Connect the video loopback cable from the decoder card to your existing video card.

13

DVD Recordable/Rewritable Drives

So far, we've talked only about DVD drives that operate on a read-only format. But DVD drives are also available in recordable and rewritable formats. Do a little research on the Internet and you will discover that there are three competing formats that allow you to record your own DVDs: DVD-RAM, DVD-R, and DVD-RW. Table 13.1 shows the differences between these three formats.

TABLE 13.1   Comparison of DVD Formats

Format	Description	Capacity/Side	Possible Rewrites
DVD-RAM	Random access storage similar to floppy disk or CD-RW.	2.6GB/side	100,000
DVD-R	Write-once. Provides sequential write, similar to CD-R. No overwrite capability.	3.95GB/side	0
DVD-RW	Limited sequential rewritability.	3.95GB/side	1,000

Needless to say, the three competing formats are not compatible. For now, most experts believe that the DVD-RAM format has the edge because of price and functionality, but you will note that this format also offers the smallest storage capacity. For now, it is best to wait a little longer and let one of the three formats rise as the dominant format, much the same way that VHS beat out Beta in the VCR wars some years ago.

Summary

In this hour, you learned about DVD drives, what features are important to look for when selecting a new DVD upgrade kit, and how to install the upgrade kit in your PC. You also learned the current status of recordable/rewritable DVD formats.

Q&A

Q Because DVD drives can also play CDs, doesn't it make sense to simply remove my old CD-ROM drive and just use my DVD drive for both CDs and DVDs?

A You could do that, but if you have a relatively new CD-ROM drive (one purchased in the last year or so), your DVD drive may be a bit slower than your CD-ROM drive. If you have a relatively new CD-ROM drive, chances are it operates at speeds around 50x–56x. Chances are your DVD drive will operate somewhere in the range of 6x–24x. However, the speeds of the two devices are not measured the same. CD-ROM 1x speed is 150Kbps/sec whereas DVD 1x speed is 1.32MB/sec. Do the math and you will see that a 56x CD-ROM drive is slightly faster than a 6x DVD drive (8.4Mbps versus 7.92Mbps). But a 12x DVD drive is almost twice as fast as a 56x CD-ROM drive (15.8Mbps versus 8.4Mbps). If you're using the drives to install software from CDs, you may gain a few seconds in your busy life. However, if your CD drive is a CD-RW, speed is not your only concern.

13

HOUR 14

Adding a Removable Media Drive

Another category of devices that remain popular with PC users is read/write removable media drives. Excluding CD-RW, optical disk drives, and floppy disk drives, there are basically two types of mainstream removable media drives: tape backup drives and removable disk drives (removable disk drives that mimic floppy or hard disk drives).

Even though we are including tape drives in this category, when we mention removable media drives, most users think of the types of drives that mimic the functionality of floppy or hard disk drives and give users a source of cheap (or cheaper), unlimited file storage and backup.

During this hour, you will learn the following:

- The different types of removable media drives and how most are used primarily as backup devices
- About the types of tape drives available for use on PCs
- How to install an internal removable media drive
- How to install an external removable media drive

Removable Hard Disk Drives

Removable hard disk drives have become extremely popular in the past several years. The price of these drives has dropped, and some models duplicate the performance of standard hard disk drives while giving the user the potential for unlimited disk storage and the ability to quickly back up data.

Two of the biggest players in the removable hard disk market are Iomega (see Figure 14.1) and SyQuest (see Figure 14.2).

FIGURE 14.1

Iomega, one of the largest manufacturers of removable hard disk drives.

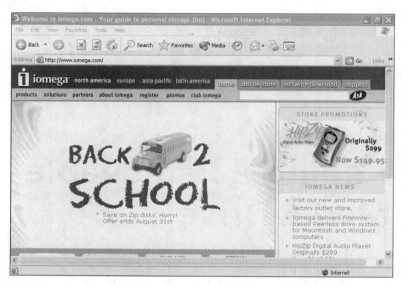

The Iomega Zip Drive

Iomega (http://www.iomega.com/) and SyQuest (http://www.syquest.com/)make the most popular removable hard disk drives. Both companies produce low-end and high-end models. Iomega produces the most popular low-end model—the Zip drive (see Figure 14.3).

Zip drive cartridges are capable of storing 100–250MB of data, and the drives are available in both internal and external models. The external models use either a SCSI, USB, or parallel port interface. The internal models use either a SCSI or IDE interface. Zip drives are typically installed as a backup device because their performance (that is, their speed and capacity) is not quite up to par with standard hard disk drives, especially the models using an IDE or parallel port interface, which are somewhat slower than the SCSI models.

FIGURE 14.2

SyQuest, another large player in the removable hard disk market.

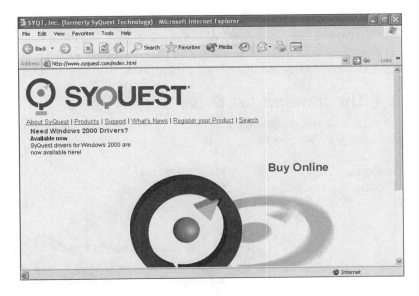

FIGURE 14.3

An external model of the new Iomega USB Zip 250 drive.

You install the SCSI models using the same procedures as you would to install a SCSI CD-ROM drive (see Hour 12, "Upgrading or Adding a CD-ROM/CD-RW Drive"). The IDE model Zip drive installs the same as an IDE model CD-ROM/CD-RW drive. To install a Zip drive with a parallel port interface (available only as an external model), you merely plug the drive into your parallel port and install the software.

14

Some computer manufacturers have started offering Zip drives as a replacement for a standard floppy disk drive. Although some users find this arrangement satisfactory, many experts think this option is still a bit premature because Zip drives still have not achieved universal status and they do not read or write existing 1.44MB 3 1/2-inch disks.

The Iomega Jaz Drive

Iomega also manufactures the most popular high-end model removable hard disk drive— the Jaz drive (see Figure 14.4).

FIGURE 14.4

The Iomega Jaz drive.

The original Jaz drive used a cartridge capable of storing 1GB of data, and its performance closely rivaled that of standard hard disk drives. To achieve this kind of performance, the Jaz drive is available with a SCSI, USB, or Firewire interface. In late 1997, Iomega released a new model of its Jaz drive to counter competition from SyQuest.

The SyQuest model, the SyJet, equals the performance of the original Jaz drive and uses a cartridge capable of storing 1.5GB of data. To regain its top position, Iomega introduced a new model of its Jaz drive, which also uses a SCSI, USB, or Firewire interface, and employs a cartridge capable of storing 2GB of data.

Because both the Jaz models and the SyJet drive equal the performance of many hard disk drives, it is possible to use them in place of standard hard disk drives. You install them the same as you would any other internal SCSI or external SCSI, USB, or Firewire device (see Hour 10, "Replacing, Upgrading, or Adding a Hard Disk Drive").

You can also install Jaz or SyJet drives as your primary hard disk drive, an option that enables you to switch operating systems as easily as you switch disk cartridges. To boot up your PC using either a Jaz or SyJet drive, you must make sure that you set the SCSI ID number to 0. And just like booting up a standard SCSI hard disk drive, you cannot combine SCSI and IDE hard disk drives in the same PC and boot up the SCSI drive.

The SyQuest SyJet 1.5 Gigabyte Drive

The SyJet (see Figure 14.5) is SyQuest's high-end drive. It comes in SCSI (external), IDE (internal), and parallel port (external) versions. Its performance is roughly comparable to the Iomega Jaz drive in the same configuration (that is, IDE, SCSI, or parallel).

FIGURE 14.5

The SyQuest SyJet removable media drive.

The SyQuest SparQ 1 Gigabyte Drive

The SparQ (see Figure 14.6) is SyQuest's middle-level drive. SyQuest manufactures the SparQ in only IDE and parallel port versions. The performance of the SparQ is roughly comparable to Iomega's IDE and parallel port Jaz models.

The SyQuest EZFlyer Drive

The third model in the SyQuest lineup of removable media drives is the EZFlyer (see Figure 14.7). The EZFlyer is SyQuest's low-end model targeted against the Iomega Zip drive. The EZFlyer comes in four different configurations:

- SCSI (internal and external)
- IDE (internal)
- parallel port (external)

14

FIGURE 14.6
FIGURE 14.6
The SyQuest SparQ removable media drive.

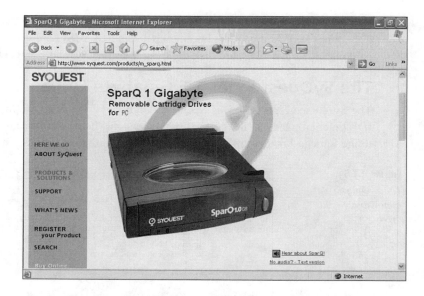

FIGURE 14.7
The SyQuest EZFlyer removable media drive.

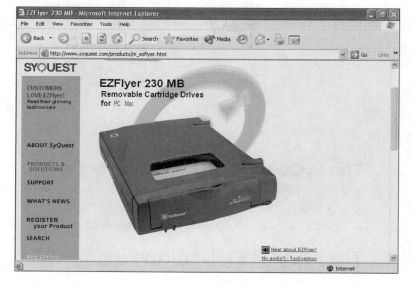

Other Removable Disk Options

Don't think for one second that if you want to add a removable disk to your PC that Iomega and SyQuest are the only games in town. They aren't, even though they do command the lion's share of removable disk market.

Other companies attempting to carve out their piece of this niche market include Sony, Castlewood Systems, and several manufacturers of the LS-120 drive.

Sony HiFD

Sony released a removable media drive positioned as a replacement for your 1.44MB floppy disk drive. Sony calls its 200MB drive HiFD (see Figure 14.8).

FIGURE 14.8
Sony's HiFD removable disk drive— a 200MB replacement for your floppy disk drive.

Sony is attempting to carve out a portion of the low-end removable disk market with its HiFD drive (http://www.ita.sel.sony.com/jump/hifd/index.html). In addition to providing 200MB of storage on each disk, the HiFD drives are also capable of reading and writing to standard 3 1/2-inch, 1.44MB floppy disk drives. So far, Sony has not made much of a dent in the Zip drive market because many analysts think the HiFD drive is over-priced despite its impressive performance.

Castlewood Systems

Castlewood Systems (http://www.castlewood.com/)is a company attempting to dethrone Iomega's Jaz drives from the top of the high-end removable disk market. The company produces the ORB, a 2.2GB removable disk drive priced considerably under Iomega's Jaz disk cartridges (see Figure 14.9).

Despite its extremely aggressive pricing, the ORB is not yet making a noticeable dent in Iomega's Jaz market most likely because Castlewood doesn't pour as much as Iomega into its advertising budget.

14

FIGURE 14.9

The Castlewood Systems' ORB removable disk drive.

The LS-120 Drive

The LS-120 is another removable media drive you may have heard about. The LS-120 is made by several manufacturers and looks very similar to a standard 3 1/2-inch floppy disk drive. The LS-120, as the name implies, uses a disk with a capacity of 120MB in addition to being able to read and write to standard 3 1/2-inch 1.44MB floppy disks. The LS-120 is mostly sold as an internal model with an IDE interface but can also be purchased as an external model that connects to a parallel port.

The LS-120 is a good replacement option for the standard 3 1/2-inch drive, considering that it is bootable. Some PC manufacturers, such as Gateway and Compaq, also offer it as a replacement for the standard floppy drive.

Tape Backup Drives

Tape backup drives currently come in an assortment of sizes and capacities. At one time, tape backup drives were almost exclusively used to back up network file servers. Now tape backup drives are growing in popularity among individual computer users. Hard disk drives have grown in size to where it is inconceivable to think of backing them up using floppy disks; tape drives have been following the lead set by hard disk drives and are also dropping in price.

Choosing a tape backup drive is largely a matter of how much you want to spend. An expensive tape backup drive won't back up any better than a cheaper model, but an expensive drive will most likely back up your hard disk faster and use fewer tapes.

Tape drives come as both internal and external models and use both IDE and SCSI interfaces; a few tape drives are available with USB and Firewire interfaces, and some come with their own proprietary interface. There are even external tape drives that plug in to the parallel port on the back of your computer in the same way as Zip drives.

Here are some of the leading manufacturers of tape backup devices:

- **OnStream**—http://www.onstream.com
- **Sony**—http://www.ita.sel.sony.com/
- **Compaq**—http://www.compaq.com/
- **Advance Digital Information Corp.**—http://www.adic.com/
- **Aiwa**—http://www.aiwa.com/
- **APS Technology**—http://www.apstech.com/
- **Artecon, Inc.**—http://www.artecon.com/
- **Exabyte, Inc.**—http://www.exabyte.com/
- **Hewlett-Packard**—http://www.hp.com/
- **IBM**—http://www.ibm.com/
- **MicroSolutions, Inc.**—http://www.micro-solutions.com/

One of the best sources for finding up-to-date information on PC hardware components is the hardware section of CNET's Computers.com (http://computers.cnet.com/hardware/0-1016.html). In addition to listing just about every tape drive (and removable media drive) you could possibly think of, this site also does comparison reviews and allows you to compare prices on the products listed. Where applicable, this site also lists specifications on the products listed and points you to the manufacturer for more information.

If you're looking for more technical information, you should make a point to bookmark Tom's Hardware Guide (http://www.tomshardware.com/).

External Tape Backup Drives

The parallel port and USB-type drives are probably the easiest types of tape drives to install because all you do is plug the drive in to your parallel port and install the tape backup software. You don't have to worry about connecting cables, running your PC's Setup program, or even taking the cover off your PC. The drawback to these types of tape drives is speed—they are among the slowest tape drives on the market. Most users

14

get around this limitation by performing their backups overnight or by dividing their backup procedure into sections that fit onto one tape.

Other external tape drives use a SCSI interface and install pretty much the same way as an external CD-ROM drive (see Hour 12). All you need to do is set the tape drive to use an available SCSI ID number and insert it into your SCSI chain. If you place the drive at the end of the chain, remember to move your terminator.

Internal Tape Backup Drives

Internal tape drives use IDE, SCSI, and proprietary interfaces. Internal drives are installed pretty much the same as internal CD-ROM drives. You must take into account the same considerations, such as an available drive bay, the reach of the interface cable, and so on (see Figure 14.10).

FIGURE 14.10

An internal tape backup drive being inserted into an empty drive bay.

Tape drive data cable

Tape drive power cable

SCSI tape drives are typically faster and more expensive than IDE drives, so take this into consideration when deciding what type to purchase. Remember, too, that with a SCSI drive you need a SCSI interface card, if you don't already have one (see Figure 14.11).

FIGURE 14.11
A SCSI interface card.

When deciding on what type of tape drive to get, pay attention to the storage capacity of the tapes each drive uses (see Figure 14.12).

FIGURE **14.12**
A typical tape backup cartridge.

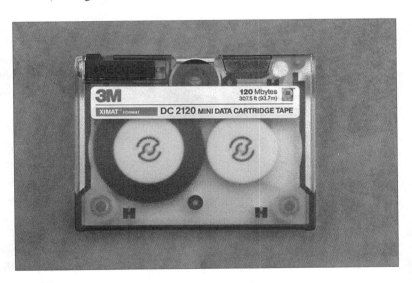

Although the general rule of thumb used to be that you should be able to back up each hard disk drive in your PC with one tape, the size of many of today's mammoth multi-gigabyte drives makes this rule a bit unreasonable. Fortunately, all tape backup software enables you to span a backup session across multiple tapes.

14

Be sure to pay attention to the cost of tape cartridges. Tape cartridge prices vary considerably from manufacturer to manufacturer, and capacity is not always an indicator of cost. Also purchase a tape head cleaner for your tape drive (and be sure to use it as recommended) to make sure that your tape backup unit is always performing in peak condition.

Installing a Removable Media Drive

Removable media drives come in two basic designs—internal models and external models. Internal models connect to either an IDE or SCSI interface inside your PC.

Task: Installing an Internal IDE Removable Media Drive

Installing an internal IDE removable media drive is no more difficult than installing an IDE hard disk drive.

> Just as you did before, when handling any delicate electrical components inside your PC, make sure that you have properly grounded yourself to protect against static electricity.

To install an internal IDE drive, follow these steps:

1. Select a drive bay in your PC that you can use to install the drive. Remove the front panel on the case covering the empty bay if there is one. Make sure that you have an unused power connector you can use to plug in to the drive. If you don't have an unused power connector, go to your local computer store and pick up a Y-connector. Unplug one of your power connectors from another device and attach the Y-connector.

2. On most PCs built in the last four or five years, you find two IDE interfaces, usually labeled *primary* and *secondary* (see Figure 14.13). Your hard disk drive (if you have an IDE hard disk installed in your PC) should be attached with a cable to the interface labeled *primary*. Make sure that you have a cable that will reach from the secondary interface to the bay in which you are installing your new drive.

3. If you have to install any guide rails on the sides of your drive, install them according to the instructions accompanying the drive (see Figure 14.14). If drive rails are not included with your device, but are needed, be sure to pick up a set from your local computer store.

Secondary IDE Interface

FIGURE 14.13
*Primary and secondary
IDE interfaces on the
motherboard.*

Primary IDE Interface

FIGURE 14.14
*Guide rails of various
sizes used for
installing removable
media drives and other
peripheral devices.*

4. Insert the drive into the drive bay and attach the ribbon cable from the secondary
(slave) IDE interface to the 40-pin IDE interface on the rear of the drive.

14

Even though IDE interfaces can accommodate two IDE devices, if you can avoid it, do not connect the removable media drive to the same interface you connect your IDE hard disk drive to. The removable media drive, which is a much slower device than a hard disk drive, will degrade the performance of the hard disk drive.

If your PC has only one IDE interface connector, don't panic. Instead, just make a quick trip to your local computer store and purchase an IDE interface card. It usually runs in the vicinity of $25–$30. Don't worry about it conflicting with any of your existing IRQs or memory addresses. Most manufacturers realize that it is added as a secondary interface and usually assign it IRQs and addresses that would be the same as a secondary interface. Just remember, when in doubt, ask the salesperson or the store's in-house technical guru.

5. After you have everything connected to your drive, go ahead and adjust your drive so that it's even with the front opening of the drive bay. Tighten the screws to secure your drive in place.

6. Just as you did when you installed your hard disk drive in Hour 10, you will probably have to run some type of software installation disk to install the appropriate driver, depending on the operating system you are running. If you are running Windows 98/2000/Me/XP, when you restart your PC, Windows should automatically detect your newly installed removable media drive and install the proper driver (a feature known as Plug and Play).

In addition to a hardware driver for your drive, the disk that comes with your removable media drive also includes a number of utilities for your drive. These utilities will vary from manufacturer to manufacturer.

Installing an Internal SCSI Removable Media Drive

Installing an internal SCSI removable media drive is almost exactly the same as installing an internal IDE drive. The cable is a bit different, and just as you do when installing a SCSI hard disk drive, you must set the SCSI ID on the removable media drive according to the instructions that came with your drive. Remember, too, that the SCSI ID of the drive (0–6) has to be unique.

> All SCSI devices, such as hard disk drives and removable media drives, leave the factory with a preset SCSI ID, which in most cases you can leave as is. Just be sure to check that the ID set on the device isn't an ID you are already using on your SCSI chain. Two devices on a SCSI chain with the same ID will not operate.

Remember to check the termination on your SCSI chain. Some SCSI removable media drives come with a factory-installed terminator. If your removable media drive is not placed at the end of your SCSI chain, you'll have to remove the factory-installed terminator or the devices on the chain after the removable media drive will not operate. Check your removable media drive documentation on how to remove the terminator. In many cases, you simply have to remove a jumper.

Installing an External Removable Media Drive

External removable media drives offer you a few more choices depending on what configuration each manufacturer decides to offer. External models can attach to a SCSI, parallel, USB, Firewire, or USB port on your PC.

> If you select a removable media drive that connects to your USB port, make sure that your operating system will support a USB port. Windows 98, 2000, Me, and XP support USB. Windows 95 supports USB ports only with the proper upgrades. Windows NT does not support USB.

14

To install your external removable media drive, simply plug it in to the appropriate connection port on your PC and then run the accompanying software to install the appropriate hardware driver. Remember, if you are installing a SCSI external removable media drive, be sure to check the SCSI ID to make sure that it is not already being used by another device on your SCSI chain. If your drive is at the end of your SCSI chain, make sure that it is properly terminated. In most cases, the drive comes with a terminator, and your documentation will explain how to activate the terminator.

Tips for Getting the Most Out of Your Backup Drive

Whether you use a tape drive or a removable media drive as your backup unit, here are a few tips for getting the most out of your backup system:

- *(Extremely Important)* After you install your backup system, be sure to test it. Make sure that you fully understand how to back up the files on your hard disk drives. Be sure to test the restore procedure as well as the backup procedure. Try restoring a few files to a temporary directory.

- If you use a backup tape drive, make sure that you purchase top-quality tapes. Remember, the tapes you buy are your only insurance against disaster. Just as you wouldn't want to trust a cheap, cut-rate parachute, don't trust cheap, cut-rate backup tapes.

- Don't overuse your tapes. Tapes are a much more fragile medium than are hard disk drives. Tapes do wear out with extensive use. Extra tapes are a lot cheaper than the time it takes to replace unrecoverable data. Ten times is probably the maximum number of times you should use a tape.

- Create a backup schedule and stick to it. This way, you know which backup tape contains the data you are looking for.

- Tape backup drives require regular maintenance. Be sure to read the documentation and perform whatever routine maintenance the manufacturer prescribes, including regularly cleaning the read/write heads of your tape drive.

Summary

In this hour, you learned about many of the options available to you if you decide to add a removable media drive to your PC. You learned about both high-end and low-end drives and about the selection of interfaces each model uses.

Q&A

Q Why are all the drives that use a parallel port interface so slow?

A Because the parallel port was not designed to pass a data stream very quickly. The parallel port was designed as a standard output port to pass data bits in parallel sequence, eight bits at a time, to devices such as printers.

Q If it is so slow, then why is the parallel port used at all?

A The parallel port is used as an interface because every PC has one and every parallel port works just like every other parallel port. It is a standard interface that does not require any configuration on the part of the user, and it works on every PC just as it comes out of the box. Attaching drives to IDE or SCSI ports requires the user to perform some degree of configuration to make them work. The parallel port is literally Plug and Play at its easiest, but you pay a price—speed.

Q Can you consider the USB port, available on most newer PCs, a good alternative interface?

A The USB port is a good alternative interface because it is now standard on newer PCs. The only problem with USB ports is making sure that you are using an operating system that supports USB.

14

PART IV

Upgrading Your Communications Devices

Hour

Hour **15**

Upgrading Your Modem

Modems are like larger monitors: items formerly considered an extravagance but that have long since been seen as standard equipment. Originally brought to prominence by online services such as CompuServe and AOL, the modem became indispensable with the rise in popularity of the Internet.

Modem technology used to be one of the fastest developing computer technologies and, consequently, one that seemed to demand a continuing cycle of upgrades. But with the development of 56K modems, this technology seems to have reached its technological limit over standard telephone lines.

If you're considering upgrading your modem, this hour should prove valuable to you in deciding whether to get a 56K modem or one of the other newer communications technologies.

During this hour, you will learn:

- How modems work
- Whether you want to upgrade your existing modem to a 56K modem
- Whether you want to try one of the alternative digital communications technologies such as ISDN, ADSL, or cable modems

Understanding Modems

Modem is short for MOdulate/DEModulate, which is what a modem does to send and receive data from one computer to another. Your computer stores data in digital form. But standard telephone lines transmit information as sound, which is an analog signal. The modem in your computer system converts the digital information in your computer to an analog (sound) signal and transmits the analog signal over telephone lines to another computer. The modem there converts the analog signal that your computer transmitted back into a digital form (see Figure 15.1).

FIGURE 15.1

How modems modulate and then demodulate signals between PCs.

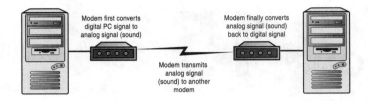

Modem first converts digital PC signal to analog signal (sound)

Modem finally converts analog signal (sound) back to digital signal

Modem transmits analog signal (sound) to another modem

Analog and *digital* are terms used quite freely and they have taken on several popular meanings. In the context of computer communications, analog refers to communicating by means of converting the signal in your computer to a measurable frequency and modulation, which happens to be sound waves. Digital refers to communicating by means of transmitting your message using a representation of the binary symbols 0 and 1 just as they are created in your PC.

Most standard modems today transmit data in the range of 28,800–56,000bps (bits per second). Don't be surprised (or disappointed) if you purchase a modem advertised to operate in this range but only get a maximum transmission speed of between 26,400bps and 50,000bps. Modem transmissions at higher speeds are largely governed by the quality of your telephone lines. Telephone lines for the most part are simply unshielded, twisted copper wire and are extremely vulnerable to interference from a variety of sources. Interference reduces the audio quality of the call you are making to your mother (whether you notice it or not), and reduces the transmission speed of your modem as well.

Selecting a Modem

Modems are available in both internal and external models. An internal modem is installed inside your PC (see Figure 15.2) and requires a slot on your motherboard. An external modem (see Figure 15.3) plugs in to one of your serial ports (using a serial cable).

15

FIGURE 15.2

An internal modem.

FIGURE 15.3

An external modem.

One question many beginning modem users continue to ask is "What type of modem do I need to access AOL (America Online)?" The answer is simple—virtually any type of modem enables you to access AOL. AOL is designed to accommodate a wide range of PC systems and modem types, and you should be able to find a communications line ranging in speeds from 9600bps up to ISDN speeds of 128,000bps (although the recommended minimum speed is 14,000bps). If you are having trouble with your modem, give AOL technical support a call. That's part of what you're paying for each month.

Functionally, you do not see any differences between an internal and an external modem; both operate exactly the same. When deciding which type to purchase, consider that an internal modem generally costs less than an external modem because it lacks a case and a power supply, but it takes up a slot in your PC. Both internal and external modems require an interrupt (IRQ) signal from your PC (the internal modem requires its own interrupt, whereas the external modem uses the interrupt signal assigned to the serial port the modem is connected to).

Again, in deciding on a brand, you might want to refer to product reviews by the popular trade magazines. Although all brands that adhere to the various international specifications for modems operate, theoretically, at the same speed, there are some differences in how certain modems handle error correction. As I mentioned earlier, modems use standard telephone lines that are subject to interference from various sources. When a transmitted signal encounters interference, the modem attempts to resend the portion of the signal that encountered the interference. Different manufacturers use different methods for detecting and correcting interference, and these methods can result in some variance in actual transmission speeds.

When you're in the market for a new modem, one of the best sources for finding up-to-date information on PC hardware components is the hardware section of CNET's computers.com (`http://computers.cnet.com/hardware/0-1016.html`). In addition to listing just about every modem you could possibly think of, this site also does comparison reviews and allows you to compare prices on the products listed. Where applicable, this site also lists specifications on the products listed and points you to the manufacturer for more information. If you're looking for more technical information, you should also make a point of bookmarking Tom's Hardware Guide (`http://www.tomshardware.com/`).

And finally, if you select an internal modem, be sure to check whether the modem must be inserted into an ISA or a PCI slot (see Hour 8, "Replacing Your Main System Board," for information on the differences between ISA and PCI slots). Internal modems used to all be designed for ISA slots, but in the last few years many manufacturers have started switching to internal modems that are inserted into PCI slots. This is mainly because many motherboard manufacturers have started to reduce the number of ISA slots installed on motherboards on their way to total elimination of ISA slots and boards.

Installing Your Modem

The only difference between installing an internal modem and installing an external modem is what you do with the hardware. The software you install with your modem—the modem hardware driver and the communications software you plan to use with your modem—is exactly the same.

Installing an Internal Modem

Installing an internal modem is fairly simple because all you have to do is insert the modem into one of your available motherboard slots and then configure your PC or operating system to recognize the modem.

> If you are running Windows 98/2000/Me/XP on your PC, make sure that any internal modem you purchase is designated Plug and Play (PnP). Plug and Play is a Windows 98/2000/Me/XP feature that enables the operating system to automatically detect and configure your modem to work with your PC. Plug and Play is not available in Windows NT 4.0.

▼ To Do

Task: Installing an Internal Modem

To install an internal modem, do the following:

1. Read the documentation that accompanies your modem thoroughly before you begin to install the modem. Check the documentation for your modem to determine whether there is a certain communications port (COM1, COM2, and so on) that your modem prefers to use. Check also to see whether there are any switches or jumpers you must set for the communications port you will be using. If you have jumpers on your modem, they are used to set your modem to use one of your two main serial ports, COM1 or COM2. If you are running Windows 98/2000/Me/XP and your modem is Plug and Play, you can skip this step. If you have to set your modem by setting a jumper, make sure that you are not setting your modem to use a serial port that is being used by another device, such as a serial mouse. This will create a device conflict and neither device will function properly. You can check for interrupt conflicts using the SysChk utility (see Hour 3,

▼

▼ "Examining Your PC's System Configuration," for information about using SysChk).

> Communications ports are connection points your computer uses for communicating with some peripheral devices. Most computers have three basic types of communications ports: serial, parallel, and USB. The major difference between the three types of ports is in how they communicate. A parallel port transmits data eight bits at a time. A serial port communicates data one bit at a time, and a USB port is basically just a faster serial port. Your computer typically uses parallel ports to communicate with printers. Serial ports are used primarily for communicating with modems (and other serial devices) and are often referred to as COM (short for communications) ports. Your computer is designed to operate with two main serial ports, COM1 and COM2, but can be configured to have more COM ports.

2. Turn off your PC, unplug the cord from the wall or power supply, ground yourself to prevent static electricity discharges, remove the cover, and insert your modem into an empty slot (see Figure 15.4).

FIGURE **15.4**
Inserting an internal modem in your PC.

3. Follow the instructions for installing any additional software that came with your modem. Make sure that you follow the instructions specifically for the operating system you are running.

▲ 4. Make a note of which communications port you use in installing your modem.

Installing an External Modem

External modems are even easier to install than internal modems.

To Do

Task: Installing an External Modem

To install an external modem, follow these steps:

1. Turn off your PC.

2. Plug one end of your serial cable into an unused serial or USB port on the back of your PC; plug the other end into the serial or USB connector on your modem.

3. Turn on your modem and then turn on your PC.

4. Follow the instructions for installing any additional software driver that came with your modem for the operating system you are running.

5. Make a note of the communications port used by your modem when you install the modem driver.

Why Doesn't My 56K Modem Transmit at 56K?

56KB modems communicate over the same phone lines as the modem you were previously using, which means that if you experienced any degree of interference with your previous modem, the interference problem only gets worse because a 56KB modem is more sensitive and susceptible to any transmission line interference.

For example, if you were previously using a 33.6KB modem but you almost always connected at 28.8KB or slower, you most likely will connect at speeds far slower than 56KB with your new 56KB modem. Another fact you need to be aware of is that in all product testing reviews I have read by the major trade journals, I have never read one where a 56KB modem was tested and achieved transmission speeds of 56KB. Most of the test reports stated transmission speeds of around 36–44KB, and this was only in one direction.

If you read the small print on the boxes of all 56KB modems, you see that 56KB transmission speeds are (theoretically) attainable only when downloading information from a host computer. When uploading, or transmitting data to a host computer, the transmission speed is only (theoretically) 33.6KB.

Alternatives to Standard Modems

One of the problems mentioned earlier with modems is that they transmit an analog signal (sound) over standard phone lines and are subject to interference, which results in a degradation of signal and transmission speed. Alternatives to modems and analog signals do exist. For example, you can get fully digital communications lines, which are not subject to the same interference and signal degradation as analog modems. If you decide you want to investigate digital communications lines, start by checking with your local Baby Bell or your cable TV provider to see whether they are providing digital or broadband service.

ISDN

A technology that has been around for a lot longer than 56KB modems, but continues to receive far less press coverage, is *ISDN*.

> *ISDN* stands for *Integrated Services Digital Network* and is a way of getting reliable communications speeds above 33.6KB using digital telephone lines, instead of the analog lines used for typical phone communication and standard modems. For connecting to the Internet at speeds of either 64KB or 128KB in both directions with the host computer, ISDN is almost universally available in the United States.

On the plus side, ISDN works over digital telephone lines instead of your standard analog, voice-grade lines, which means they are not susceptible to interference as are analog lines. Being digital means that, on an ISDN line, you will always get speeds of 64KB (or 128KB)—in both directions!

On the minus side, however, ISDN has a lot that has kept it from being widely embraced. For starters, you need to have a special ISDN communications line installed by your telephone company. The actual line is the same copper wire the phone company uses for standard telephone lines, but it is connected differently at your end and at the phone company's switching office. Prices for ISDN have been steadily coming down over the past few years, but prices still vary around the country and can be expensive for installation and monthly service. You can expect to pay in the range of $50–$250 for installation of your line. Monthly charges also vary considerably. Some Baby Bells charge you a flat monthly rate; some offer you a tiered system of varying flat rate for a certain maximum number of hours; and some simply charge you by the minute for actual usage. ISDN is now almost exclusively available from the Baby Bells because most other ISPs that provide digital service are opting for DSL or cable modems (see

Hour 16, "Adding a Cable or DSL Modem"); for this reason, ISDN has sort of fallen out of favor and may soon disappear except for some special or niche applications.

You also need a special ISDN interface—either an internal card or an external device—to access your ISDN line.

> ISDN interface cards and devices are often incorrectly called ISDN modems, but they are not true modems because they do not convert a signal from digital to analog (or vice versa) as modems do. The term *modem* is used because it is almost universally understood as being a type of communications device. The same misnomer has been applied to "cable modems" and "DSL modems."

ISDN interface cards and devices have also been dropping in price and currently range between $100 and $300. If you have an empty slot in your case, it is best to get the internal interface card. The internal ISDN devices are cheaper because the external devices need a case or power supply. In addition, internal ISDN devices attain a slightly faster speed than do the external devices. The external ISDN device plugs into a serial port (the same way an external modem does), but standard serial ports can achieve speeds of only 115KB, which means that your ISDN device can achieve speeds of only 115KB rather than the advertised 128KB.

ISDN has been extremely popular in small offices because at speeds of 128KB, ISDN connections make it possible to provide Internet connections to multiple users simultaneously. For small offices, ISDN devices are combined with devices used to form small networks.

ADSL

ADSL is another digital service that continues to get a lot of press. ADSL stands for *Asymmetrical Digital Subscriber Line* and is a digital technology providing up to 7.1Mbps of transmission speed from the host computer to your computer and 64Kbps of speed from your computer to the host.

As is ISDN, ADSL is a digital signal that is not subject to line noise or interference, which means you always have a transmission signal operating at 7.1Mbps (downstream) and 64Kbps (upstream).

ADSL, most often marketed as simply DSL, is still not widely available in most parts of this country, but availability is expanding. My phone service provider, Verizon, is still providing spotty ADSL coverage in its service area, but at least it is here.

ADSL works over your existing phone lines but requires some additional hardware. The first device you need is called the ADSL Terminal Unit-Remote (ATU-R)—a unit often referred to as the "ADSL modem." You also need an Ethernet network interface card installed in your PC to connect to your ADSL modem. Note that there is a distance limitation to connecting ADSL to your home. You must live within about 12,000 feet (about 2 miles) of your local telephone switching office (the distance limitation for ISDN is about 3 miles). For more on ADSL and connecting an ADSL modem to your PC see Hour 16.

Cable Modems

Cable modems are an attempt by the cable TV industry to cash in on the phenomenal popularity of the Internet. The cable modem system is a shared system operating at a reported 10Mbps.

If you work on a networked computer at work that is connected to the Internet, you are already familiar with the downside of a shared system. Regardless of how fast the transmission is, you are sharing it with other users, which means your communications begin to slow down as more people simultaneously log in to the system.

The "shared" nature of the cable modem communications line also means that additional security problems exist unless the provider takes some steps to eliminate or remove them.

Regardless of security issues, the cable modem guys seem to be doing a booming business providing coverage in areas inaccessible (because of distance) by DSL providers. Chances are cable modem will be available in your area before DSL is.

For more on cable modems and connecting a cable modem to your PC, see Hour 16.

Summary

In this hour, you learned how modems work, were presented with information you'll need to make a selection on an upgrade modem, and should have decided whether you want to upgrade to a 56KB modem. You also learned about some of the digital communications alternatives to analog modems, such as ISDN, ADSL, and cable modems.

Q&A

15

Q How can 56KB modems be sold as 56KB modems if they cannot achieve 56Kbps transmission speeds?

A As the technology was being developed, the design engineers did achieve speeds of 56Kbps, but these were under laboratory conditions—that is, pristine copper wires, absolutely no line interference, and so on. Unfortunately, the real world does not work that way, and in the real world, we have interference, line noise, and 30–40-year-old copper wires still being used by the phone companies. In other words, they developed the technology under conditions that don't exist in the real world.

Q Which is better, ADSL or cable modems?

A Both have their pluses and minuses. Cable modems are generally cheaper and don't have the distance limitations of ADSL. ADSL, on the other hand, offers you a connection line that isn't being shared by your neighbors and is generally more secure. If you have the choice and the cost of ADSL won't break your budget, you may be happier with ADSL.

HOUR 16

Adding a Cable or DSL Modem

Most motorists, if given the opportunity, would gladly trade in their Geo Prisms or Volkswagen Beetles for a 16-cylinder Ferrari Barchetta. The analogy is the same when PC users are asked to choose between continuing with an analog (56K) modem or upgrading to a cable or DSL modem-based, high-speed Internet connection.

Here's the way most users describe their Internet sessions when they switch from an analog modem to a cable or DSL modem: *it's like going from first gear to warp ten!*

It's easy to understand the burst of enthusiasm!

Instead of puttering along the Internet at 40–50Kbps with your old analog modem, you can be warping through cyberspace at somewhere between 640–10,000Kbps! Pages that once took 10–20 seconds to load now appear almost instantly. Files that once took more than an hour to download now download in a few minutes. But quickly downloading pages and files is not the only reason to upgrade to a cable or DSL modem. The high speeds available with cable and DSL modems also make high-bandwidth Web site animation viewable and enjoyable and make it feasible to enjoy the higher resolutions required for streaming video and audio.

But enough about how fast you can go and how fast things will happen after you upgrade to a high-speed Internet connection. We're here to discuss what you have to do to get the high-speed connection up and running with your system.

During this hour, you will learn the following:

- How cable modems and DSL modems work
- How to select a cable or DSL broadband Internet service
- How to install your high-speed Internet connection
- What additional security measures you have to take with a high-speed Internet connection

Understanding a High-Speed Internet Connection

Cable and DSL modems and the high-speed connections they originate from are what we call *broadband communications*. *Broadband* is a type of data transmission in which a single transmission medium can carry multiple channels. Cable modems are attached to the same coaxial (coax) cable that brings cable TV into your living room; DSL modems are connected to the same copper wires that provide your basic telephone service.

Both cable and DSL broadband providers use the term *modem* to describe their communications device even though they do not actually modulate and demodulate digital signals to analog sound as true modems do. Because "modem" is a term familiar to most computer users as a type of communications device, the name has stuck.

Just as you can watch cable TV at the same time you can surf the Web with a cable modem connection, you can likewise talk on the telephone at the same time you surf the Web using your DSL connection.

The diagram in Figure 16.1 shows the basic setup for both cable and DSL broadband services. As the diagram shows, broadband service is provided from either your cable TV provider or your local telephone company.

FIGURE 16.1

How cable and DSL broadband services connect to your PC.

Internet   Broadband Service Provider   Standard telephone cable or coax cable   Cable or DSL Modem   Ethernet cable   PC with Ethernet Card

16

 Even though several companies might be offering to provide DSL service in your area, ultimately those companies are purchasing the service from the phone company, repackaging it, and then selling it to you.

With both DSL and cable service, you must install an Ethernet card in your PC and connect it to either the cable modem or DSL modem using what is called an Ethernet or *Cat5 (Category 5) cable*.

 A Cat5, or Category 5, cable meets the electrical specifications for conducting network data communications up to 100Mbps. Simply put, it is an unshielded, twisted-pair cable consisting of eight wires twisted together with an RJ-45 connector on each end. Although it may sound very technical and possibly expensive, it's not. You can purchase a Cat5 cable for a few dollars at any computer store such as CompUSA, Best Buy, Circuit City, or Radio Shack.

How a Cable Modem Works

The cable TV system was originally designed to be a one-way system—the cable TV company would send a multi-channel television signal downstream to each customer's home. Coax cable was originally chosen as the medium for the cable TV signal because a single coax cable has sufficient bandwidth to carry several hundred megahertz of broadcast (television) signals. Each television channel requires only a 6MHz slice of the available bandwidth to reach the TV in your home.

To include Internet capability over that same coax cable, the cable companies have to include equipment that allows two-way communications over the system. The cable company has to upgrade the cable system to include a Cable-Modem Termination

System (CMTS) at the provider's end of the cable system. The company also has to include a cable modem on the customer's end of the cable system. To send data downstream to the customer, the cable company simply packages the signal into one of the available 6MHz slices of bandwidth in the coax cable. The Internet signal looks like just another channel on the cable TV system. To transmit the return signal (the upstream signal from the customer), only a 2MHz slice of the available bandwidth is reserved. The cable company assumes that most customers will be downloading a lot more data than they will be uploading—a fairly safe assumption for most home users. Just remember that even though the upload signal is slower than the download signal, the upload signal here is still considerably faster than the typical dial-up signal.

The majority of cable modems in use in the United States follow the Data Over Cable Service Interface Specifications (DOCSIS) protocol. The cable modem contains a small tuner to separate the channel carrying Internet (network) traffic from the remaining cable TV channels and electronics to convert the RF (radio frequency) cable signal back into a digital signal. The cable modem also keeps the downstream and upstream channels and traffic separate.

How a DSL Modem Works

Digital Subscriber Line (DSL) can be offered in several different service configurations:

- **ADSL**—Asymmetric Digital Subscriber Line
- **R-ADSL**—Rate-Adaptive Digital Subscriber Line
- **HDSL**—High Bit-rate Digital Subscriber Line
- **VDSL**—Very High Bit-rate Digital Subscriber Line
- **SDSL**—Symmetric Digital Subscriber Line

The vast majority of the home DSL service in this country is offered as ADSL service because the upstream transmission rate is usually considerably slower than the downstream transmission rate. DSL providers make the same assumptions about customer usage as do their cable broadband service counterparts—that customers typically download a lot more data than they upload.

DSL broadband service uses the same lines as your normal telephone service, which means that you will not need to have a new line installed to your home to subscribe to DSL service.

The telephone service you use in your home every day comes in over a simple pair of copper wires. This pair of copper wires is capable of supporting much higher-quality audio than is currently provided, but because the phone service is not overly concerned with providing high fidelity in the audio quality of normal voice conversations, not much of the available bandwidth is used. DSL takes advantage of the unused bandwidth available in twisted-pair copper wires to literally piggy-back its signal on the same telephone line used for normal voice conversations.

There are two competing and incompatible standards for delivering ADSL broadband service—the official ANSI standard, Discrete Multitone (DMT), used by the vast majority of DSL broadband providers, and Carrierless Amplitude Phase (CAP), used by a few early ADSL providers. Both types of ADSL service work by converting data to higher frequency signals than those used for voice communications (which is why when you subscribe to DSL broadband service for your home, your provider supplies you with line filters to attach to all the lines with telephones). The line filters filter out the higher frequency data signal.

Differences and Similarities in Cable and DSL Broadband

In addition to the faster communication speeds available with both broadband services, the major similarity between the two services is that both are always on. You do not have to dial in to your provider as you do with your older analog 56K modem—broadband connections are always connected to your Internet Service Provider.

There are major differences in the communications speeds available with each type of service. Cable modems offer the highest theoretical speed. Depending on your cable provider, speeds can range from 10–30 megabits per second downstream (what you receive) to 0.128–10 megabits per second upstream (what you send). I say the speed is "theoretical" because your transmission speeds largely depend on how many of your neighbors also have cable broadband service. Cable broadband has what is called *shared bandwidth*, meaning that the downstream and upstream speeds—or more precisely, the amount of data that can be transmitted each second—is shared by all the cable broadband subscribers. What this means is that as more cable broadband subscribers access the Internet simultaneously, your transmission speeds will slow down.

DSL broadband service is not shared, but it does have its own set of limitations. DSL has a distance limitation. Optimally, your home should be no more than 3.4 miles (5.4 kilometers) from the telephone company central switching office. Within this distance limitation, you can transmit at speeds of 1.5–8 megabits per second downstream (what you receive) to 0.090–1.544 megabits per second upstream (what you send). ADSL providers will often offer several different subscription packages that differ in the maximum transmission speeds available.

How to Obtain Cable or DSL Broadband Service

Whether or not you can get cable or DSL broadband service depends on whether it is available in your geographic area. Cable broadband service is available only through your cable TV provider. This means that you have only one choice for cable broadband service because local municipalities award cable TV franchise rights to only one cable TV provider (read "exclusivity"—there's no competition).

DSL broadband service, which ultimately comes from your telephone company, can be offered by a variety of companies because of federal law that forces the Regional Bell Operating Companies (RBOCs), otherwise known as the "Baby Bells," to resell DSL service. Because you can have several companies offering competing DSL packages, you can shop around for your best deal. Just remember that despite who you mail your check to each month, the service is ultimately coming from the phone company. In some cases, this arrangement can be a plus because the phone company may offer you certain incentives to purchase directly from them. For example, I purchase my DSL service directly from Verizon (which used to be Bell Atlantic). Part of the package I have is that Verizon is also my ISP. As part of the inducement to get me to purchase DSL and ISP service from the same company, Verizon charges me $39 a month for DSL service and only $10 a month for ISP service.

> The company that provides you with broadband service does not necessarily have to be your ISP. The company that provides the broadband service is only providing a physical connection to the Internet. Your ISP provides the actual Internet services, such as WWW, e-mail, Usenet (newsgroups), and so on.

Before you pull out your checkbook, you should address one other consideration before getting DSL. As mentioned earlier, DSL has a distance limitation: You have to live within 3.4 miles of the telephone company's central switching office. Some companies will install DSL beyond this distance but will advise you that your connections speeds will be slower.

You can consult several Web sites to see whether DSL service is available in your area. All the Baby Bells allow you to check their sites to see whether DSL service is available for you, but they don't mention any competing companies that may be reselling DSL. Here is a short list of Web sites you can check for DSL and cable broadband availability and miscellaneous information:

- `http://www.dslplus.com/`
- `http://compnetworking.about.com/cs/dslavailability/`
- `http://www.teamits.com/internet/?/internet/dsl/dslform.html`
- `http://www.k2net.cc/dsl/dslinquiry.htm`
- `http://www.catv.org/`
- `http://www.cable-modem.net/`
- `http://cable-dsl.home.att.net/`
- `http://www.cablemodeminfo.com/`

There are numerous other sites you can check. Just go to your favorite search engine and enter "**dsl availability**". You can also check the Web site of your Regional Bell Operating Company.

Providers of both types of service often include the actual cable or DSL modem (usually as a rented item) in their subscription packages along with the Ethernet card required to connect the modem to your PC. It is usually cheaper to purchase these items separately. Cable modems can range in price from $100–300. DSL modems are similarly priced. You will also need an Ethernet card to connect either device to your PC, which you can purchase for $10–20.

Installing a Cable or DSL Modem

As just stated, it is usually cheaper to purchase your cable or DSL modem rather than rent one from your provider (which isn't yours to keep after so many rental payments). You can usually purchase these devices online or from stores such as CompUSA, Best Buy, Circuit City, or Radio Shack. You don't have to purchase a modem with a lot of bells and whistles; just make sure that it conforms to the standards used by your provider—DOCSIS (Data Over Cable Service Interface Specifications) for cable broadband service or Discrete Multitone (DMT) for ADSL broadband service.

Contact your broadband service provider and order the service you want. For ADSL broadband service, a visit to your home for installation is not required. DSL service can be turned on from the telephone company's central office. For cable broadband service, however, an installation visit is required because a splitter must be installed at the point where the actual coax cable enters your house to place your cable TV service and broadband service on separate cable lines inside your house. Don't worry; there is still only one cable coming to your house.

Task: Installing an Ethernet Card in Your PC

The first thing you have to do is to install the Ethernet card in your PC. You will need an Ethernet card for both cable and DSL broadband service. To install your Ethernet card, follow these steps:

1. Unplug your PC, remove the cover, and install the Ethernet card into one of the vacant slots on your PC's motherboard (see Figure 16.2).

FIGURE 16.2
Installing an Ethernet card into a PC slot.

If your PC does not have any vacant slots, don't despair. Many Ethernet card manufacturers also make external cards that plug into a USB port. These Ethernet "cards" work just as well as a card installed in a slot on your motherboard.

2. Replace the cover and turn on your PC. If the operating system supports Plug and Play, when your PC boots, it should detect the newly installed Ethernet card and begin the hardware installation of the new card (see Figure 16.3). Simply follow the instructions on the screen to install the driver for your Ethernet card.

3. If the Add Hardware Wizard does not start automatically, follow the instructions that came with your Ethernet card to install the Ethernet driver.

FIGURE 16.3

Windows is shown here installing an Ethernet card using the Add Hardware Wizard.

16

If your Ethernet card comes with an installation CD, the Windows XP Hardware Wizard will recommend that you cancel the wizard and proceed with the installation using the installation CD.

4. After you install the hardware driver for your Ethernet card, you must install the TCP/IP protocol. In Windows XP, select Start, Control Panel, Network Connection; Windows should list the Ethernet card you just installed. Right-click the Ethernet card listed and select Properties to open the Properties dialog box for your Ethernet card (see Figure 16.4).

FIGURE 16.4

The Properties dialog box for your newly installed Ethernet card.

5. Click Install, select Protocol, and then select Add. When the choices for available protocols to add are listed, select Internet Protocol (TCP/IP) and click OK.

Finally, you must configure TCP/IP for your broadband service. Your service provider should supply you with the following information:

- Your IP address, subnet mask, default gateway, and whether these configuration settings are static or dynamically assigned.

> Many broadband service providers dynamically assign your IP address and other TCP/IP configuration parameters because dynamically assigned parameters are easier to manage (for them, not you).

- The IP address(es) of your provider's DNS (Domain Name Service) server(s).

Task: Configuring Your TCP/IP Settings

To add and configure the TCP/IP protocol for your broadband connection, do the following:

1. In Windows XP, select Start, Control Panel, Network Connection; Windows should list the Ethernet card you just installed. Right-click the Ethernet card listed and select Properties to open the Properties dialog box for your Ethernet card.

2. Scroll down the This Connection Uses the Following Items box and select Internet Protocol (TCP/IP). Click the Properties button to open the Properties dialog box (see Figure 16.5).

FIGURE 16.5

The Properties dialog box for TCP/IP settings.

▼ 3. If your service provider provides you with a dynamically assigned IP address, select the Obtain an IP Address Automatically option. If your service provider gave you a static IP address, select the Use the Following IP Address option and enter the IP address, subnet mask, and default gateway IP addresses provided by your provider.

4. Repeat step 3 for the DNS server address section of the dialog box.

5. Click OK, and continue closing all the dialog boxes and screens you previously
▲ opened.

Depending on how your broadband provider and service provider have configured their hardware and network, you may or may not have to install software provided by these service providers. If you do, insert the CD you received and install the software following the instructions provided.

Task: Connecting Your PC to the Cable or DSL Modem

Now that you've finished configuring your PC, it's time to connect your PC to your cable or DSL modem. The procedure is the same regardless of which type of service you subscribe to.

To connect your PC to your broadband modem, follow these steps:

1. Plug one end of the Ethernet cable (the Cat5 cable) into the Ethernet card in your PC. Plug the other end of the cable into your cable or DSL modem. Look for a plug labeled "Ethernet."

2. If you are using a cable modem, connect the coax cable from the splitter (connected by your cable provider) to the cable modem. If you are using a DSL modem, connect a standard telephone cable to the modem and plug the other end into a phone jack. If you are using a DSL modem, make sure that you connect RF filters (see Figure 16.6) to all other phone lines connected to telephones in your home.

FIGURE 16.6
Two types of RF filters used with DSL connections.

▼

3. Turn on your cable or DSL modem.

4. To test your connection, start your Web browser (Internet Explorer, Netscape Navigator, or whichever Web browser you use) and see whether you can connect to a Web site. If you can't, make sure that all your cables are properly connected and that you followed all the previous instructions for installing and configuring your Ethernet card.

Security Concerns

You may think that you're done with your broadband communications connection if you were able to successfully connect to a Web site using your Web browser. But there's one more important task you have to perform: You must secure your PC from *hackers* or *attackers*.

Some people argue over the use of the term *hacker* to describe someone who might break in or attack your PC. Some prefer the term *cracker* (someone who illegally cracks into computer systems) instead of *hacker* (someone with extraordinary computer skills). Regardless of the term you choose to use, you still should protect your PC from a potential *attacker*.

PCs connected to broadband services are frequently attacked and used to launch Denial of Service (DoS) attacks against large online organizations, companies, and universities. PCs on broadband service are targeted because the broadband service is always on and provides a high-bandwidth (high-speed) connection the attacker can use in an attack. The attack scenario works like this: The attacker scans known ranges of IP addresses used by broadband service providers for their customers, looking for vulnerable PCs. A "vulnerable PC" is a PC the attacker can easily access and install software that allows him to control that PC remotely. When the attacker has accessed several hundred PCs which he can control, he then uses them to launch a Denial of Service attack.

A *Denial of Service* attack is an attack in which the attacker commands the hundreds of PCs he now controls to send an unending stream of data to a single Internet site. Controlling several hundred PCs on broadband connections makes a Denial of Service attack easier because the high-speed connections allow each commandeered PC to send a tremendous volume of data to the site being attacked.

The site being attacked is overwhelmed with data, usually much more than the site is equipped to handle. The result is that legitimate users to the attacked site cannot access it because of the constant bombardment of useless data. Attacks like this have been known to continue for hours or days without end. The Internet Service Provider for the site being attacked can make adjustments in the hardware (network routers) to fend off the attack, but usually not before the attacked site has not been able to service its regular customers for hours or days.

To prevent your PC from being commandeered and used in a Denial of Service attack, you must install either software or hardware designed to prevent the attacker from accessing your PC. Such programs or devices are collectively known as *firewalls*. A firewall is a program or device used to prevent some type of intrusion or attack.

> PC firewalls are by no means an absolute guarantee that your PC will not be attacked and commandeered, but they usually are enough of a deterrent to send the attacker off in search of easier prey. By some estimates, roughly 26–40 percent of all broadband users have some type of firewall installed. In the time it would take an attacker to defeat even the weakest firewall product, he could easily have commandeered 20–30 unprotected PCs from the 60–74 percent of broadband users with no firewall protection. Time is on your side; the attacker would much rather spend his time on more fruitful pursuits.

Software firewall products are typically less expensive than hardware devices, and there are numerous to pick from. Here's a list of the best known:

- ZoneAlarm from Zone Labs (www.zonelabs.com)
- BlackICE Defender from Network ICE (www.networkice.com)
- Symantec Desktop Firewall (www.symantec.com)
- McAfee Personal Firewall (www.mcafee.com)
- Sygate Personal Firewall (www.sygate.com)

You can download and purchase all of these products online.

> Of the personal firewall products listed here, which is not by any means a total list of the products available, ZoneAlarm and Sygate are free for personal and home use.

> Windows XP users have a firewall option included in the new operating system. To activate this option, open the Properties dialog box for your Ethernet card (described previously) and click the Advanced button. In the Advanced dialog box, select the option to turn on your XP firewall.

Task: Installing Personal Firewall Software

Of the products listed here, BlackICE Defender is probably the easiest to install and configure. To install BlackICE Defender, follow these steps:

1. Purchase and download the program from the Network ICE Web site at `http://www.networkice.com/products/blackice_defender.html` (see Figure 16.7).

FIGURE 16.7

The Network ICE Web site where you can purchase and download BlackICE Defender.

2. Run the program `bidef.exe` and follow the prompts to install BlackICE Defender.

When BlackICE Defender is installed, you will see a small icon in the taskbar to indicate that it is actively protecting your PC. *When* (not *if*) you see it flashing, this indicates a possible attack on your PC. Click the icon to open BlackICE Defender to examine the nature of the attack (see Figure 16.8).

> If you are unsure of the meaning of the warning issued by BlackICE, click the advICE link in the lower-right corner of the BlackICE window.

You can also purchase and install hardware firewall products to protect your PC. Some security experts consider hardware firewall products superior to their software cousins when it comes to protecting your PC, but most users don't begin considering hardware firewalls until they have more than one PC to protect, such as when several PCs are connected together in a home (or small office) network (see Hour 17, "Adding a Home Network").

FIGURE 16.8

A list of possible attacks on a PC repelled by BlackICE Defender.

Several companies have been marketing hardware firewall devices to cable and DSL broadband users. These multifunction devices contain small network hubs or switches and routers, as does the Linksys device shown in Figure 16.9. If you are connecting only a single PC to your broadband connection, then you obviously don't need a device designed for small networks, so save your money and don't buy hardware devices with functionality you don't need.

FIGURE 16.9

A cable/DSL firewall/router from Linksys.

Summary

In this hour, you learned about the two main types of broadband Internet services available in this country: cable modem service and ADSL. You also learned the how these services work and some major advantages and disadvantages in each service. You learned how to select and install each service so that you can connect to the Internet.

Finally, you learned about the precautions you should take, such as installing a firewall, to make sure that your PC is safe from possible attacks over the Internet.

Q&A

Q Is there really any difference between a $125 cable modem and a $300 cable modem? Shouldn't I just go with the cheapest model I can find?

A If all you're buying is a cable modem, you are probably better off buying the least expensive model you can find; just make sure that it is compatible with the standard used by your cable provider. Most likely, if it meets the DOCSIS standard, it is okay. But some manufacturers are combining cable modems with other devices such as firewalls, routers, hubs, and switches. If you have only one PC and absolutely no plans to get another PC or create a small home network, then stick with the least expensive models.

Q Cable broadband seem so much faster than DSL broadband. Why would anyone settle for a maximum speed of 10Mbps (DSL) when they can get a maximum speed of 30Mbps with cable and pay a lot less for it?

A Although it may look as if cable is always a better buy than DSL, remember that the speed advertised by a cable broadband provider is the maximum speed possible by subscribers—provided that not too many subscribers are using the service at the same time. Cable broadband is a shared service; as more subscribers in your neighborhood attempt to use the service simultaneously, the slower it gets. Depending on how saturated your cable segment gets, that blazing cable modem speeds can literally be reduced to a crawl. On the other hand, DSL is not a shared system. If you subscribe to 1.8Mbps DSL service, that's the speed you'll get—all the time.

HOUR 17

Adding a Home Network

With PC prices continuing to drop and more and more users hanging on to their older PCs, it's becoming more common to find users with more than one usable PC in their homes. And sooner or later, after staring at those two PCs, most users will have thoughts of networking them together.

A few years ago, the idea of networking two or more PCs in your home would have been a costly and tedious procedure. Now it can be done with nothing more than a little planning and a trip to your local computer store to purchase a $100 kit.

PC users cite many reasons for networking their PCs: to share a printer, to play head-to-head games, or to share a high-speed Internet connection such as a broadband cable or DSL connection (see Hour 16, "Adding a Cable or DSL Modem"). There are a few options available to users who want to set up a small, home network.

During this hour, you will learn the following:

- How to install a simple home network using a home networking kit
- How to share a high-speed Internet connection on your home network

Why You Might Want to Install a Home Network

If you rummage through your basement or attic and dig out the old computer magazines and catalogs from the last few years, chances are you will find ads for several devices that allow you to share a printer between two or more PCs. Long before anyone gave any thought to setting up a home network, users were looking for ways to share peripherals, and the first peripheral they were likely to share was a printer.

Nowadays, printers may just be one item on a short list of shared peripheral devices and resources you want to make available to users on multiple PCs. in addition to printers, PC users are also inclined to share hard disks and other mass storage devices, modems or other communications devices, and files.

Users have found other novel reasons for networking two or more home PCs. For example, if you are really into gaming, networking your PCs is a great way to play head-to-head competitions.

If you've recently purchased a digital camera, you've undoubtedly run into a problem that can be solved by networking your PCs. Depending on the resolution of your digital camera and photos, you may have experienced the problem of creating files that don't fit on a floppy disk drive. You may have tried zipping (compressing) the files to move them from one PC to another; if this failed, you may have settled for using a lower resolution to make the files small enough to fit on a floppy disk. However, if your PCs were networked together, you'd have no trouble moving your files from one PC to another regardless of their resolution or file size.

Installing a Simple Home Network

In recent years, several companies have started offering home networking kits. Most of these are fairly simple starter kits consisting of a small network *hub*, two or more network cards, and some Ethernet cables (see Figure 17.1).

A *hub* is a device used to connect PCs together on a network. In large corporate networks, hubs may have several dozen or even several hundred connections, called ports, used to connect PCs to the network. In small home networks, hubs generally have from 4–8 ports you can use to connect your PCs together. To connect a PC to a network using a hub, you plug one end of the Ethernet cable into the hub and the other end of the cable into the Ethernet card installed in your PC.

Many hardware-based firewall products (discussed later in this chapter) have a built-in network hub called a network *switch*. If you already have or are planning to purchase a hardware-based firewall containing a network switch, there is no need to purchase a standalone hub. Use the firewall switch in place of the hub.

FIGURE 17.1

The components in a typical home networking kit.

Before you rush right out and purchase one of these kits, which average around $100–150, you should know that you can easily purchase the same items separately for less. Check your local computer store or office supply superstore; you can pick up a 10/100Mbps Ethernet card for $10–15, a 4 or 5 port hub for $30–40, and two 25-foot Ethernet Cat5 cables for $15 apiece:

2	10/100Mbps Ethernet cards	$20–30
1	5-Port Ethernet hub	40
2	25-foot Ethernet Cat5 cables	30
	TOTAL	$90–100

I'm not guaranteeing that you can beat the price of every networking kit you find, but just do a little comparison shopping before you part with your hard-earned cash. All you need are the specifications for each device you want to purchase.

Make sure that you purchase a hub designed for an Ethernet network (it's actually difficult to purchase a hub for a type of network other than Ethernet), with an advertised
speed of 10/100Mbps for each of the ports. Make sure that each port is "auto-sensing."
You can purchase a hub with 4, 5, or as many ports as the manufacturer supplies. What
all this means is this:

- *Ethernet* is the type of network you will be creating; the other type of network you
  could create is token ring, but most manufacturers don't make token ring components
  for home use.

- *10/100Mbps* is the minimum and maximum speed your network will use when
  communicating with the various devices on your network such as the PCs and
  possibly the communications device you probably will be attaching later in this hour.

- *Auto-sensing* means that each port in your hub will automatically sense whether it
  is attached to a device operating at 10Mbps or 100Mbps and adjust the speed of
  the specific port accordingly.

The network cards you purchase should be Ethernet cards designed to operate at speeds
of 10/100Mbps. You might also want to purchase Ethernet cards that fit into a PCI slot.
Almost all PCI Ethernet cards are newer cards, which means they will almost definitely
be Plug and Play cards, which ultimately means they will be easier for you to install.

You can purchase network cables of any length you need. Just make sure that they are
rated as Category 5, often just called Cat5, Ethernet cables.

Task: Installing an Ethernet Card in Your PC

To install your Ethernet card, follow these steps:

1. Turn off and unplug your PC, remove the cover, and install the Ethernet card into
   one of the vacant slots on your PC's motherboard (see Figure 17.2).

> If your PC does not have any vacant slots, don't despair. Many Ethernet card
> manufacturers make external cards that plug into a USB port. These Ethernet
> "cards" work just as well as a card that is installed in a slot on your
> motherboard.

2. Replace the cover, plug in, and turn on your PC. If your operating system supports
   Plug and Play, it should detect the newly installed Ethernet card when it boots and
   begin the hardware installation of the new card (see Figure 17.3). Simply follow
   the instructions on the screen to install the driver for your Ethernet card.

FIGURE 17.2
Installing an Ethernet card into a PC slot.

FIGURE 17.3
Windows installing an Ethernet card using the Add Hardware Wizard.

3. If the Add Hardware Wizard does not start automatically, follow the instructions that came with your Ethernet card to install the Ethernet driver.

If your Ethernet card comes with an installation CD, the Windows XP Hardware Wizard will recommend that you cancel the wizard and proceed with the installation using the installation CD.

After you install the hardware driver for your Ethernet card, you must install the TCP/IP protocol. TCP/IP is the most common network protocol used today to allow devices on a network to communicate with each other. You will definitely need TCP/IP if you plan to share an Internet communications device on your network.

Task: Installing TCP/IP on Your PC

To Do ▼

To install TCP/IP on your PC, follow these steps:

1. In Windows XP, select Start, Control Panel, Network Connection; Windows should list the Ethernet card you just installed. Right-click the Ethernet card listed and select Properties from the shortcut menu to open the Properties dialog box for your Ethernet card (see Figure 17.4).

FIGURE 17.4

The Properties dialog box for your newly installed Ethernet card.

2. Click Install, select Protocol, and then click Add. When the choices for available protocols to add are listed, select Internet Protocol (TCP/IP) and click OK.

▲

Finally, you must configure TCP/IP for use on your network. For a network with only two or three PCs, configuring TCP/IP settings is fairly simple. If you don't have a registered set of IP addresses, you will have to use what are called "private network" IP addresses (IP addresses that are not routed over the Internet and are reserved for use on private networks). The range of IP addresses you should use is from 192.168.0.1 through 192.168.0.254. For example, on your first PC, use the IP address 192.168.0.1. On the second PC, use 192.168.0.2. On the third PC, use 192.168.0.3, and so on.

Task: Configuring Your TCP/IP Settings

▲ To Do

To install and configure TCP/IP on your PC for the card you just installed, follow these steps:

1. In Windows XP, select Start, Control Panel, Network Connection; Windows should list the Ethernet card you just installed. Right-click the Ethernet card listed and select Properties from the shortcut menu to open the Properties dialog box for your Ethernet card.

2. Scroll down the box labeled This Connection Uses the Following Item and select Internet Protocol (TCP/IP). Click Properties to open the Properties dialog box shown in Figure 17.5.

FIGURE 17.5

The Properties dialog box for TCP/IP settings.

17

3. Select the Use the Following IP Address option and type the IP address **192.168.0.1** for your first PC; type **192.168.0.2** for the second PC; type **192.168.0.3** for the third PC, and so on for as many PCs as you have to network.

4. Leave the entry for default gateway blank because you don't have one.

The default gateway is typically the device used to connect your network to another network, such as the Internet. If or when you connect your network to a communications device such as a cable modem or DSL modem, you will enter the IP address you set for that device as your default gateway.

▼

▼
5. Windows should automatically fill in the appropriate subnet mask based on the IP address you enter.

6. Leave the entry for your DNS server blank, because you don't have one of these, either (yet!).

7. Click OK and continue closing all the dialog boxes and screens you previously
▲   opened.

Task: Turning on File and Print Sharing

The last task you must perform to make your small network fully operational is to turn on File and Print Sharing. This feature allows you to share files and peripherals such as a printer.

To turn on File and Print Sharing, follow these steps:

1. In Windows XP, select Start, Control Panel, Network Connection; Windows should list the Ethernet card you just installed. Right-click the Ethernet card listed and select Properties from the shortcut menu to open the Properties dialog box for your Ethernet card.

▲   2. Make sure that the File and Print Sharing for Microsoft Networks option is selected.

Sharing Your High-Speed Internet Connection

One of the main reasons for networking your PCs together is so that you can share a single communications line for the Internet. If you upgraded to a cable or DSL modem back in Hour 16, "Adding a Cable or DSL Modem," this is the ideal communications line to share across a small home network.

> Because of the complexity and variety of home network configurations, many cable and DSL broadband providers do not support access over a home network. Keep in mind one other possible support headache: Most providers also won't support you if you are not running some version of Windows or Mac OS (that is, no Linux).

Back in Hour 16 when you connected a cable or DSL modem to your PC, you plugged a Cat5 Ethernet cable into the network card in your PC. You will use this same cable to connect your cable or DSL modem to your network. After you connect the cable from your cable or DSL modem to your network, you must also set the default gateway setting on each PC.

Task: Connecting a Cable or DSL Modem to Your Network

To connect your cable or DSL modem to your network, follow these steps:

1. Locate the Cat5 Ethernet cable you used back in Hour 16 to connect your modem to your PC. Leave the cable connected to the modem and plug the other end of the cable into one of the ports in your hub.

2. At each PC, you must set the default gateway entry in your TCP/IP settings. In Windows XP, select Start, Control Panel, Network Connection; Windows should list the Ethernet card you installed in the PC. Right-click the Ethernet card listed and select Properties from the shortcut menu to open the Properties dialog box for your Ethernet card.

3. Scroll down the box labeled This Connection Uses the Following Item and select Internet Protocol (TCP/IP). Click Properties to open the Properties dialog box.

4. In the default gateway field (which you left blank when you previously configured TCP/IP on your PC), type the IP address you entered for your cable or DSL modem.

5. Turn on your cable or DSL modem.

6. To test your connection, start your Web browser (Internet Explorer, Netscape Navigator, or whichever Web browser you use) and see whether you can connect to a Web site. If you can't, make sure that all your cables are properly connected and that you followed all the previous instructions for installing and configuring your Ethernet card.

17

Network Security Concerns

As was true back in Hour 16, you still must be concerned with possible security violations on your PCs now that they are connected to a network—especially since you've turned on file and print sharing.

There are two ways to solve this problem on your network. You can use the same software option you used back in Hour 16—that is, you can install a software-based firewall program on each PC. Alternatively, you can install a hardware-based firewall product which many users actually find a lot easier to configure.

Because we covered how to install a software firewall product back in Hour 16, in this hour we will explain how to install one of the many hardware-based firewall products marketed at cable and DSL users.

Hardware-based firewall products, often called *cable/DSL firewall routers*, are not only simpler to set up and use than the software versions, but most also offer other advantages. Many hardware firewalls include a network hub or *switch* and *router* as part of the configuration, meaning that you don't have to purchase a separate hub to create your network.

Many hardware-based firewall products show what looks like a built-in network hub but refer to it as a network *switch*. A switch and a hub perform the same function on a network; the difference is that a switch performs it a little better. You could describe a switch as a "smarter" hub. A switch contains a few more electronics than a hub; these extra electronics are used to improve performance on your network. So don't be confused if you see a cable or DSL firewall advertised with a switch. Likewise, don't be alarmed when the manufacturer refers to the device as a *router*. The router function built-in to the device just allows you the ability to expand your home network later if you are so inclined.

One of the first manufacturers to offer cable and DSL users a combined firewall/hub/ router product was Linksys (http://www.linksys.com/). Their product line continues to be one of the best sellers (see Figure 17.6).

FIGURE 17.6

A Linksys cable/DSL firewall router in operation.

Linksys offers a combined firewall/hub/router device in configurations with 1, 4, and 8 network ports for connecting PCs to your network. If you have already purchased a hub for your network, you can save money by selecting the 1-port Linksys model.

Other companies offering similar and comparably priced products are NetGear (www.netgear.com) and D-Link (www.dlink.com) products.

To connect your cable/DSL firewall/router to your network, you will need one more Cat5 cable. Make sure that you have one before you begin because many manufacturers don't always include one with the cable/DSL firewall router. Before you purchase the cable, check your hub to see whether it has a port designated as an "uplink" port. If your hub has an uplink port, you can purchase a standard Cat5 cable. If your hub does not have an uplink port, make sure that the Cat5 cable you purchased is a "crossover cable."

Task: Connecting a Cable/DSL Firewall Router to Your Network

To connect your cable/DSL firewall router to your network, follow these steps:

1. Locate the Cat5 cable connecting your cable or DSL modem to your network hub. Unplug this cable from the hub and plug it instead into the network port on your cable/DSL firewall labeled WAN. WAN stands for wide area network.

2. Take a second Cat5 cable and plug one end into one of the ports on your cable/DSL firewall router and the other end into the port on your hub labeled uplink (see Figure 17.7). You may have to press the uplink button on your hub to activate the port as an uplink port. If your hub does not include an uplink port, make sure that the cable connecting your hub and the cable/DSL firewall router is a Cat5 crossover cable.

FIGURE 17.7

An uplink port on a network hub.

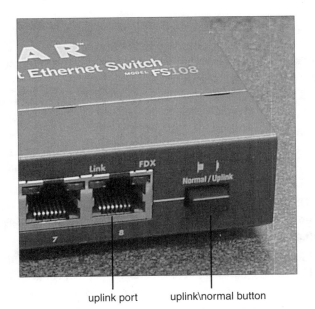

uplink port   uplink\normal button

3. Using one of the PCs on your network, follow the instructions included with your cable/DSL firewall router to configure the device. You will probably have to set IP addresses for both the WAN (wide area network) side and LAN (local area network) side of your cable/DSL firewall router. Many of these devices also allow you to run what is known as *DHCP* on your network so that you don't have to individually set IP addresses on each networked PC.

DHCP stands for *Dynamic Host Configuration Protocol*. This network service automatically provides IP addresses and other configuration information to each networked PC.

Summary

In this hour, you learned how to connect your PCs together in a small home network so that you can share peripherals and resources. You also learned how to share one of the most important resources over your network: your Internet connection. Finally, you learned about a hardware option for providing security on your network to protect against possible security violations and attacks over the Internet.

Q&A

Q Why don't many cable and DSL broadband providers support operations on a home network?

A Many providers simply don't want to provide you the extra support necessary to set up a network. It is simply easier for them to say that you can't do it and eliminate the extra support headache. Many also don't want users to set up their own Web servers, which tend to increase the amount of traffic over the provider's network. This is especially true with cable broadband providers because you're sharing the available bandwidth with other cable subscribers.

Q My DSL provider doesn't give me a static (permanent) IP address. Instead I get an IP address assigned dynamically. Can I still use the cable/DSL firewall router?

A Absolutely. In fact, using a cable/DSL firewall router may make it easier to network your PCs and share your broadband Internet connection. Most cable/DSL firewall routers allow you to set the WAN port to be a DHCP client, meaning that you receive your IP address dynamically from your provider while at the same time you provide dynamically assigned IP addresses to your networked PCs. This is exactly how my home network is set up.

Hour 18

Expanding Your Home Network by Using Phone Lines or Going Wireless

In the last hour, you learned how you can network two or more PCs together into a small home network so that you can share resources such as hard disk drives and other mass storage media, printers, and high-speed Internet connections.

Networking two or three PCs that are in close proximity to each other is a rather simple task, but what do you do when you want to network Dad's PC down in the game room, Mom's PC in the family room, and Junior's PC upstairs in his bedroom? If you're handy at pulling cables through walls and floors, you can dig out your drill and fish tape. But if you balk at the idea of putting holes through your walls, floors, and ceilings, you'll look for alternatives. During this hour, we will present two alternatives for setting up your home network that do not require you to string cables through your walls and ceilings.

During this hour, you will learn:

- How to set up a home network that uses your in-house phone lines instead of standard Ethernet cables
- How to set up a wireless home network

Creating a Home Phoneline Network

Back in Hour 15, "Upgrading Your Modem," you learned that DSL broadband service works because there is additional bandwidth available over your phone line that broadband service can easily share with normal voice communications. This is essentially the same principle that home phoneline networks make use of.

Phoneline networks are incredibly simple to set up—and not just because you don't have to drill holes and pull cables. They can also be some of the least expensive networks to install. Essentially, all you have to purchase is a phoneline network interface card kit for each PC you intend to network (see Figure 18.1).

FIGURE 18.1

A typical phoneline network card kit.

After you install the network cards and install the driver, all you do is plug the cards into your phone jacks, and you're done.

Although the major advantages of a phoneline network are ease of installation and cost, phoneline networks do have a few drawbacks. The phoneline network cards are not compatible with standard Ethernet cards or networks; if you ever decide to upgrade to a home Ethernet network, you will have to ditch all your phoneline equipment. Phoneline equipment is also slower than standard Ethernet equipment, but even at 10Mbps for phoneline networks versus 100Mbps for standard Ethernet networks, the speed is more than adequate for home use.

Because phoneline network software tends to be somewhat proprietary, you will most likely purchase all your hardware products from the same vendor, which actually should not be much of a problem as long as the company is still around when you need technical support.

Task: Installing a Home Phoneline Network

To install your phoneline network, follow these steps:

1. Purchase a phoneline network card kit for each PC you intend to network.

2. Turn off and unplug your PC, remove the cover, and install the phoneline card into one of the vacant slots on your PC's motherboard.

> If your PC does not have any vacant slots, don't despair. Many phoneline card manufacturers also make external cards that plug into a USB port. These phoneline "cards" work just as well as a card that is installed in a slot on your motherboard.

3. Replace the cover, plug in, and turn on your PC. If your operating system supports Plug and Play, it should detect the newly installed phoneline card when it boots and begin the hardware installation of the driver for the new card (see Figure 18.2). Follow the instructions on the screen to install the driver for your phoneline card.

FIGURE 18.2
Installing the driver for your phoneline card.

18

▼   4. If the New Hardware Wizard does not start automatically, follow the instructions
          that came with your phoneline card to install the hardware driver.

> If your phoneline card comes with an installation CD, the Windows XP New
> Hardware Wizard will recommend that you cancel the wizard and proceed
> with the installation using the installation CD.

   5. Finally, you must install the networking software provided by your card's manu-
      facturer (see Figure 18.3). The networking software will check your PC to make
      sure that you have the correct settings for file sharing with other PCs on your phone-
      line network. Make sure that you run the software on each PC you network.

FIGURE 18.3

*Installing the network-
ing software for your
phoneline card.*

▲

The installation procedures and software will vary from one manufacturer to another, so
follow the instructions that come with your network card kit. In addition to the driver,
you will also get software utilities that allow you to share peripheral devices such as
printers and modems.

Bridging to Ethernet

Even though standard Ethernet equipment is not compatible with phoneline equipment, at least one manufacturer who is serving both markets has come up with a way to allow the two technologies to coexist. NetGear (www.netgear.com) produces an Ethernet-to-phoneline bridge (see Figure 18.4).

FIGURE 18.4

NetGear's Ethernet-to-phoneline network bridge.

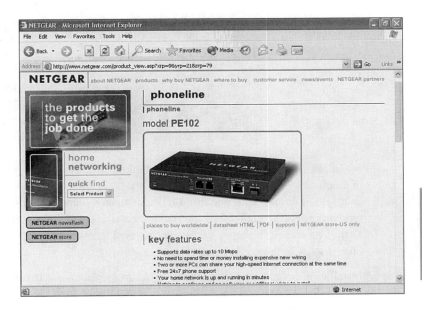

To use the Ethernet-to-phoneline bridge, you simply plug a phone line with an RJ-11 plug into one side of the bridge, plug an Ethernet Cat5 cable into the other side, and then turn it on.

Wireless Networking

Wireless networking components for home networks are fairly versatile, and manufacturers have designed them to function either as the heart of your network or as simply a part of it. The key to wireless networking is what is known as the Wireless Access Point such as the one shown in Figure 18.5.

18

FIGURE 18.5
A Wireless Access Point device from Linksys.

A typical configuration for which a user might employ one or more wireless components in a network is a standard Ethernet network set up in a basement or home office using a small Ethernet hub with one or more PCs connected and perhaps a cable modem or DSL modem providing high-speed Internet connectivity. A Wireless Access Point device such as the one shown in Figure 18.5 might be used to connect several other PCs located in other rooms in the house to this Ethernet network.

Installation is fairly straightforward. You simply plug the Wireless Access Point device into one of the ports on your Ethernet hub and then follow the manufacturer's instructions to configure the device. Typically, configuration amounts to little more than assigning the device an IP address.

The only other device that is needed to complete this configuration is a wireless network card for each PC connected to the network.

Wireless Ethernet cards typically are designed for laptop computers because just about all of them are manufactured as *PCMCIA*-type devices (see Figures 18.6 and 18.7). A few are also manufactured as USB devices.

PCMCIA is a specification for devices manufactured to work with laptop computers. PCMCIA devices are designed to fit into the two small slots typically located on the sides of laptop computers.

FIGURE 18.6

A typical wireless PCMCIA network card.

FIGURE 18.7

A wireless PCMCIA network card being inserted into a laptop PCMCIA slot.

18

Many manufacturers have realized that even though wireless network cards were originally designed with laptop users in mind, there might also be a market for desktop users. Therefore, many manufacturers also offer a type of low-cost conversion card that enables you to use a laptop PCMCIA card in a desktop computer. As you can see in Figure 18.8, the conversion card is simply a PCI (or ISA) card with a built-in PCMCIA slot that allows you to insert the wireless laptop card into the slot, and then insert the entire card into a desktop computer.

FIGURE **18.8**

A conversion card for a wireless PCMCIA card with the card inserted.

Using a conversion card/wireless card combo is no different than using any other type of Ethernet card in a PC in your network. You simply insert the card into a slot in your PC, install the hardware driver for the card, and then install and configure the TCP/IP protocol.

Task: Installing a Conversion Card/Wireless Card Combo

To Do ▼

To install a wireless Ethernet card in your PC, follow these steps:

1. Turn off and unplug your PC, remove the cover, and install the wireless Ethernet card in the conversion card into one of the vacant slots on your PC's motherboard.

2. Replace the cover, plug in, and turn on your PC. If your operating system supports Plug and Play, it should detect the newly installed Ethernet card when it boots and begin the hardware installation of the new card. Follow the instructions on the screen to install the driver for your Ethernet card.

3. If the New Hardware Wizard does not start automatically, follow the instructions that came with your Ethernet card to install the Ethernet driver.

▲

> If your Ethernet card comes with an installation CD, the Windows XP New Hardware Wizard will recommend that you cancel the wizard and proceed with the installation using the installation CD.

After you install the hardware driver for your Ethernet card, you must install the TCP/IP protocol. TCP/IP is the most common network protocol used today to allow devices on a network to communicate with each other. You will definitely need TCP/IP if you plan to share an Internet communications device on your network.

Task: Installing TCP/IP for Your Wireless Ethernet Card

To install TCP/IP on your PC, follow these steps:

1. In Windows XP, select Start, Control Panel, Network Connection; Windows should list the Ethernet card you just installed. Right-click the Ethernet card listed and select Properties from the shortcut menu to open the Properties dialog box for your Ethernet card.

2. Click Install, select Protocol, and then click Add. When the choices for available protocols to add are listed, select Internet Protocol (TCP/IP) and click OK.

Finally, you must configure TCP/IP for use on your network. For a network with only two or three PCs, configuring TCP/IP settings is fairly simple. If you don't have a registered set of IP addresses, you will have to use what are called "private network" IP addresses, IP addresses that are not routed over the Internet and are reserved for use on private networks. The range of IP addresses you should see are 192.168.0.1 through 192.168.0.254. For example, on your first PC, use the IP address 192.168.0.1; on the second PC, use 192.168.0.2; on the third PC, use 192.168.0.3, and so on.

Task: Configuring Your TCP/IP Settings

To configure the TCP/IP settings for your network, follow these steps:

1. In Windows XP, select Start, Control Panel, Network Connection; Windows should list the Ethernet card you just installed. Right-click the Ethernet card listed and select Properties from the shortcut menu to open the Properties dialog box for your Ethernet card.

2. Scroll down in the box labeled This Connection Uses the Following Items and select Internet Protocol (TCP/IP). Click Properties to open the Properties dialog box (see Figure 18.9).

FIGURE 18.9

The Properties dialog box for TCP/IP settings.

▼   3. Select the Use the Following IP Address option and type the IP address **192.168.0.1** for your first PC; type **192.168.0.2** for the second PC; type **192.168.0.3** for the third PC, and so on for as many PCs as you have to network.

     4. Leave the entry for default gateway blank because you don't have one.

> The default gateway is typically the device used to connect your network to another network, such as the Internet. If or when you connect your network to a communications device such as a cable modem or DSL modem, then you will enter the IP address you set for that device as your default gateway.

     5. Windows should automatically fill in the appropriate subnet mask based on the IP address you enter.

     6. Leave the entry for the DNS server blank because you don't have one of these, either (yet!).

     7. Click OK and continue closing all the dialog boxes and screens you previously
▲   opened.

Task: Turning on File and Print Sharing

The last task you must perform to make your small network fully operational is to turn on File and Print sharing. This feature allows you to share files and peripherals such as a printer.

To turn on file and print sharing, follow these steps:

     1. In Windows XP, select Start, Control Panel, Network Connection; Windows should list the Ethernet card you just installed. Right-click the Ethernet card listed and select Properties from the shortcut menu to open the Properties dialog box for your Ethernet card.

     2. Make sure that the File and Print Sharing for Microsoft Networks option is
▲   selected. Click OK.

Security Concerns

Security for a phoneline network is no different than security for any other type of network that is connected to the Internet. Make sure that you have anti-virus software installed and properly updated on each PC. You should also use personal firewall software on each PC as described in Hour 17, "Adding a Home Network."

On wireless networks, however, you have a different set of security concerns. Wireless transmissions can be intercepted because they are essentially radio frequency transmissions. Most wireless devices allow you to turn on and use what is known as the Wireless Encryption Protocol (WEP). WEP sets up an encrypted communications link between communicating wireless devices so that even if the transmissions are intercepted, they appear as gibberish so that anyone intercepting them will not be able to decrypt the transmissions. Don't worry about having to take any extra steps to use a wireless encryption device. The encryption-decryption is done automatically by the communicating devices after the devices are configured for the same network. Follow the manufacturer's instructions for configuring WEP on your wireless devices.

Summary

In this hour, you learned how to create a network using the phone lines in your home as an alternative to using standard Ethernet cables. You also learned how to create a wireless network that does not require cables to connect your PCs to the network.

Q&A

18

Q How do wireless devices and phoneline devices compare in transmissions speeds to standard Ethernet devices?

A Both phoneline and wireless devices still lag behind their standard Ethernet cousins in transmission speeds. Ethernet devices—even those used in the home—achieve speeds of 100Mbps (in corporate networks, you can get 1Gbps Ethernet speeds) while phoneline networks currently top out at 10Mbps and wireless networks hit their peak at 11Mbps. But don't be discouraged that phoneline and wireless can't keep pace with standard Ethernet. In a home setting, these speeds are more than adequate because most of the traffic on your network will likely consists of Internet traffic (Web pages and e-mail messages) and your phoneline and wireless devices can easily keep pace with cable and DSL modems. Unless you plan to set up room-to-room videoconferencing, I wouldn't worry about the speeds of phoneline and wireless devices.

Q Are these speeds likely to increase any time soon?

A Absolutely. It was only a year or two ago that the HomePNA (Home Phone Network Associations) specifications for phoneline networks were upgraded from 1Mbps to 10Mbps. Some experts theorize that home phoneline networks could possibly achieve speeds of 80–100Mbps. A few years ago, the wireless standard 802.11b was released which upgraded these devices from 2Mbps to 11Mbps. As with any technology that is largely driven by consumer demand, wireless manufacturers are looking ahead and hoping to upgrade speeds here as well. Many scientists are working on bumping up wireless transmissions to the 80–100Mbps range.

Part V

Upgrading Other Peripherals

Hour

Hour 19

Upgrading Your Keyboard, Mouse, and Other Input Devices

After reading the title of this chapter, you may start wondering what's wrong with your keyboard and mouse. Actually, the keyboard and mouse you are now using may be fine, but over the course of this hour (well actually, maybe in a little less time) you will learn about some better alternatives for the common keyboards and mice usually shipped with PCs.

During this hour, you will learn:

- About ergonomic design
- That most keyboards are not ergonomically designed
- How to select an ergonomically designed keyboard
- How to select a more comfortable and useful mouse or other pointing device

Is Anything Wrong with My Keyboard or Mouse?

The title of this lesson might prompt you to skip it because nothing is wrong with your keyboard or mouse. Well, the idea is not that anything is wrong with the keyboard and mouse that came with your PC, but that replacement keyboards and mice can make long hours of PC use easier and much more pleasant.

Keyboards and mice have improved considerably over the past few years—in design, functionality, and *ergonomics*.

> *Ergonomics* is the study of the relationship between people and their work environments. In simpler terms, it means producing tools in the workplace, such as chairs, desks, keyboards, and so on, that conform more to the way human bodies are designed and how they function rather than making human bodies conform to workplace tools. The idea is to increase comfort and reduce the possibility of injuries or stress.

Functionally, probably nothing is wrong with your keyboard, or at least we hope nothing is mechanically or electronically wrong with it. Like thousands of other PC keyboards, however, yours may be contributing to a physical problem that hundreds of orthopedic surgeons are seeing more and more of each year. You may have encountered the terms *repetitive stress injury* and *carpal tunnel syndrome*. These medical terms are used to describe an extremely painful and sometimes disabling condition brought on by continuously repeating a physical action that places your hands, arms, or legs in an unnatural position. Whether you are aware of it or not, most of us do this every time we use our keyboard.

Although we can absolutely in no way offer a diagnosis on whether you've suffered a repetitive stress injury or whether you've actually developed carpal tunnel syndrome, we can offer you some advice that may help you avoid problems down the road. Now that we've gotten the legal stuff out of the way (which should make the lawyers and suits happy), let's move right along.

The average flat keyboard forces you to bend your wrist outward so that your fingers are in position to reach all the keys. If you're a hunt-and-peck typist, this problem may not be so bad. If you are a touch typist, however, your wrists are probably angled outward at about 30 degrees. If you extend the legs on your keyboard to lift the back of your keyboard upward, you are putting more strain on your wrists because now you are also hyper-extending them backwards another 30–40 degrees.

This unnatural bending of your wrist for long periods of time, day in and day out, eventually can place stress on the nerves in your arms, hands, and wrists. You may have noticed after using your keyboard for several hours that you experience some tingling or numbness in your wrists or fingers. This could be the start of more serious problems.

After studying this problem for several years, designers have come up with what they call the ergonomic keyboard. Although several manufacturers have come up with various styles on the basic design of a keyboard split in the middle with the keys positioned in a more natural position, the Microsoft keyboard remains the most popular seller (see Figure 19.1).

FIGURE 19.1

A typical ergonomic keyboard.

The basic idea behind the ergonomic keyboard is that it places your wrists and hands into a more comfortable and natural position, with your palms facing more toward each other. This position places much less stress on the nerves and ligaments in your wrists and hands.

Ergonomics, however, is not the only direction keyboard makers are going. Added functionality is another. Keyboards are no longer just keyboards. You can now purchase keyboards with additional devices such as scanners (see Figure 19.2), trackballs, or touchpads built in.

Whether you purchase a keyboard for more comfort and functionality, or if you are just looking for a keyboard with a better feel than the one you are currently using, make sure that you get a keyboard with the correct type of plug for your PC. Most PCs today are manufactured with ports for the newer, smaller 6-pin PS/2-style keyboard plugs shown on the left in Figure 19.3.

19

Figure 19.2

A keyboard with a built-in sheet-feed scanner.

AT Style Keyboard Plug

Figure 19.3

A 6-pin PS/2-style keyboard plug on the left and an older AT-style keyboard plug on the right.

PS/2 Style Keyboard Plug

This PS/2 type of plug is easy to identify because it is the same size as the plug used on mice. The other type of keyboard plug is the original AT-style plug, which is noticeably larger than the PS/2 plug.

Don't panic if, when you purchase a new keyboard and attempt to plug it in to your PC, you discover that your new keyboard has the wrong size plug. Most computer stores sell keyboard plug adapters for $5–$10 that convert PS/2 to AT and vice versa (see Figure 19.4).

FIGURE 19.4

Keyboard adapters for converting PS/2- to AT-style plugs.

Another option to consider is a wireless keyboard. These are keyboards with a small built-in radio transmitter/receiver. Another small radio transmitter/receiver is plugged into the keyboard receptacle on your PC (see Figure 19.5). The radio transmitters in these devices are usually good for a distance of about 2 meters. Wireless keyboards are a good way to eliminate the bother of having another cord to deal with—especially if you like to recline in your easy chair while computing.

FIGURE 19.5

A typical wireless keyboard.

19

Fixing a Keyboard?

Even though some texts attempt to explain how to fix your keyboard, depending on the type of keyboard you have, you could start tearing it apart only to discover that it's about as difficult to put back together as grandpa's old pocket watch. I hate to lump keyboards into the category of being just another throw-away commodity, but if your keyboard goes bad, the trash bin is usually its fate. But this doesn't mean you can't occasionally perform some routine maintenance to help keep your keyboard clean.

Keyboards are great for attracting and collecting dust. And if you're like me and occasionally catch a quick snack while working, you'll find that your keyboard is also quite good at attracting and collecting crumbs. Later in this hour, I'll give you some handy tips on how to clean your keyboard and mouse.

Mice and Other Pointing Devices

For many users, the mouse is purely a functional device; either it is functioning, or it isn't! Mice and other types of pointing devices today, however, offer a lot more than mere functionality. Ergonomic mice have been designed to fit your hand. Cordless mice eliminate the cord's getting in your way. Some mice have two buttons; some have three; some are left-handed; and some mice even have built-in gyroscopic mechanisms that you can wave through the air instead of dragging across a pad. Another mouse innovation for people who surf the World Wide Web a lot is a mouse with a special scrolling wheel placed between the two buttons. The scrolling wheel enables you to scroll up and down long Web pages quickly and smoothly. A lot of applications now also support this scrolling action, including Microsoft's Office suite.

Several manufacturers are also producing optical mice. Instead of a ball, an optical mouse scans your desktop with a laser that produces a tracking precision much greater than a typical mouse with a roller ball (see Figure 19.6).

One main advantage optical mice have over other types of mice is that because there are no ball and rollers to attract dust and dirt; you don't have to clean them.

And if you don't like cords getting in your way, you can even get a cordless optical mouse (see Figure 19.7). The transmitter/receiver units on these devices have about the same distance limitations as with cordless keyboards—about 2 meters. One downside to using a cordless optical mouse is that the laser is quite a drain on the batteries. Expect battery life to be about 3–4 weeks with typical use.

FIGURE 19.6
A typical optical mouse.

FIGURE 19.7
A cordless optical mouse.

19

If you have limited desktop space and prefer to move your hand rather than move your pointing device, you should opt for a *trackball* rather than a mouse (see Figure 19.8).

A *trackball*, simply stated, is a mouse turned upside down. The ball inside the pointing device is not moved across a pad, but instead your hand motions move the ball (which is usually much larger than the ball in a mouse).

FIGURE 19.8
A typical trackball pointing device.

Another pointing device that can help you save desktop space is a touchpad. A touchpad is about the same size as a trackball, but instead of a large ball that you move to position the pointer, you touch a touch-sensitive pad with your finger to position the pointer. Just like a trackball, a touchpad can take a little getting used to, but it is another pointing device you may want to consider.

Just as you can purchase a keyboard with the wrong type of plug, mice also come out of the box with one of two types of connectors—a 6-pin DIN connector and a 9-pin serial connector. To give you the option of using either type connector, most manufacturers now include a mouse plug adapter with their mice (see Figure 19.9).

What's most important when selecting a new pointing device is comfort and ease of use. In other words, the mouse or trackball should move smoothly. Many large computer stores have a selection of mice on display that you can try to see how they feel and operate. Take this opportunity to try different sizes and styles of mice to see which type you prefer.

If you're in the market for a new keyboard or mouse, one of the best sources for finding up-to-date information on PC hardware components is the hardware section of CNET's computers.com Web site (`http://computers.cnet.com/hardware/01016.html`). in addition to listing just about every keyboard and mouse you could possibly think of, this site also does comparison reviews and allows you to compare prices on the products listed. Where applicable, this site also lists specifications on the products listed and points you to the manufacturer for more information.

FIGURE 19.9

A mouse plug adapter.

Tips on Cleaning Your Input Devices

Over time and with normal usage, your keyboard, mouse (provided you did not opt for an optical mouse), and other input devices attract dirt and dust on the ball and rollers. The best way to tell when your devices are dirty and need to be cleaned is when they start to behave erratically, such as your mouse pointer not moving in the direction you are trying to position it, or your keyboard keys becoming hard to press.

Cleaning Your Keyboard

Over time, your keyboard accumulates dust, crumbs (if you eat and work, as many computer users do), and other small bits of debris, which can cause keys to stick or make your keys slightly harder to press. The easiest method you can employ to clean your keyboard of these small bits of debris is simply to turn it over so that the keys are facing down toward your desktop and shake your keyboard firmly. Don't shake it hard enough to jar loose your keys, but give it a few good shakes to clear out the crumbs and other small particles.

If you have the misfortune of accidentally spilling a liquid on your keyboard, such as a soda or other soft drink, you may quickly discover that the sugar or other sweetener causes your keys to become sticky. If this happens, immediately stop what you're doing.

19

Save any work you're doing and shut down your PC. Unplug your keyboard and take it to an empty sink. Soda and other liquids can be easily removed using simple alcohol (the rubbing type, not the drinking type). Take a bottle of alcohol out of your medicine cabinet and slowly pour it into the keyboard in about the same area where the spill occurred. The alcohol does not harm the electrical contacts in your keyboard and does a fairly good job of cleaning the spilled liquid. You may need to use more than one bottle of alcohol. You can usually tell when you have completely cleaned your keyboard by simply pressing the keys to check whether they still feel sticky. Just make sure that you allow sufficient time for the alcohol to dry (evaporate) before you plug your keyboard back in to your PC and begin using it again.

Don't use any cleaning products commonly used to clean your kitchen or bathroom because some can damage the plastics in your keyboard and others can leave residues, which can cause more damage. Isopropyl alcohol is about the safest (and often cheapest) cleaning product you can use.

Although some professionals advocate opening and dismantling a keyboard, I generally don't make this recommendation because it can be extremely difficult to reassemble all the small pieces. If you find that a good cleaning with alcohol does not clean anything you might accidentally spill on your keyboard, you are probably better off pitching the keyboard and purchasing a new one.

Cleaning Your Mouse

Mice also get dirty. Usually the parts that get dirty are the rollers inside the mouse, which come in contact with the ball. Just as you did with your keyboard, reach for your bottle of alcohol. This time, instead of pouring the alcohol over the ball and rollers, you want to remove the ball and, using a cotton swab soaked with alcohol, clean the rollers of any build-up of dirt and grease, which can accumulate over time. The instructions that came with your mouse can explain how to open it and remove the ball. Usually, it is just a matter of sliding or twisting a panel holding the ball in place. Just make sure that you understand how to replace the ball before you remove it.

Again, just as with your keyboard, don't use common household cleaning products that can damage your mouse.

Summary

In this hour, you learned how to select a better and more comfortable keyboard and mouse and how important comfort and ergonomics can be when using them. You also learned how to overcome the problem of purchasing a mouse or keyboard with a plug that doesn't match your PC mouse and keyboard connections.

Q&A

Q **What can be done to prevent repetitive stress injuries such as carpal tunnel syndrome short of purchasing a new ergonomic keyboard?**

A Actually, you can do several things. First, make sure that your keyboard is lying flat. If you have the legs on your keyboard extended, fold the legs back down so that you can work without your wrists bending upwards. Second, give yourself frequent breaks when typing. Stop every 10–15 minutes for a minute or two and let your hands and wrists relax. You might also consider purchasing a keyboard and/or mouse rest pad. These are soft, gel-filled devices that provide additional support and comfort for your hands and wrists. Also make sure that the chair you're using is high enough so that your wrists don't bend upwards.

Q **If I develop a repetitive stress injury such as carpal tunnel syndrome, what can be done?**

A You have to see your doctor for proper diagnosis and treatment. Some cases that have not progressed too far can be treated with some of the corrective actions mentioned in this chapter. If the injuries are severe, however, often the only treatment is surgery.

Q **Why do cordless optical mice go through batteries so fast?**

A For a while, there was some doubt that cordless mice could even be made to work considering the amount of voltage needed to run a laser. But a very low voltage laser was developed that could run off two AA batteries. When you add the radio transmitter/receiver, that's a fair amount of drain on a pair of batteries. It's remarkable that the first generation of these devices will last as long as 3–4 weeks. Like everything else, expect improvements as time goes on.

19

Hour **20**

Upgrading Your Video Card and Monitor

For most users, upgrading a video card is like getting your appendix taken out—you don't do it until you need to. Most users make do with whatever video card came with the PC when it was purchased.

There's actually nothing wrong with this video card philosophy. Chances are the video card installed in your PC by the manufacturer is more than adequate for 98 percent of the applications you run. So, why should anyone want to upgrade their video card? The answer is the same for any decision to upgrade a component in your PC—to get better performance!

Better performance in a video card can mean several things—higher video resolution, faster screen refreshes, better graphics, or more colors on your screen. For most users, the need for better performance in a video card is usually driven by a specific application: a high-end graphics art program, a CADD or engineering design program, or even a game using enhanced 3D graphics.

But if you are still using the same old 14- or 15-inch monitor, you're cheating yourself out of the very benefits you sought when you upgraded your old video card with a new one. The main reason most users upgrade their video cards is to gain higher resolution, which enables them to see more on their screen. But resolutions of 1024×768 and 1280×1024 are nearly unreadable on 14- and 15-inch monitors unless you have a passion for squinting.

In the past, the biggest deterrent for most users interested in purchasing larger monitors was cost. As recently as three years ago, most 21-inch and larger monitors hovered in the $2,000–$2,500 range. Nowadays, these same monitors are advertised with prices in the $600–$800 range, in part because of competition from the newly released 19-inch monitors in the $300–$600 price range. For the average PC user, selecting an upgrade among this glut of lower-priced, larger monitors can be confusing.

Regardless of your reasons for wanting to get better video performance out of your PC, during the next hour you will learn:

- What features are currently being touted in video cards
- What to look for in selecting a video card upgrade
- How to install a new video card in your PC
- What monitor features such as "dot pitch," "refresh rate," and "viewable area" are and how important they are in selecting a larger monitor
- What other features are important to look for in selecting a new monitor

What's Currently Available in Video Cards

Nowadays, it is extremely difficult to purchase a bad video card. Video cards have been one of the fastest developing technologies in the computer industry in recent years, and surprisingly, this advancement has been driven largely by the computer gaming industry.

Video cards are also referred to as *video adapters*, *graphic adapters*, and *graphic cards*. These terms all refer to the same device—the interface card installed in your computer that controls and produces video on your monitor. Although the term mostly applies to separate interface cards installed in your PC, the term video card can also refer to video display circuitry built in to the motherboard.

For years, computer gaming software has been pushing the display envelope for faster and more complex graphics and animation. Consequently, the entire computer industry has benefited from this small but demanding segment of the industry because these same video cards also deliver improved graphic performance for the more mainstream business application uses of computers.

Most of what's been happening with video cards for the last 2–3 years can be summed up in two words: speed and memory. Video cards have gotten faster and manufacturers are building them with more (and faster) video memory. On average, expect to see most if not all new video cards with 32MB or more of memory.

What to Look for in a Video Card

It's fairly easy to determine how much memory each video card has installed. The amount of memory installed on the card is usually printed in big, bold letters on the outside of the box. Video memory is usually referred to as VRAM.

VRAM, short for *Video RAM* (Random Access Memory), is a special type of high-speed memory designed for use in video cards. VRAM is typically not upgradeable because it is permanently installed in video cards.

How Important Is Video RAM?

Video RAM or video memory is important because it directly controls video resolution and the number of colors you can display on your monitor. Resolution is defined as the number of *pixels* (short for picture elements) displayed on your screen. A pixel is the smallest video display unit that can be displayed on your screen.

In standard VGA mode, there are 640 pixels displayed horizontally across your screen by 480 pixels displayed vertically, for a total of 307,200 pixels (640×480=307,200).

When you increase your resolution to 800×600 (800 by 600), the number of pixels increases to 480,000 (800×600=480,000). The number of pixels displayed on your screen, however, is only half the story. Each pixel is made up of a color. In 16-color mode, the lowest number of colors for VGA, each pixel can be 1 of 16 possible colors. You need 4 bits of memory to support 16-color mode, and if you do the math, you'll see that you need 153,600 bytes of memory to support 16-color mode:

```
640×480=307,200
307,000×4=1,228,800(bits)
```

To convert bits to bytes, divide by 8:

`1,228,800(bits)/8=153,600(bytes)`

Unfortunately, 16-color mode does not produce very brilliant colors. A better color mode is 256 colors. To produce 256-color mode, however, you need to jump from 4 to 8 bits per pixel, or 307,200 bytes of memory. Your display is getting better but it is still not great. An improvement would be to increase your color or color depth to 65,536 colors. To jump to a color depth of 65,536 colors, however, you need 16 bits of memory for each pixel, for a total of 614,400 bytes of memory.

No video card manufacturer ever produced video cards with 614,400 bytes of memory. Instead, they rounded this number up to a more convenient 1MB of memory. So, to display VGA resolution at 65,536 (64KB) colors, you needed 1MB of memory on your video card. If you increased your resolution up to 1,024×768 at 64KB (65,536) colors, you needed 2MB of memory on your video card, and if you increased your resolution to 1,280×1,024 or the number of colors displayed to 16.8MB (16,777,216), then you needed 4MB of memory on your video card. Table 20.1 lists video memory requirements at various resolutions and color depths on cards you will typically see on the market these days.

TABLE 20.1   Video Memory Requirements

Resolution	Color Depth	Colors	Video RAM	Memory Required (bytes)
640×480	4-bit	16	256KB	153,600
640×480	8-bit	256	512KB	307,200
640×480	16-bit	65,536	1MB	614,400
640×480	24-bit	16,777,216	1MB	921,600
800×600	4-bit	16	256KB	240,000
800×600	8-bit	256	512KB	480,000
800×600	16-bit	65,536	1MB	960,000
800×600	24-bit	16,777,216	2MB	1,440,000
1024×768	4-bit	16	512KB	393,216
1024×768	8-bit	256	1MB	786,432
1024×768	16-bit	65,536	2MB	1,572,864
1024×768	24-bit	16,777,216	4MB	2,359,296
1280×1024	4-bit	16	1MB	655,360
1280×1024	8-bit	256	2MB	1,310,720
1280×1024	16-bit	65,536	4MB	2,621,440

TABLE 20.1 continued

Resolution	Color Depth	Colors	Video RAM	Memory Required (bytes)
1280×1024	24-bit	16,777,216	4MB	3,932,160
1600×1200	4-bit	16	512KB	960,000
1600×1200	8-bit	256	2MB	1,920,000
1600×1200	16-bit	65,536	4MB	3,840,000
1600×1200	24-bit	16,777,216	8MB	5,760,000

If all you're working on are spreadsheets and text documents, you're not going to see much difference between 16 colors and 65,536 colors displayed on your screen. If you are a graphic artist, however, the increase in color depth from 4-bit color to 24- or 32-bit color (16.8MB colors) is essential.

Task: Demonstrating Video Resolution and Color Depth

▼ To Do

To demonstrate video resolution and color depth using your existing video card, follow these steps:

1. Use SysChk or SiSoft Sandra (see Hour 3, "Examining Your PC's System Configuration") to determine how much video memory you have installed on your existing video card (see Figure 20.1).

FIGURE 20.1
SiSoft Sandra displaying video information.

2. If your current video mode is not VGA (640×480 resolution) and 16 colors (color depth), change to this particular resolution and color depth: Right-click your desktop to open the display shortcut menu, select Properties, and then select Settings to open the Display Properties dialog box (see Figure 20.2). Make the appropriate change to Color Palette and Desktop Area.

▼

▼

If your display adapter does not immediately give you the option of changing to VGA, 640×480 resolution, click the Advanced button on the Properties page, select Adapter, select List All Modes, and then select 640×480,16 Colors.

FIGURE 20.2

The Display Properties dialog box in Windows XP.

3. If you have Internet access, start your Web browser and proceed to the following Web page:

   `http://www.felixnet.com/wolfpark/wolftrip.htm`

   Select the second group of pictures and click the first picture to display it full-sized (see Figure 20.3). This picture has fairly vivid colors and good resolution when viewed at something better than 16-color VGA mode.

4. Repeat step 2, staying in VGA mode (640×480 resolution), but select a better color depth (such as 256 colors or 65,536 colors). Go back and view the test picture again and note the change in appearance. Take a few minutes to try various screen resolutions and color depths to see which combination produces the best results using your video card and monitor.

▼

FIGURE 20.3

A test picture for comparing various video modes and color depths.

Video Speed

Video speed is often referred to as *refresh rate*, the speed at which the video card can redraw or refresh your display screen at certain resolutions. Most experts agree that your video card should have a minimum refresh rate of 72Hz at every resolution to avoid flicker, which can cause eye strain and fatigue. Although the type of memory installed on your video card can definitely affect refresh rate, the other factor controlling refresh rate is the speed of the Digital Analog Converter (DAC). You should look for a video card with a DAC speed of at least 250MHz.

Ultimately, speed is important for a video card because a faster card can redraw or refresh your display screen and produce smoother animation when you are displaying moving objects on your screen. Again, this is a feature more important to graphic art programs, Web design applications, CADD engineering software, and video games than to a word processing program. But video speed is also important if you are working in any type of business graphic program or if you are viewing graphics or animation on the Internet. The bottom line is that any application benefits from a higher quality video card and eventually you will be faced with using some sort of graphical application.

Video card speed is a little hard to accurately test. Often it takes sophisticated testing programs to determine the relative speed of a particular video card. Most users lack the

20

testing software and resources to test numerous video cards, so we must rely on the various computer industry journals to test and publish their results. These testing reviews can often be valuable sources of information that you as a consumer and computer user should regularly check before making any computer purchase.

A few magazines you might want to browse for product reviews on video cards are *PC Magazine*, *PC World*, and *Windows 2000 Magazine*.

So, what does all this mean when deciding whether you need a new video card? If you are an ardent game player and are trying to keep pace with the latest gaming technology, you most likely want the fastest video card you can get—one with 32MB of memory or more and one that can display ultra-fast 3D graphics.

If you are using any type of sophisticated graphics or animation software, you also want to consider upgrading to a video card that fits the same bill. However, an even less demanding reason technologically for upgrading your video card is purchasing a larger monitor. Although VGA mode (640×480 resolution) is perfectly acceptable on a 14- or 15-inch monitor, if you are looking at a 17-, 19-, or 21-inch monitor, you'll want to crank up the resolution to a higher level to take advantage of the larger display. For 17-inch monitors and larger, it is fairly common to use a resolution of 1024×768 to 1600×1200 or higher. If you look back at the preceding section, you see that higher video resolution and higher color depth require a video card with more memory. Once again, refer to Hour 3 and use SysChk to determine the specifics of your existing video card.

Although SysChk indicates the basics of your video card, if you are serious about expertly testing your video card and tuning your monitor, you should look into a professional testing utility such as DisplayMate from Sonera Technologies, located at http://www.displaymate.com (see Figure 20.4).

FIGURE 20.4

Sonera Technologies, the developer of DisplayMate, a professional video-testing utility.

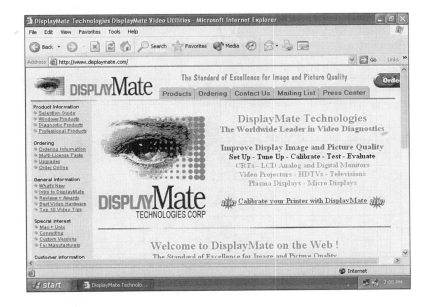

Installing a Video Card

There is very little setup involved when installing a new video card.

> Regardless of which version of Windows you are using, before you remove your existing video card and install a new one, do this: Set your video mode to VGA and your colors to 16. This ensures that Windows, with the standard VGA driver installed, will definitely work with your new video card.

Task: Installing Your New Video Card

To install a new video card, follow these steps:

1. From the Start menu, select Control Panel and then select System to open the System Properties dialog box.

2. Select the Hardware tab and then choose Device Manager to access the Hardware Device Manager.

3. Click Display Adapters and then select the adapter in your PC. Right-click Uninstall to uninstall the driver for your display adapter (see Figure 20.5). Windows replaces the driver with the standard generic (and low resolution) VGA driver.

To Do

20

FIGURE 20.5

Uninstalling your video driver in Windows XP.

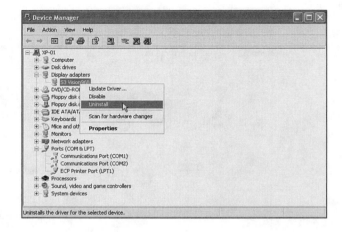

4. Click OK to reboot your PC.

> If you install a new video card that requires a video driver that is incompatible with the driver required by your previous video card, it is possible that your PC will not start Windows. To prevent this from happening, you can install the generic VGA video driver, which should work with just about every video card on the market.

5. Turn off and unplug your PC. Ground yourself and then remove the cover.

6. Unplug the cable from your monitor, which is connected to your current video card.

7. Remove your current video card and insert the new video card into the same slot on your motherboard (see Figure 20.6). If you are removing a card from an ISA bus slot and the new card requires a PCI bus slot, be sure to insert the new card into the proper slot. If you are removing a card from a PCI slot and the new card requires an AGP slot, be sure to insert the new card into the proper slot.

> *AGP (Accelerated Graphics Port)* refers to a special graphics slot designed by Intel, which began appearing about 2-1/2 to 3 years ago in PCs with Pentium II motherboards. Read the next section for more details on AGP.

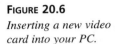

FIGURE 20.6
Inserting a new video card into your PC.

Some motherboards have built-in video cards, which you must disable before adding an upgraded video card. To disable a built-in video card, consult the documentation that came with your PC. In many instances, you can disable a built-in video card by running the hardware Setup program used to configure your PC. To disable some built-in video cards, however, the manufacturer might have included a special video configuration utility.

8. Replace your PC's cover and attach the video cable to your new card. Plug your PC in and turn it on.

9. Install the video driver for your new card, following the instructions accompanying the new card. Because of Plug and Play, most versions of Windows (except NT 4.0) should detect your new video card and begin the driver installation for you. Just follow the prompts to install the new video driver.

What About AGP?

If you regularly read the computer trade journals, another term you may have seen is *AGP*, which stands for *Accelerated Graphics Port*. Strictly speaking, it is not an upgrade item. You cannot add AGP to your existing computer.

20

In addition to the 440LX motherboard *chipset*, you also need to be running either the Windows 95 OEM Service Release 2.1 or Windows 98/2000/Me/XP because these are the only versions of Windows that fully support AGP. You also need a video card that is AGP compliant and software that is written to use AGP's advanced capabilities.

A *chipset* is nothing more than a specialized processor or group of processors designed for a specific task. In references like this, it refers to a chipset installed in a particular series of motherboards.

So what does all this AGP hardware and software buy you? Amazing graphics texture and silky smooth animation, but surprisingly no additional display speed. In tests conducted on similar computer systems using an AGP video card and a PCI video card, the AGP card was not significantly faster, and in some tests, the AGP turned in the same or lower speed as the PCI.

Another drawback to AGP is that Intel set a rather relaxed standard. The only real qualification for AGP is that the AGP card fit into the proprietary AGP slot. In early models released by several manufacturers, some cards did not fully implement the full texturing features for enhanced 3D graphics. There are even different implementations of display speed on the so-called compliant video cards. Some cards operate at 66MHz and provide 264 megabytes per second of display video data, whereas other cards are able to effectively double these numbers. Reportedly, some manufacturers are working on cards that quadruple these figures.

Finally, little software has been written to take full advantage of AGP. The largest category, as you might guess, is games. Even the best AGP video cards do nothing to improve existing graphics software.

Upgrading Your Video Monitor

The main reason most users decide to upgrade their video cards is to gain higher resolution, which enables them to see more (often, a lot more) on their screen. But resolutions of 1024×768 and 1600×1200 are nearly unreadable on 14- and 15-inch monitors unless you have a passion for squinting.

In the past, the biggest deterrent for most users interested in purchasing larger monitors was cost. As recently as a few years ago, most 21-inch and larger monitors were in the $2000–$2500 range. Nowadays, these same monitors are advertised with prices in the $500–$800 range, in part because of competition from the newly released 19-inch monitors in the $300–$500 price range. For the average PC user, selecting an upgrade among this glut of lower priced, larger monitors can be confusing.

Why You Should Purchase a Larger Monitor

Plain and simple, the reason you want a new, larger monitor is that it enables you to see more of what is displayed on your screen. For example, if you are currently using a 15-inch monitor, upgrading to a 17-inch monitor may not seem like a big deal, but a 17-inch monitor gives you about 30 percent more onscreen viewing area. Upgrading from a 15-inch monitor to a 21-inch monitor gives you more than 50 percent more onscreen viewing area because you can comfortably set your display to a higher resolution. Table 20.2 shows the recommended resolution for 15-, 17-, 19-, and 21-inch monitors. Keep in mind that these are just recommendations, not chiseled-in-stone guidelines.

TABLE 20.2   Optimal and Acceptable Display Resolutions

15-inch	17-inch	19-inch	21-inch
640×480	640×480	640×480	640×480
800×600	*800×600*	*800×600*	800×600
1024×768	**1024×768**	**1024×768**	*1024×768*
	1280×1024	**1280×1024**	**1280×1024**
		1600×1200	**1600×1200**
			1800×1440

Optimal, *Useable*, Not advisable

To give you an idea how resolution can affect how much you can view onscreen, take a look at Figures 20.7, 20.8, and 20.9. These three figures display the same information onscreen, but as you can see, as the resolution increases, so too does the amount of information visible onscreen.

Prices of larger monitors have continued to drop in the past year. A good 17-inch monitor can be purchased now in the range of $200–$400. A good 21-inch monitor can be purchased now for between $400 and $600.

Purchasing a larger monitor has a downside. Larger monitors are just that—larger monitors! They take up more room on your desktop, and more importantly, larger monitors weigh a lot more. Some 21-inch models can tip the scales at 25–30 kilograms. You also shouldn't place a large monitor on top of your PC case since a mass weighing 25×30 kilos can bow or crack your PC's case.

20

FIGURE 20.7

*Resolution set at
640×480.*

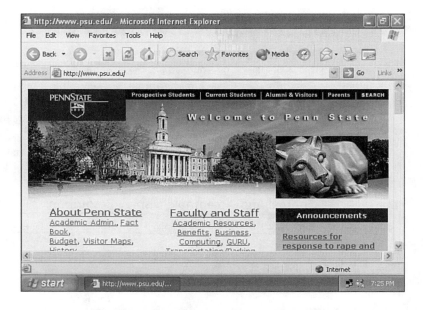

FIGURE 20.8

*Resolution set at
800×600.*

FIGURE 20.9

Resolution set at 1024×768.

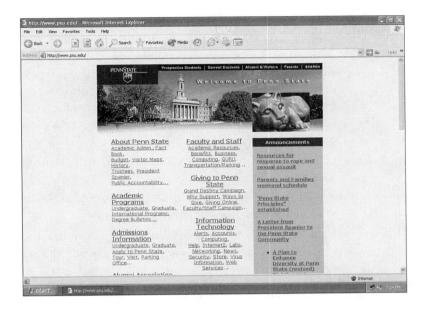

Another reason to upgrade to a newer monitor is that monitor technology has improved in the last few years. Monitors are not just bigger, they are also better. Monitors now produce clearer, sharper images with less distortion and flicker on the screen, which means if you regularly spend hours in front of your PC, you are less likely to suffer eye strain (or at least less eye strain than before). Newer monitors also generally are equipped with better controls (such as horizontal and vertical controls, contrast, brightness, and so on), which enable you to do a better job of fine-tuning your monitor to your own personal preferences.

Selecting Your New Monitor

Before you head out and plop down your hard-earned cash for a new monitor, there are a few guidelines you need to know about selecting a monitor:

20

- **Be careful of dot pitch claims.** A few years ago, the big buzzword for monitors was dot pitch. A computer monitor's screen is composed of thousands of very small dots called pixels (short for picture elements), which when set to the correct color, create the appearance of images. Dot pitch is the measurement between these dots. Unfortunately, not every manufacturer measures dot pitch the same way, so using dot pitch to compare one monitor to another quickly becomes a comparison of apples and oranges.

Another problem with using dot pitch to compare monitors is that it only works on monitors using the dot-trio shadow-mask picture tube. In the dot-trio shadow-mask picture tube, a thin sheet of perforated metal coated with light-sensitive phosphor is what creates the actual dots. On monitors using this type of picture tube, you want to measure the shortest distance between the perforated dots. Some manufacturers measure the distance from the center of one dot to the center of an adjacent dot, but not every manufacturer uses the dot-trio shadow-mask picture tube in their monitors.

Some manufacturers use what is called the aperture-grille picture tube. The aperture-grille picture tube uses an array of stretched wires coated with phosphor instead of a sheet of perforated dots.

A third method is called the slot-mask picture tube, which combines portions of shadow-mask and aperture-grille technologies.

- **Look for a high refresh rate.** Another important factor to consider in selecting a new monitor is the monitor's refresh rate. The refresh rate is the speed at which the monitor can refresh or redraw the onscreen display. You want a monitor with a fast refresh rate because this tends to reduce onscreen flicker. Refresh rates are not determined by the type of picture tube the manufacturer uses, so refresh rate turns out to be a more legitimate gauge for comparing monitors. Refresh rates do vary according the resolution used on the monitor. Select a monitor with a refresh rate of at least 72Hz (which means the screen is refreshed about 72 times a second) for the highest resolution you intend to use.

- **How much control you have over your monitor.** As strange as this may sound, many experts also suggest that you check to see the number of controls available on the monitor. A monitor with a lot of controls gives you greater latitude in fine-tuning your monitor.

While we're on the subject of controls, if you can select a monitor with all the controls on the front rather than on the back, adjusting your monitor will be a lot easier.

- **Check the actual size of the viewing area.** The advertised size of the monitor is not the size of the display screen. Table 20.3 shows you approximately what you can expect for your display size (measured diagonally) when you purchase a certain size monitor. Keep in mind that, just like with your television set, the measurement is made diagonally.

- **Is it a flat screen monitor?** Having a flat screen as opposed to the slightly rounded screen will display images with less distortion. But be prepared to pay a little extra for a flat screen.

TABLE 20.3 Monitor Display Sizes

Monitor Size in Inches	Approximate Viewing Area
14	12.5
15	13.5
17	15.5–16
19	20.5–18
20	20.5–19
21	19.5–20

You really don't need a degree in electrical engineering to compare monitors and select the best one for your needs. If you really want to get down to a low-level technical comparison between monitors, a number of good software programs are available that you can use to test monitor performance. Two of the best are the WinBench series from ZD Labs (www.zdnet.com) and a program mentioned earlier in this hour, DisplayMate by Sonera Technologies (www.displaymate.com).

For many users, however, the best way to choose one monitor over another is by performing a few simple tests in a local computer store.

When you're in the market for a new monitor, one of the best sources for finding up-to-date information on PC hardware components is the hardware section of CNET's Computers.com (http://computers.cnet.com/hardware/0-1016.html). In addition to listing just about every monitor you could possibly think of, this site also does comparison reviews and allows you to compare prices on the products listed. Where applicable, this site also lists specifications on the products listed and points you to the manufacturer for more information. If you're looking for more technical information, make a point of bookmarking Tom's Hardware Guide (http://www.tomshardware.com/).

LCD Monitors

Another type of monitor you might want to consider when deciding to purchase one is the LCD monitor (see Figure 20.10).

LCD stands for *liquid crystal display*, and is the type of monitor you see on laptop computers. You can also purchase freestanding LCD monitors to attach to your desktop PC. LCD monitors have low-glare screens and consume considerably less power than their CRT cousins (5 watts versus about 100 watts). LCD monitors excel when it comes to color quality and are actually better than many standard monitors.

20

FIGURE 20.10

A typical LCD monitor from Samsung, one of the leading manufacturers of LCD monitors.

LCD monitors are still limited in size—you don't see many larger than 15 inches and they cost a bit more than CRT displays, even though their prices have been coming down in the last year or so. You can purchase a 15-inch LCD monitor for under $600.

Despite the slightly higher price tag, LCD monitors have one indisputable advantage over CRT displays—size. LCD monitors can easily be $1/10^{th}$ the depth of CRT displays and weigh on average between 2 and 14 kilos.

If you've got a little extra cash in your monitor budget, then by all means go for an LCD monitor.

Setting Up Your New Monitor

As mentioned earlier, a larger monitor takes up more room on your desktop, so make sure that you have the available desktop real estate before you unbox your new monitor.

Task: Setting Up Your New Monitor

To set up your new monitor, follow these steps:

1. Turn off and unplug your old monitor. Turn off the power to your computer. Then disconnect your old monitor from your PC and remove it from your desktop.

2. Unbox your new monitor and carefully examine it for any signs of transit damage. Examine the video cable and connector that plugs into your PC.

3. Place your new monitor on your desktop. Do not place it on top of your PC. If a separate base accompanies your monitor, follow the instructions for assembling and placing your monitor on the base.

4. Adjust the height of the monitor so that the approximate center of the screen is at eye level.

5. Plug your monitor's video cable into your PC and connect the monitor's power cable.

6. Turn on your monitor and your PC.

There is still a lot of controversy over whether you should turn on your monitor or your PC first, or whether you should plug them both into a combination surge protector/power strip and turn them both on together. I have heard so-called experts recommend each method. Personally, I previously owned a PC for which the instructions stated to turn the monitor on first, so I always turn my monitor on first and then turn on my PC.

7. Your new monitor should come with a disk containing drivers for Windows. These drivers enable your Windows operating system to properly adjust certain settings to those required by your monitor. Follow the instructions that come with your monitor for installing these drivers.

If you are running Windows 95/98/2000/Me/XP and your monitor is Plug and Play, these versions of Windows will attempt to make these adjustments for you. Just follow the onscreen prompts.

Plug and Play is a combination hardware and software feature that enables an operating system such as Windows 95/98/2000/Me/XP to identify and configure hardware you add to your PC. To work, the hardware item must have special chips built in that identify the hardware item. Also, the operating system must be Plug and Play–enabled so that it can read those chips and use the information contained within the chips to configure the hardware.

20

After your monitor is installed and correctly set up, be sure to adjust the resolution to the optimum setting, as recommended in Table 20.2. If you are installing a 17-inch monitor, adjust the resolution to at least 1024×768. If you have a 19-inch monitor, set your resolution to 1024×768 or 1280×1024. If you have a 21-inch monitor, adjust the resolution to either

1280×1024 or 1600×1200. Keep in mind that these are merely suggestions for what many experts consider the optimum settings for certain size monitors. Your own preferences may dictate a higher or lower resolution. The best judge is what feels comfortable to you.

Summary

In the past hour, you learned about selecting a new video adapter and a new, larger monitor. You learned about some of the factors to consider when selecting a new video subsystem.

Q&A

Q What about monitors larger than 21 inches? I don't see them mentioned very much.

A There are monitors larger than 21 inches, but they mainly fall into two categories that have prevented them from being widely used. The first category is monitors larger and more costly than the current batch of 21-inch monitors. These are extremely high-resolution monitors that can adequately display 1600×1200 resolution. They are also extremely costly, usually in the range of $2500–$4000. The second category is large home-use monitors usually in the size of 28–32 inches. To keep the cost down for the home market, these monitors are usually limited in the resolution they support. Most display a maximum of only 800×600.

Q Are there video resolutions higher than 1280×1024? If so, what are they used for?

A The highest advertised video resolution I have ever seen is 1800×1440. Resolutions this high are typically used in CAD/CAE (Computer Aided Design/Computer Aided Engineering) and usually require 21-inch or larger monitors.

Q Is it possible to install two video cards in a PC, attach two monitors, and view different information on each monitor?

A Yes, but to do so requires either special software or an operating system (Windows 2000/Me/XP, Linux) that supports this type of operation. Also, unless your software is designed for multiple views, you will see the same display on both monitors.

Hour 21

Upgrading or Adding a Sound System to Your PC

Computers aren't just for crunching numbers and composing text. In the last few years, large high-resolution monitors, CD-ROM and DVD drives, and digital sound systems have literally brought a multimedia explosion to PCs. Even the once conservative and staid Internet is now buzzing with dazzling animation, graphics, and thundering digital audio.

Although most of the emphasis in multimedia has been placed on animation and dazzling graphics, sound and digital audio have been steadily making inroads into the multimedia paradigm. Back in Hour 20, "Upgrading Your Video Card and Monitor," you learned that the gaming industry is largely responsible for many of the advancements seen in video cards because of the demands placed on the hardware by advanced 3D graphics. Well, the computer gaming industry has also been largely responsible for the advancements in multimedia audio. Just as games have placed demands on PC video systems, they have also placed demands on your PC's audio system. Another reason some users have added audio to their PCs is the proliferation of MP3 files and DVD players.

But enough about what led to the advancements in PC audio; we're here to discuss what you need to do to get the best, or at least better, audio from your system.

During this hour, you will learn the following:

- How to select a sound card for your computer
- How to select audio speakers to complement your sound card
- How to install your sound system in your PC
- How to connect and use your home stereo as your computer's sound system

Your PC's Current Sound System

Most PCs sold today still go mainly to large corporations for general business use. Although they are potentially capable of producing a multimedia frenzy of vivid graphics, dazzling animation, and thundering sound, the vast majority of these computers are sadly lacking many of the key multimedia ingredients, especially a decent sound system.

Once PCs were sold with a sound system no better than what was originally placed into the original IBM PCs sold back in 1981. In the last few years, many manufacturers have begun offering sound systems as an option. But many consumers either don't know enough about audio to choose a good system, or choose to save a few bucks by eliminating an audio system.

Two buzzwords you've probably heard in the same breath with multimedia are *MMX* and *DirectX*. MMX stands for Multi Media eXtensions, and is the term coined by Intel to describe the multimedia functions included in some of its Pentium-class processors. The MMX instructions are designed to enable faster processing of sound and graphics, and thus produce a richer multimedia experience. DirectX is a series of technologies licensed by Microsoft and incorporated in Windows 95/98/NT/2000/Me/XP that allow for a more robust display of graphics, 3D animation, and sound. Although MMX and DirectX were designed primarily for games, we are starting to see some of these technologies incorporated into Web designs and presentation business applications.

If you did not purchase a multimedia-equipped PC, don't despair. You do not have to settle for the pipsqueak audibles now emanating from your PC. By the end of this hour, you will have all the information you need to turn your PC into a big, mean sound machine that will do justice to Carnegie Hall.

Selecting a Sound Card for Your PC

Sound card usage basically falls into one of two categories: using your sound card to listen to prerecorded audio in the form of games and CDs, and using your sound card with additional equipment to create computer-generated audio or music. The vast majority of users fall into the first category, which is the one we concentrate on in this hour.

If the most you plan to do with your audio is listen to music and sound that someone else has recorded, such as audio tracks on games and educational CD-ROMs or the occasional Duke Ellington music CD, you need to understand that most of the audio computer world is SoundBlaster-compatible (see Figure 21.1).

FIGURE 21.1
SoundBlaster is the number one selling sound card for PCs.

You don't really need a sound card that is SoundBlaster-compatible to listen to music CDs. In fact, you don't even need a sound card of any type in your PC to listen to music CDs. Virtually all CD-ROM players today include a head-phone jack into which you can plug a set of headphones and listen content-edly for hours. If you want to hear booming bass drums, however, you likely want to channel your audio through a sound card and out to a good set of speakers, and for this, any sound will card suffice.

21

SoundBlaster sound cards currently have the lion's share of the computer audio market, a dominance that largely grew out of its early adoption by the computer gaming industry as its (so-called) standard and the SoundBlaster's early compatibility with the AdLib (a pre-SoundBlaster model) sound card.

Some of the earliest 8-bit SoundBlaster sound cards weren't really good for much except games, which really wasn't a problem for most computer users because games comprised better than 90 percent of all software with any type of sound or audio track. Today, however, SoundBlaster 64-bit sound cards are considered by some to be near the top of the line for both games and serious music composition using *MIDI* devices and electronic synthesizers.

MIDI (Musical Instrument Digital Interface) is an interface and a file format that enables you to connect a musical instrument to a computer and store musical instrument data. This data can then be enhanced, edited, and played back. MIDI is not recorded sound but instructions to your computer's sound system on how to electronically reproduce certain sounds.

If you purchase a SoundBlaster sound card, or any model of a compatible sound card, you should not have trouble playing any type of computer audio file or software that you encounter.

Just remember the old computer maxim: "Compatibility is in the eyes of the beholder." Although some sound cards may claim to be SoundBlaster-compatible, there is no absolute guarantee. If you want to ensure 100% SoundBlaster compatibility, make sure that you purchase a genuine Sound-Blaster sound card.

SoundBlaster compatibility, however, is not the only prerequisite for a good sound card. Following are a couple other features you might want to look for in a sound card:

- If you're interested in creating MIDI audio files, make sure that your sound card has several megabytes of onboard memory and can be expanded.
- For improved sound quality in many of the newer games, make sure that your card provides support for the Microsoft Windows API DirectX—including DirectSound.

When you're in the market for a sound card, one of the best sources for finding up-to-date information on PC hardware components is the hardware section of CNET's computers.com (`http://computers.cnet.com/hardware/0-1016.html`). Besides listing just about every sound card you could possibly think of, this site also does comparison reviews and allows you to compare prices on the products listed. Where applicable, this site also lists specifications on the products listed and points you to the manufacturer for more information.

If you're looking for more technical information, you should make a point of bookmarking Tom's Hardware Guide (`http://www.tomshardware.com/`).

Selecting Speakers

Selecting speakers is largely a matter of what your budget can afford. In general, the old saying that "you get what you pay for" applies to speakers. Your selection of speakers is not limited to companies that produce speakers for only the computer industry. The demand for higher quality audio has tempted several of the traditional stereo speaker makers to produce models specifically for computers:

- **Sony**—`http://www.ita.sel.sony.com/products/av/`
- **Cambridge SoundWorks**—`http://www.cambridgesoundworks.com/`
- **Bose**—`http://www.bose.com/`

The following companies produce top-quality speakers only for computers:

- **Altec Lansing**—`http://www.altecmm.com/`
- **Labtec**—`http://www.labtec.com/noflash/gear/speakers.cfm`
- **Benwin**—`http://www.benwin.com/`

Just make certain that you purchase amplified speakers designed for use with computers; computer speakers are shielded to prevent the magnetic coils in the speakers from causing distortion or damage to your monitor if you choose to place the speakers next to your monitor.

Most computer stores that sell speakers usually have some sort of display enabling you to compare one model against another. Before you purchase, try to decide what type of audio you will be listening to. Will you mostly be playing games with your PC, or will you mostly use your sound card and speakers to listen to relaxing music CDs while you work? Having an idea of the type of audio for which your speakers will be used can help you decide how much you want to spend on speakers.

Although speakers have traditionally been sold in pairs, one on each stereo channel, the configuration that seems to be growing in popularity now is a pair of speakers with a third speaker operating as a subwoofer, which produces deeper, richer bass tones.

21

A good set of PC speakers can usually be purchased for between $100 and $200, but if you're interested in top-quality audio for your PC's sound system, high-end speakers can set you back between $500 and $700.

Some manufacturers are also making speakers that plug in to your USB port. If you are using an operating system that supports USB, such as Windows 98/2000/Me/XP, consider this as another factor in your selection of speakers.

Installing a Sound Card and Speakers

Very little setup is involved to install a sound card in your PC. The sound card comes preconfigured with default settings, which work well in most PCs. If your sound card does not work after you complete the installation, there is a chance that one of the settings is conflicting with another device in your PC that is already using that setting.

The most common problem is that your sound card's default settings are using the same interrupt request (IRQ) that another device in your PC is already using. If this is the case, simply follow the instructions that accompany your sound card to change the interrupt request used by the sound card. Usually, changing an interrupt on a sound card is accomplished by running a Setup program for the sound card. (See Hour 3, "Examining Your PC's System Configuration," for more information on your IRQ settings.) Check also to see whether your sound card has to use a specific interrupt.

Task: Installing Your Sound Card

To install a sound card in your PC, take the following steps:

1. Read all the installation instructions that came with your sound card. In addition to instructions for installation, you often see cautions or warnings about potential problems that other users may have encountered. Make sure that you familiarize yourself with the various connectors on your sound card. Look for microphone connectors, line-out connectors for speakers, line-in connectors for auxiliary sound devices such as CD players, and joystick or MIDI connectors (see Figure 21.2).

2. Turn off and unplug your PC. Ground yourself and then remove the cover of the computer.

3. Locate a vacant slot on your motherboard in which you can install the sound card.

4. Insert the sound card into the slot (see Figure 21.3).

FIGURE 21.2

The connectors typically found on most sound cards.

Microphone connector

Audio out connector

Joystick or MIDI connector

FIGURE 21.3

Inserting your sound card into an available slot on the motherboard.

21

▼   5. If you have a CD-ROM drive installed in your PC, attach the audio cable from
        the audio connector on the sound card to the audio connector on the back of the
        CD-ROM drive (see Figure 21.4). You may have to remove your CD-ROM drive to
        access the audio connector. If you don't have an audio cable (see Figure 21.5), you
        can pick up one from your local computer store for less than $10. Make sure that
        you write down the model of the CD-ROM drive you have installed and the type of
        sound card you just installed before you go shopping for a cable.

FIGURE 21.4

*The rear connectors
on a CD-ROM drive
showing the audio
connector for your
sound card.*

Sound card   40-pin IDE   4-pin power
connection   interface   connector

6. Replace your PC's cover and turn on your PC.

7. Depending on which operating system you are using on your PC, you have to run
   the appropriate software to configure your operating system to recognize your new
   sound card and to load the audio drivers. If you are running Windows 98/2000/Me/XP
   and your new sound card is designed as Plug and Play, Windows should automatically recognize your sound card and begin the configuration process for you. If this
   happens, just follow the onscreen prompts to complete the configuration. Make
   sure that you have your Windows CD and the driver disks that accompanied your
▼   sound card.

FIGURE 21.5

A variety of audio cables used for connecting a CD-ROM drive to a sound card.

▲

When you complete the configuration process, the configuration software should include a procedure to test your newly installed sound card.

Make sure that your speakers are plugged into the correct connector (labeled "audio out" or "speakers" on the back of your sound card) and that they are turned on.

If the audio test fails, review the instructions for your sound card and make sure that you followed each step correctly. If you still haven't found the cause of the problem, rerun the PC checklist program from the SysChk utility, as described in Hour 3 to check your interrupt settings and make sure that your sound card is not in conflict with another device in your PC. After you have uncovered and resolved the problem, retest your sound card and enjoy the new dimension you've just added to your PC.

If you have a CD-ROM drive installed in your PC and you connected the audio cable from your CD-ROM drive to your sound card, you might want to try playing an audio CD in your drive. Check the software that accompanied your sound card to see whether it includes a CD player program. If it does not, you can use the Windows Media Player to play audio CDs.

21

Connecting Your Sound Card to Your Stereo

If you have your PC set up in the same room where you have your home stereo, it is possible to use your sound card with your stereo system. All you need is a cable connecting your sound card to your stereo amplifier or receiver. One end of the cable plugs into the same output connector on your sound card that you would normally use for your speakers and the other end plugs into an auxiliary input jack on your stereo amplifier or receiver.

The cable you need to purchase is carried by most good electronics stores and can be purchased for between $5 and $10. (Figure 21.6 shows the type of cable you need to purchase.) It has two RCA-type plugs on one end, which connect into the left and right input connectors on your stereo receiver, and the cable has what is called a "miniature stereo plug" on the other end, which plugs into your sound card.

FIGURE 21.6

A cable used for connecting your sound card to your stereo amplifier or receiver.

Task: Connecting Your Sound Card to Your Home Stereo

Connecting your sound card to your home stereo is simply a matter of connecting a cable. To connect the two, do the following:

1. Purchase the cable described earlier in this section. Try to purchase a cable that is long enough to reach from your sound card to your stereo but that does not have too much slack. The cables usually come in lengths of 3, 6, 10, and 20 feet. If the distance from your sound card to your stereo is 7 feet, don't purchase a cable 20 feet in length because audio signals diminish as cable lengths increase.

2. Plug the miniature stereo plug into your sound card. Plug this cable into the connector used for speakers.

3. Make sure that your stereo is turned off. Plug the two RCA-type plugs into a spare auxiliary input connector on your stereo. It does not matter which plug you plug into the left jack or the right jack.

4. Make sure that the volume control is turned down on your stereo. Turn your stereo on again, and using your stereo controls, select the auxiliary input source to which you connected your sound card.

5. Generate some type of audio on your PC (for example, start a game or play a music CD in your CD-ROM drive). Adjust the volume on your stereo to your liking.

Precautions When Using Your Stereo

You need to be aware of only two precautions when using your stereo with your PC sound card:

- Be careful when adjusting the volume levels; it is very easy to blast the room you're in.

- Make sure that your stereo speakers are not placed close to your PC monitor because stereo speakers typically are not shielded. Magnetic interference is generated by speakers. Unshielded speakers can potentially damage your monitor; shielded speakers prevent the damage from occurring.

If you exercise these two cautions, you can safely play your sound card through your home stereo.

Summary

In this hour, you learned how to select and install a sound card into your PC. You also learned about selecting and installing speakers to accompany your sound card and how to use your home stereo with your sound card in place of dedicated PC speakers.

21

Q&A

Q I was listening to a MIDI file the other day and it sounded okay but did not sound like real musical instruments. Why?

A Unlike waveform (WAV) files, MIDI files are digital representations of sound events, not actual recordings of sound. MIDI sound events are played back through a MIDI synthesizer, so what you are hearing is an electronic synthesized version of the music, not a digital recording of the music. This is another reason why MIDI files of entire songs are so much smaller than waveform files of the same musical score.

Q What about listening to MP3 files? How will they sound?

A Even though there is a slight degradation in quality because of the way the files are compressed, many users cannot tell the difference between MP3 audio and audio CDs. MP3 files sound virtually identical to the original source and do not have that "electronic synthesized" quality of MIDI files.

Hour **22**

Selecting and Installing a Printer, Scanner, or Digital Camera

One of the basic peripherals for a PC used to be a difficult installation task for many users, but as you will see in this hour, it is now a fairly simple procedure. Desktop printers have been around as long as PCs and still connect to PCs pretty much the same as they did back in 1981.

On the other hand, a new technology that seems to be making as big a splash with many computer users as printers originally did is digital imagery. In the past few years, many PC users have had the opportunity to dabble with digital imagery largely because of the availability of better quality and less expensive digital scanners and digital cameras. Scanners have never been less expensive, more available, or easier to set up and use. And digital cameras are slowly approaching the quality of film cameras while inching toward the price range considered affordable by most PC users.

In this hour, you will learn the following:

- How to install a printer to work on your PC with Windows 98/NT/2000/Me/XP
- How to install a second printer to work with your PC
- How to set up your PC to select between two printers
- About the types of scanners available for the PC industry
- How to install and set up your scanner
- How to select a digital camera

Understanding the Types of Printers

All printers fall into one of two broad categories: impact or nonimpact printers. *Impact* printers employ some type of mechanical process to form characters or images by physically striking (or impacting) paper or some other printable medium. Some examples of impact printers are

- Dot-matrix printers
- Daisy-wheel printers

Nonimpact printers use a nonphysical (or nonimpact) process to transfer characters or an image to paper. Some examples of nonimpact printers are

- Laser printers
- Inkjet printers
- Thermal printers

Many years ago, dot-matrix printers reigned supreme primarily because of their speed and the fact that they were relatively inexpensive. Some of the better quality dot-matrix printers could also produce a relatively high-quality text, what was then called "near letter-quality text."

Today, however, dot-matrix printers have declined significantly in popularity and have practically gone the way of the dodo now that laser and inkjet printers have dropped dramatically in price and have made true typeset-quality and color text affordable to the masses.

How to Select a Printer

For many users, price is ultimately the deciding factor in choosing between a laser and an inkjet printer. Laser printers (see Figure 22.1) are still slightly more expensive to

22

purchase but cheaper to operate than their inkjet counterparts. By "cheaper" I mean that the average per-page cost is lower. Keep in mind also that, among laser printers, the average cost per page can vary significantly because of the differences in laser printer toner cartridge prices.

FIGURE 22.1

A typical desktop laser printer.

Inkjet printers (see Figure 22.2) are less expensive but still command a higher per-page cost to operate because of the cost of ink cartridges. Laser printers still average about one-half cent per page, whereas inkjet printers can range anywhere from about 2–10 cents per page depending on whether you are printing in monochrome or color. It doesn't sound like much initially, until you begin to multiply these costs by several hundred or several thousand pages.

FIGURE 22.2

A typical desktop inkjet printer.

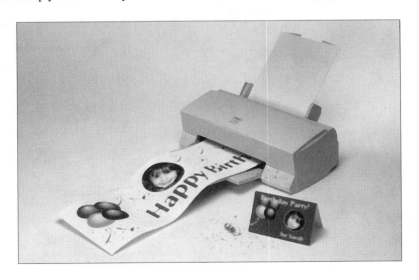

Price, however, should be only one of several factors you use in deciding what type of printer is best for your needs. In addition to price, other factors you should consider before purchasing a printer are

- Print speed
- Print quality
- Color versus monochrome
- The demand you plan to place on your printer—that is, the number of pages you think you will print each month
- The versatility of the printer; some manufacturers combine printers, scanners, copiers, and fax machines in one complete package

Comparing Various Printer Models

One of best places to begin looking when you want to start comparing printer features is the Computers.com site run by CNET at `http://computers.cnet.com/hardware/0-1016.html`. CNET maintains a fairly up-to-date listing of available printer models and will periodically review printers for you and make suggestions in various categories (see Figure 22.3).

FIGURE 22.3
CNET comparison categories for its reviewed printers.

You might also consider going directly to some of the major printer manufacturers' sites for more detailed information when you have narrowed down your choices. Here are a few sites to consider:

- **Hewlett Packard**— `http://www.pandi.hp.com/seg/printers.html`
- **Epson**— `http://www.epson.com/cgi-bin/Store/index.jsp`
- **Brother**—`http://www.brother.com/usa/printer/info/hl1240/`
  `hl1240_oth.html`
- **Lexmark**—`http://www.lexmark.com/`
- **Kyocera**—`http://www.kyocera.com/KEI/printers/index.htm`
- **Tektronics**—`http://www.tek.com/Color_Printers/`
- **Okidata**—`http://www.oki.com/english/Home.html`

Print Speed

Laser printers lead the race over inkjet printers when it comes to churning out a large number of pages per minute, but the inkjet is rapidly closing the speed gap. Most personal laser printers print in the 6–8 ppm (pages per minute) range, whereas many inkjet printers can print monochrome text (one color text, usually black) in the 4–6 ppm range.

Print Quality

Print quality is measured in resolution, similar to video resolution. Remember from Hour 20, "Upgrading Your Video Card and Monitor," that video resolution is measured by pixels (picture elements) on the entire screen measured horizontally and vertically (for example, 640×480 or 800×600). Printer resolution is also measured horizontally and vertically, but instead of the entire screen or page, the resolution is measured within a one-inch (1×1 inch) square. Instead of pixels, printer resolution is measured in dots per inch (abbreviated dpi—printers still have not adopted the metric system). For example, most laser printers now print at a resolution of 600×600 (or 1200×1200) dpi.

The dots-per-inch resolution of a printer should be described using both the horizontal and vertical measurements (600×600 dpi), but often, if the measurements are the same, the description is shortened. For example, a resolution of 300×300 dpi is shortened to simply 300 dpi. Therefore, when you see the common resolution of 600 dpi, you know that the resolution is in fact 600×600 dpi.

Although most laser printers seem to have standardized on a resolution of 600×600 dpi, in contrast, inkjet printers run the gamut from about 600×300 dpi to 720×1440 dpi. When printing text, laser printers seem to still have a slight quality edge over inkjet printers. However, when printing graphic images, many inkjet printers can produce much higher quality printouts than laser printers.

If you use dpi as one of your determining factors in choosing a printer, consider these suggestions:

- When printing text such as letters or manuscripts, 300 dpi is adequate. Most users cannot distinguish between text printed at 300 dpi and text printed at 600 dpi.
- When printing graphics, however, higher resolution almost always means higher quality output. Most users can distinguish between a graphic image printed at 300 dpi and the same image printed at 600 dpi.

Color Versus Monochrome

In deciding between color and monochrome, the decision is usually much simpler to make. If you need to print in color, you purchase an inkjet. If you are satisfied with printing only in black and white, get a laser printer.

> Color laser printers are available, but unfortunately, they are still in the $2,000–$3,000 price range. Most users who require color still opt for inkjet printers, which can produce output at nearly the quality of color laser printers, and at a fraction of the cost.

Keep in mind that with an inkjet printer, you can also choose to print in just black and white. Many inkjet printer users produce draft copies of their output in black and white and print the final output in color. Doing so can save on color cartridge costs.

Installing a Printer to Work with Your PC

Printers are among the easiest peripherals to install, especially if you are running Windows 98/2000/Me/XP because any of these versions of Windows will practically install the printer for you. Most printers today are designed to connect to your PC through the parallel port, so basically all you need to connect your PC and printer is a standard *Centronics parallel cable*.

A *Centronics parallel cable* is a simple communications cable with a 36-pin Centronics male connector on one end and a 25-pin female connector on the other. You can purchase a Centronics parallel cable in most computer stores in lengths ranging from 6 to 15 feet. And don't believe that myth about parallel cables having to be less than 10 feet in length. If you need a 15-foot cable, go ahead and purchase one. Many stores now carry printer cables in lengths of 25 feet and longer.

Connecting the Hardware

Connecting your printer is a two-step process. The first step is connecting the hardware, and the second step is installing the correct printer driver.

Task: Connecting a Printer to Your PC

Here's what you have to do to connect a printer to your PC:

1. Unpack and set up your printer according to the manufacturer's instructions. Be sure to carefully remove all the packing materials and restraints.

2. Plug the 36-pin male Centronics connector of your parallel cable into the parallel port on your printer (see Figure 22.4).

FIGURE 22.4
The Centronics parallel port on a printer.

3. Plug the other end of your printer cable (the end with the 25-pin female connector) into the parallel port on the back of your PC. If you're not sure which port is the parallel port, refer to Hour 2, "Understanding the Components in Your PC."

4. Turn on your PC and your printer.

Installing Your Printer Driver

If you are running Windows 98/2000/Me/XP, the installation of your printer driver begins as soon as you restart the operating system, provided that your printer is designed as a Plug and Play peripheral. Just about all printers made in the last few years are Plug and Play. Simply follow the onscreen prompts and insert the printer driver disk when instructed.

> Before you can use your printer, you must install the appropriate printer *driver*. A printer driver is simply a small program that enables your PC to communicate with your printer.

Task: Installing a Printer Driver

Windows 98/2000/Me/XP begin installing your printer driver as soon as the operating system restarts, but if it doesn't, follow these steps to start the driver installation:

1. Click the Start button to open the Start menu.

2. Select Printers and Faxes to open the Windows Printer Control section (see Figure 22.5).

FIGURE 22.5
The Printer Control section under Windows XP.

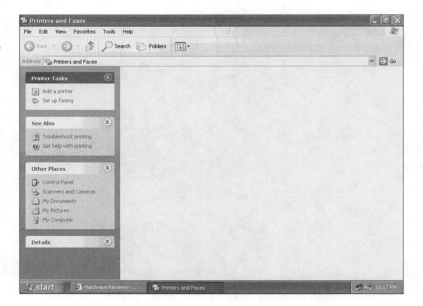

▼   3. Click the Add Printer icon to start the Add Printer Wizard (see Figure 22.6) and
        follow the prompts to install your printer driver.

FIGURE 22.6
The Windows XP Add
Printer Wizard used to
install printer drivers.

▲

Installing a Second Printer to Work with Your PC

So far, we have discussed how to install only one printer to your PC. What if you have
one PC but need to connect two printers? It's not uncommon for many users to have both
a laser and an inkjet printer.

You can connect two printers to your PC in the following ways:

- You can set up the second printer next to the first printer and switch the printer
  cable from one printer to the other.

- You can purchase and install a second parallel port in your PC and connect the
  second printer to this second port using a second printer cable.

- You can purchase a hardware device called an A/B switch and use it to switch the
  communication signal from one printer to the other.

- If your second printer and your PC both have USB ports and you are using
  Windows 98/2000/Me/XP, you can connect one printer to the parallel port
  and one printer to the USB port.

> Years ago, you could connect one printer to the parallel port and the other
> printer to your serial port. This option is not usually possible nowadays
> because very few printers are now equipped with a serial interface.

Method One: Switching the Cable

To connect two printers to one PC, switching the printer cable is the easiest but not necessarily the most convenient way to connect your two printers. You need to install printer drivers for both printers, and when you want to switch from one printer to the other, you simply unplug the cable from the back of one printer and plug the cable into the parallel port of the other printer. You don't have to turn the printers on and off and you don't even have to reboot your PC.

> Regardless of which of the possible multiple-printer solutions you choose, remember that you need to select the appropriate driver in Windows for the printer you are attempting to use. In most Windows applications, you can select a different printer driver from the Print dialog box.

Method Two: Installing a Second Parallel Port

Installing a second parallel port in your PC for a second printer is perhaps the most convenient of your options. You can purchase a second parallel port on an interface card from most computer stores for $35 or less and install it in less than 10 minutes.

> The interface card you purchase for your second parallel port might contain one or two serial ports as well. To prevent any possible conflicts with your existing serial ports, simply follow the instructions that come with the card to disable the two serial ports.

If you purchase a second parallel port, you must check a few settings on the interface card before you install it in your PC. First, make sure that the parallel port on the interface card is set to function as LPT2 and not set to function as LPT1. The parallel port in your PC is set to function as LPT1 by default. If both ports are set to LPT1, the two ports create a conflict and you will be unable to print to either port. Most add-on second parallel port cards are almost always set to LPT2 at the factory, so you shouldn't have a problem with conflicts. Most manufacturers seem to understand that you are adding an additional parallel port; however, make sure that you check the settings before you install the card.

Also check the memory address and the interrupt request (IRQ) that the parallel port on the interface card is set to use to make sure that they are not in conflict with the memory address and interrupt used by the parallel port (LPT1) in your PC.

Use the SysChk program you became acquainted with in Hour 3, "Examining Your PC's System Configuration," to check the memory address and interrupt in use by the parallel port in your PC. The interrupt is most likely 7 because this is usually the default interrupt used for LPT1. The memory address looks something like 3BC or 2BC. Just make sure that you check which settings your existing parallel port uses and set the new parallel port to use different settings.

Task: Installing a Second Parallel Port

To install a second parallel port in your PC, follow these steps:

1. Turn off and unplug your PC, ground yourself, and then remove the PC cover.

2. Insert the interface card in an empty slot in your PC.

3. Replace the cover, plug in your PC, and turn it on.

4. Run your PC's hardware Setup program and install or enable LPT2. If you have to include the interrupt and memory address in the setup process, enter the settings the same as they are on the card.

You now can connect the second printer just the same as you connected the first printer earlier in this hour. When you install the driver for the second printer, remember to designate the output port as LPT2, the second parallel port in your PC.

Method Three: Installing an A/B Switch

An A/B switch is like a fork in the road—it enables you to travel in one of two directions. In this case, the A/B switch is a device that enables the signal from your PC to travel to one of two connected printers.

Essentially, the A/B switch is a device or electrical connector box with one cable attached to your PC and two cables attached to each of your two printers. The device is called an A/B switch because a physical switch enables you to select printer A or printer B.

The A/B switch is just a hardware device—meaning that you have no setup program to run. To install, just plug one cable from your PC into the input port on the switch. You then connect the remaining two cables from each output port to each of your printers. Now when you want to print to the printer connected to the first output port, you move the selector on the switchbox to the A position. When you want to print to the printer connected to the second output port, you move the selector on the switchbox to the B position. The biggest problem in using an A/B switch is making sure that you get the input and output cables installed correctly. But most A/B switches usually ship with more than enough documentation to walk you through the connections. An estimate of the price of an A/B switch is anywhere from about $35 to $75. You can purchase an A/B switch from most computer or office supply stores and from many electronics stores.

Some laser printer manufacturers warn against using an A/B switch because of a possibility of damage to the printer with the sudden loss of signal (when you switch from one printer to the other). Check to make sure that your printer will safely work with an A/B switch before attempting to use one.

Method Four: Using Both Parallel and USB Ports

If your computer has both a parallel and a USB port, and you have printer that use both types of interfaces, it is a simple matter to plug each printer into its respective port. From the Print dialog box, select the printer to which you want to print.

Learning About Scanners

For basic home use, you can choose from three different types of scanners: flatbed, handheld, and sheet feed. Handheld scanners were designed basically for computer users with very limited funds to devote to a scanning device. A handheld scanner is a small device about the size of large TV remote control unit. You scan with it by slowly (and manually) sliding the scanner over the picture you are scanning. No one recommends purchasing a handheld scanner because the images they produce are almost always distorted—it is nearly impossible to move the scanner over the object you are scanning at a constant speed.

Because sheet-feed scanners were developed as a less expensive alternative to flatbed scanners, and because prices for flatbed scanners have been dropping steadily, it's likely that handheld scanners will all but disappear very soon. If you see one for sale, even at an unbelievably low price, don't waste your money.

Although there are three types of scanners you can still purchase for home use, my recommendation for a home scanner limits your selection to just two types—flatbed and sheet-feed models.

Sheet-Feed Scanners

Sheet-feed scanners are the less expensive of the two types recommended and have virtually replaced handheld scanners as the low-end model.

Besides being less expensive than flatbed scanners, one major advantage sheet-feed scanners have is that they occupy much less desktop space. The typical flatbed scanner takes up a desktop area approximately 14×20 inches, whereas the typical sheet-feed scanner only takes up an area approximately 12×4 inches (see Figure 22.7).

FIGURE 22.7
A typical sheet-feed scanner.

Although sheet-feed scanners are capable of scanning pictures and converting them to digital images the same as their flatbed cousins, most users who purchase sheet-feed scanners use them for *Optical Character Recognition (OCR)*.

Optical Character Recognition (OCR) is a way of using your scanner and special software to scan a page of text, such as a newspaper or magazine article, and convert what is being scanned into a text file. Some OCR programs can also convert the scanned document into several popular word-processing formats, such as Microsoft Word and Corel WordPerfect. Keep in mind that several good OCR programs are on the market, and even the best is not 100-percent perfect.

Sheet-feed scanners can scan pictures and photos and convert them to digital images, but most sheet-feed scanners have a lower optical resolution than their flatbed counterparts. Most sheet-feed scanners have a maximum optical resolution of around 300×600 dpi (dots per inch).

Just like printers that measure their output in dots per inch, scanners also measure their input in terms of dots per inch.

Flatbed Scanners

Of the two types of scanners recommended here, flatbed models (see Figure 22.8) are the more versatile because they allow you to scan single sheets, pages, or photos. You can also place larger, bulkier objects such as books and magazines on the flatbed for scanning. On many models of flatbed scanners, you can also attach optional sheet feeders for scanning multi-page documents (an excellent arrangement if you plan to do a lot of OCR scanning).

Flatbed scanners also tend to have a slightly higher optical scanning resolution than sheet-feed versions. Most home-use flatbed scanners have an optical resolution of 600×600 dpi.

Scanner manufacturers often present flatbed scanner resolution in two sets of numbers. They list the maximum optical resolution and they list a higher resolution value called the interpolated resolution. *Interpolation* is a means of guessing certain color values during the scanning process. Interpolation values can in some cases be fairly accurate. Nevertheless, you should never rely on the interpolated resolution as the maximum resolution your scanner is capable of achieving. Always use the optical resolution when comparing resolutions between scanner models.

FIGURE 22.8
A typical flatbed scanner.

Selecting a Scanner

Now that you know about the types of scanners available, you're ready for a few helpful hints on how to select a scanner.

First, decide what you want to do with your scanner. If you just plan to scan a few documents and occasionally scan a few family photos, you can probably get by with a sheet-feed scanner. If you need a scanner for doing a lot of document OCR scanning, however, you probably will do better with a flatbed scanner with an optional sheet-feeder to save you the time and effort of lifting the flatbed cover and replacing documents.

If you need to scan pictures, photos, or artwork for direct transfer to a Web site, a sheet-feed scanner is probably satisfactory. Web artwork does not have to be of very high resolution. Currently, 72 dpi is good enough for Web work.

> You should not attempt to scan antique or irreplaceable photographs through a sheet-feed scanner because these devices tend to curl or bend the photos during scanning.

However, if you want to scan pictures, photos, or artwork and plan to use some type of digital editing software on the scanned image—such as PhotoShop, CorelDraw, or Paint Shop Pro—you probably need the slightly higher optical resolution offered by a flatbed scanner.

Keep in mind how much scanning you plan to do. If you will be doing a lot of scanning, you probably will want to purchase a scanner with a SCSI interface because a SCSI interface is faster than a parallel (or proprietary) interface (see Hour 10, "Replacing, Upgrading, or Adding a Hard Disk Drive," for more information on SCSI interfaces).

> Originally, if you wanted a scanner attached to your PC, your choices of interfaces began and ended with SCSI. But with scanners now achieving the status of commodity items, many manufacturers have not only made scanners less expensive, but also a lot easier to connect and use. Many scanners also come with a parallel port interface. Most newer scanners can also be purchased with a USB interface.

> Of the available interfaces for scanners, in most cases a SCSI interface will deliver the fastest performance, and the parallel port interface is the slowest. USB scanners fall somewhere in between.

Although this may begin to sound like a broken record, before you purchase any peripheral, check several of the major PC journals for product reviews. It's not difficult to find a product review on scanners every other month or so, especially with the abundance of lower-priced scanners coming onto the market in recent months.

As with most of the other PC peripherals covered in this book, when reviewing scanners or digital cameras, one of the best places to begin for product information and product comparisons is CNET's Computers.Com Web site at `http://computers.cnet.com/ hardware/0-1016.html`. Some other sites worth considering for more detailed information include:

- **Umax**—`http://www.umax.com/`
- **Hewlett-Packard**—`http://www.pandi.hp.com/seg/scanners_di_photo.html`
- **Agfa**—`http://www.agfa.com/`
- **Canon**—`http://www.usa.canon.com/`
- **Epson**— `http://www.epson.com/cgi-bin/Store/index.jsp`

Installing Your Scanner

Four to five years ago, it was next to impossible to purchase a scanner that did not use a SCSI interface. Now you can purchase scanners that connect to your PC using SCSI, parallel, serial, USB, or proprietary interfaces. Serial interfaces have all but disappeared on scanners, so for all intents and purposes, you only have to choose between SCSI, parallel, USB, and proprietary interfaces.

A few scanner manufacturers still use a proprietary interface and supply their scanners with a proprietary interface card. Most experts, myself included, recommend against purchasing any device that uses a proprietary interface because such an interface usually offers no significant advantage over other available interfaces, and they take up space in your PC (by using one of your motherboard slots) that cannot by used by other devices.

Task: Installing a Scanner to Your PC

Because scanners are external devices, you connect them to your PC much the same as you would connect a printer, external CD-ROM drive, or an external tape backup drive. To install your scanner, follow these steps:

1. Unpack and set up your scanner, following the instructions supplied by the manufacturer. Make sure that you allow sufficient space on your desktop. Be sure to "unlock" the scanner arm in your scanner. The instructions will explain how to unlock the arm, which is shipped in a locked position to protect it from possible damage. The arm must be unlocked before you can use your scanner.

2. If you have to install an interface card (SCSI or proprietary) for your scanner, turn off and unplug your PC, ground yourself, remove the cover, locate an empty slot, and install the interface card into the empty slot.

22

Some scanner manufacturers include a SCSI interface card with their scanners, eliminating the need to purchase a separate SCSI card if you don't already have one. Sometimes, however, these supplied SCSI cards are designed to work only with the scanner they are shipped with and will not function with other SCSI devices. In effect, you are getting a proprietary interface card. If your scanner came with a card, use it instead of an existing SCSI card.

3. Connect your scanner to your PC using the cable shipped with the scanner. Follow the manufacturer's instructions. If you install the scanner into an existing SCSI chain (see Hour 10), make sure that you maintain the integrity of the chain by ensuring that it is still terminated at both ends.

Virtually every scanner manufacturer supplies a cable with the scanner. If, however, your scanner does not include a cable, you can usually purchase one at your local computer store. Parallel cables are in the $10–$15 range, SCSI cables are in the $30–$50 range, and USB cables are in the $10–$20 range.

4. Insert the driver disk supplied with your scanner and follow the instructions to install the scanner software and hardware driver for your particular operating system. The scanner software consists of the hardware driver needed to allow your PC to communicate with your scanner and usually also several utility programs supplied by the manufacturer.

Bundled software is also supplied by virtually every scanner manufacturer. In addition to the basic scanning software, some of the items they supply often include an OCR program, a copy utility, and a fax utility. The copy utility can be extremely useful because it allows you to use your scanner like a photocopier, which automatically sends the output to your printer. The fax utility is similar to the copy utility, but instead of sending the output to your printer, it sends faxes of the items scanned (provided that you have a fax modem).

5. Start your scanning software so that you can test your scanner by scanning a document or a picture. If you get an error message or the scanner fails to scan, go back and check all your cable connections. Also check to make sure that the hardware driver is properly installed and configured and that your scanner is turned on.

Considering Digital Cameras

If you are interested in producing digital images for Web site composition or digital editing, a digital camera can save you a few steps and a lot of time over using a traditional film camera. You don't have to worry about getting your film developed and then scanning the photographs.

A digital camera is just what the name suggests—a photographic camera that produces digital images. A digital camera (see Figure 22.9) does not use film. Instead, it contains memory or some type of storage medium where images you take are stored until you download them to your PC.

FIGURE 22.9

A typical digital camera.

A digital camera is highly convenient, especially when you consider that your images are almost immediately available for use and you don't have to stop to have your film developed. Nevertheless, digital cameras do have their drawbacks:

- Digital cameras are still expensive. A good digital camera costs between $400 and $700. Lesser-quality digital cameras can be purchased for $200–$400.

- Digital cameras still cannot produce images at the same quality of standard film cameras. Even a moderately priced 35mm film camera can produce photos superior to digital cameras. Film can produce images with a much higher resolution than the best digital cameras, even digital cameras costing several thousand dollars.

- The quality of printed photos taken by digital cameras still does not rival actual photographic prints; printed digital photos also tend to fade a lot faster than traditional photos.

With all these negatives, you might wonder why anyone would ever bother using a digital camera. The primary reason is simple—convenience. The primary uses of digital cameras are in areas where the lower resolution produced by digital cameras is not a problem, namely Web-based graphics. Because Web-based graphics do not have to be any greater than 72 dpi, the convenience and lower resolutions offered by digital cameras make producing Web-based graphics a cinch.

Many users also purchase digital cameras because it is a lot easier to send photos as e-mail attachments to friends and relatives than to reprint and mail photos in snail mail. It's also true that digital colors (while they are safely stored on your computer) never fade.

Selecting a Digital Camera

Digital cameras can range in price from a few hundred dollars to several thousand dollars. But don't get the impression that you can't get a usable digital camera without taking out a second mortgage. There are several dozen very good digital cameras priced in the $300–$500 range (what most photographers would call "point-and-shoot" models), and several manufacturers are hard at work making more.

Just like every other product mentioned in this book, you need to check the popular PC journals for product reviews to get an idea how the various models of digital cameras in your price range compare. Just like scanners, the quality of digital cameras can vary considerably for models in the same price range. And just like scanners, because this is a hot market, manufacturers are constantly coming out with new and improved models, so it pays to check often.

You should begin your selection process by comparing current models at CNET's Computers.Com at http://computers.cnet.com/hardware/0-1016.html. You might also want to look at the sites of some of the top manufacturers, such as:

- **Kodak**—http://www.kodak.com/US/en/nav/digital.shtml
- **Canon**—http://www.canon.com/
- **Epson**— http://www.epson.com/cgi-bin/Store/index.jsp
- **Fuji**—http://www.fujifilm.com/
- **Olympus**—http://www.olympusamerica.com/p.asp?s=12&p=16
- **Nikon**—http://www.nikonusa.com/usa_home/home.jsp
- **Sony**—http://www.sel.sony.com/SEL/consumer/ss5/generic/digitalstillcameras/

You also need to be aware of what add-on products are available for various digital cameras. Some cameras allow you to add additional memory to boost the number of photos you can take before you have to download images to your PC. Some cameras come equipped with the same type of peripheral slots found on laptop computers and allow you to use the same memory and hard disk peripherals available for laptop computers. There are also digital cameras that allow you to use floppy disks the same as you would use film in a traditional camera. When you take the maximum number of photos that will fit on a disk, you simply remove the disk, insert another, and continue shooting.

Most digital cameras come with a cable and software to allow you to connect to your PC and download the photos stored in your camera. The number of photos you can take with a digital camera varies considerably depending on the amount of memory or storage in the camera and the resolution of the photos you take.

If you are thinking of purchasing a digital camera, here are a few features to consider:

- At what resolutions can you take pictures? The minimum now for most entry-level digital cameras is 640×480. Many manufacturers are offering lower-cost models that take photos at resolutions of 1024×768 and 1152×864.
- Does the camera include a built-in flash? You need a flash of some type if you plan to take photos indoors. Does the camera have any type of flash mode? Backlight reduction? Red-eye reduction? Effective range?
- How much memory or storage capacity does the camera have? Is it expandable? The amount of memory determines how many pictures it can store at one time.
- Is the lens fixed focus, or can you zoom? What is the equivalent sized 35mm lens? Is it auto-focus or manual focus? Does it have a macro mode for taking close-up shots?
- What types of batteries does the camera use and (approximately) how long will they last (or how many photos can you take)?
- How long is the setup time between taking photos?
- Can you print directly from the camera? Does the manufacturer offer a companion printer?
- What is the color depth? 24-bit? 30-bit? More?
- Does the camera save images in the standard JPG format, or does it use a proprietary image format? If it uses a proprietary format, does it include a utility for converting that format to a standard format?
- Some cameras also allow you to include a few seconds of audio to help you catalog your photos. Do the cameras you are reviewing have this feature?

Although these aren't the only features that you should be concerned with in selecting a digital camera, this list will at least give you a start in making your selection.

Summary

In this hour, you learned how to select and install a printer to your PC. You learned what criteria to use to judge printers and what steps you need to follow to connect your printer and install the appropriate printer driver. You also learned the various methods of connecting two printers to your PC.

You also learned about scanners and digital cameras, what features you need to be concerned about when selecting either a scanner or a digital camera, and how to install a scanner to work with your PC.

Q&A

Q Are there any maintenance tips I should know about for my printer?

A Just like PCs, printers do tend to attract their share of dust. Periodically—about every six months or so—open the cover and blow out as much dust as you can. It's also a good idea to have laser printers serviced about once a year. The only other maintenance advice is to use quality paper, toner, and ink cartridges.

Q I read that digital cameras last year outsold 35mm cameras. Doesn't that suggest that the quality of digital and film cameras is about the same?

A Not really. What this suggests to me is that many people are willing to pay for convenience. For the same money, digital cameras still have a long way to go to match the quality of film cameras, especially considering the broad range of film types available. To get the maximum benefit out of a good film camera, however, you have to learn a little about photography: f-stops, film speeds, macro and telephoto lenses, composition techniques with lighting, and so on. Most people just don't want to be bothered.

Go on the Web and find sales figures for companies such as Polaroid and Kodak and compare them to sales figures for companies such as Nikon and Leica. Most people who take pictures are still using point-and-shoot type cameras and don't want to be bothered with having to make settings on their camera before taking a picture. The majority of digital cameras sold are still in the point-and-shoot category.

Add to this the fact that digital cameras eliminate another headache for users—having to purchase and then take the film to a camera store or some type of processing facility before the user can see the pictures taken. Many digital cameras have not only a viewfinder for lining up the picture you want to take, but also a way to display the picture immediately after taking it. The increased sales of digital cameras in the last few years clearly points out that many consumers are more than willing to pay more for convenience even when it means sacrificing some quality.

Hour 23

Upgrading to a New Operating System

The past 22 hours have dealt exclusively with upgrading the hardware in your PC. But the latest and greatest hardware will not live up to its full potential if you are still using an antiquated operating system that is five to seven years old.

Strange as it might sound, 20–30 percent of all PC users are still using either the DOS/Windows 3.1 combination or Windows 95. In the PC world, this is tantamount to purchasing a Lamborghini Countach and never taking it out of first gear.

Now we're going to talk about upgrading your operating system. During this hour you will learn:

- About the limitations of Windows 3.1 and 95
- Why you should upgrade your operating system
- How to decide between Windows 98, 2000, Me, and XP, or another operating system such as Linux

Limitations of DOS/Windows 3.1 and Windows 95

If you are still using DOS, you are using an operating system that has been around in some form since 1981. Without going through the history or evolution of DOS, its biggest limitations include the following:

- DOS was written essentially for the 80286 processor, which means that DOS cannot address more than 16MB of memory for program execution.
- DOS lacks any type of system or file security.
- DOS uses the 8.3 filename convention (the filename can be 1–8 characters and the file extension can be 1–3 characters).
- DOS uses the FAT16 formatting structure for formatting hard disks, which means that DOS cannot create hard disk partitions larger than 2GB (2048MB).
- DOS is a single-tasking operating system, which means that you can run only one program at a time.
- DOS is text only and does not include a GUI (Graphical User Interface).

Windows 3.1 is an operating *environment*—not an operating system—that resides on top of DOS and still maintains most of DOS's limitations. Windows 3.1 was written to work on an 80386 processor.

But perhaps the biggest reason to upgrade from Windows 3.1 is that software is no longer being developed for it!

Windows 95 was Microsoft's first attempt at a 32-bit GUI-based operating system. To aid in the transition to it from Windows 3.1, Windows 95 included a lot of 16-bit programming code to maintain as much compatibility with existing software that was written for Windows 3.1. All that 16-bit programming code meant that Windows 95 was not a true 32-bit operating system. As it attempted to straddle the fence between the 16-bit and 32-bit worlds, a host of problems were uncovered, such as memory management and memory leakage problems.

Now you're probably thinking that you're using Windows 3.1 and you surf the Net and use the latest versions of Netscape and Internet Explorer, so what do I mean when I say that "software isn't being developed for Windows 3.1"? The Netscape and Internet Explorer browsers you're using were originally developed for Windows 95 and NT. The Windows 3.1 versions you're using are scaled-back versions created for people like you who have not upgraded yet. They are not functionally equivalent to the Windows 95 and NT versions (and are also about 3–4 versions behind what your Windows 98/NT/2000/Me/XP brothers and sisters are using).

Speaking of the Internet, let's use it to further illustrate the point about Windows 3.1. One of the premier World Wide Web animation tools is a program called Flash by Macromedia. Go to the Macromedia Web site (http://www.macromedia.com) and see whether you can download a version of the Flash player for Windows 3.1. See whether you can download a Windows 3.1 version of *any* of the popular Internet-distributed plug-ins or add-ons such as WinZip, Adobe Acrobat, or the Real Audio Player.

Go to a few other sites and see how many programs, plug-ins, and utilities are available for Windows 95/98/NT/2000/Me/XP:

- http://www.tucows.com
- http://www.download.com
- http://www.shareware.com

Still need more convincing? Here is the *coup de grace*. In late 1997, Microsoft announced that it was no longer selling Windows 3.1. This announcement officially made Windows 3.1 obsolete.

In case you're wondering about IBM's OS/2 operating system, it is actually just a little better than Windows 3.1. I used to be an ardent OS/2 user and supporter, but OS/2 lacks the capability to run 32-bit Windows applications, which means that whatever applies to Windows 3.1 also applies to OS/2 in regards to software and availability (except, of course, for native OS/2 applications). You don't have to take my word for it. Go to your local software store and see how much software you can find for OS/2.

The argument against Windows 95 may seem a bit less conclusive. The best argument against Windows 95 is that you have so many better options. Windows 98 was essentially released as an interim operating system to solve many of problems present in Windows 95. Windows 98 is definitely an improvement over Windows 95, but all the versions of Windows to follow 98 simply do a much better job of managing your PC's memory, providing security, and running your applications.

While we're on the subject of obsolete, or near-obsolete, operating systems, if you're still using Windows NT 4.0, you're also overdue for an upgrade. When the choices were Windows 95/98 or Windows NT 4.0, Windows NT 4.0 always edged out the competition especially in the area of security. Now however, Windows 2000 and XP offer more security than Windows NT 4.0 and also provide USB support, Plug and Play, better memory management, and improved overall stability.

Why You Should Upgrade

Now that I've told you why you should stop using Windows 3.1 and Windows 95, I need to spend a few minutes telling you why you should upgrade to Windows 2000, Me, or XP. If you are considering an upgrade from Windows 3.1 to Windows 2000/Me/XP, you can set aside your number one fear: that you will have to abandon all your favorite software titles and learn new application programs. It is a pretty safe bet that all your favorite programs *will* be available in versions that run under Windows 2000/Me/XP, but you can expect a slight learning curve to become familiar with the new features. If you are still using software designed for Windows 3.1, you should consider it just as old and obsolete as the old 486 you hate to part with and strongly consider upgrading your software, too.

Crash Protection

If you are an active Windows 3.1 user, undoubtedly you've experienced the dreaded GPF—General Protection Fault. A GPF occurs when Windows 3.1 allows two programs to use the same area of memory. GPFs do not exist in Windows 2000/Me/XP because of how well each of these incarnations of Windows manages memory usage.

> This is not to say that Windows 2000/Me/XP will never crash because of errant programs. If you are looking for crash protection, however, Windows 2000/Me/XP have the best. Windows 2000/Me/XP will not let a problem with one program affect the performance of another program. If a program crashes under 2000/Me/XP, only that program is affected and Windows 2000/Me/XP allow you to "gracefully" shut down the bothersome program (and then restart it if you like) without affecting the rest of your work. How many of you Windows 3.1 and Windows 95 users have lost hours of unsaved work because another program you had open crashed and brought down the entire system?

Internet Access and Built-in Networking Capabilities

Since Windows 95, all versions of Windows have come with all the tools you need to access the Internet. With Windows Me and XP, it is now easier than ever to access the Internet (see Figure 23.1).

All versions of Windows also still come equipped with all the tools you need for network setup, including setting up a peer-to-peer network (see Hour 17, "Adding a Home Network"); Windows XP also includes more Internet security in the form of a built-in firewall (see Figure 23.2).

FIGURE 23.1

The Internet Setup Wizard in Windows XP.

23

FIGURE 23.2

Activating the built-in firewall in Windows XP.

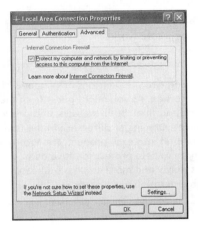

To reiterate, here are some of the pluses and minuses of Windows 3.1/95 versus Windows 2000/Me/XP:

- Windows 3.1/95 have very limited memory management capabilities; Windows 2000/Me/XP have extensive memory management capabilities.

- Windows 3.1 has no file or system security; Windows 95 has minimal system security; Windows 2000/Me/XP have extensive file and system security.

- Windows 3.1/95 will run your existing (16-bit) applications; Windows 2000 will probably run your existing (16-bit) applications (and prevent them from crashing into each other) and will also run the more advanced 32-bit applications. (Note that you're better off ditching the older software along with your old PC and OS and upgrading your software as well.)

- Windows 3.1 does not include applications or utilities for accessing the Internet; since Windows 95, all versions of Windows have included utilities and applications for accessing the Internet. With Windows Me and XP, these utilities and applications are easier than ever to use.

Windows Me, 2000, or XP?

So, which operating system should you upgrade to? Windows Me, Windows 2000, or Windows XP? Well, it depends on what you need a new operating system for, what you intend to do with your new operating system, what your level of computer experience is, and how much horsepower you have in your PC. Right now, Microsoft is marketing Windows Me and the Home Edition of Windows XP as the operating system for most home users; it's marketing Windows 2000 or the Professional version of Windows XP as the operating system for the corporate workplace.

Microsoft is marketing two user versions of Windows XP: a Home Edition and a Professional version. As you might guess from the names, one version is targeted at home and small business users, and one version is targeted at the corporate market. One major difference in the two versions is the amount of security built into each product. The Professional version offers much tighter security to help protect sensitive data. The Home Edition offers less emphasis on security and more emphasis on ease of use and greater compatibility with entertainment software.

If you are planning to upgrade your home computer, odds are you'll be better off upgrading to Windows Me or Windows XP Home Edition because the needs and demands (especially in the areas of file and system security) of home users are typically not as pressing as those of the user in the corporate environment.

Upgrading to Windows Me or Windows XP Home Edition

Microsoft did provide an upgrade path for upgrading from Windows 3.1/95/98 to Windows 2000/Me/XP. Although installing one version of Windows on top of an existing installation of Windows is possible, my advice is *don't!* The installation of a newer version of Windows will not be done cleanly because many of the files from the older version of Windows will be left on your hard disk during the installation, and these files can potentially interact with similar (newer) Windows files and be a potential source of problems.

For best results, back up all your existing data files, delete your old version of Windows entirely from your hard disk drive (delete the `C:\WINDOWS` directory), and then install the new version of Windows. Afterwards, re-install all your existing software applications—unless they are Windows 3.1 versions.

> If you decide to start with a really clean slate and reformat your hard disk, make sure that you back up your files first.

Also make sure that you have upgraded the memory in your PC. The minimum amount of memory you should have for Windows 2000/Me/XP is 64MB, but you will find that these newer versions of Windows perform best for most home users when your PC has 128MB or more of RAM.

Upgrading to Linux

There *is* an alternative to Windows. Many users have successfully switched to the Linux operating system and have never looked back. Linux is a *UNIX* operating system clone and is not directly compatible with Windows or Windows-based software (even though there are a few utility programs that allow you to run some Microsoft products). But in the past few years, many software manufacturers (except Microsoft, of course) have produced Linux versions of their applications and games. There are easily more than 10,000 software titles and utilities available for Linux, so finding software to run should not be a major concern.

> *UNIX* is an operating system that actually predates Windows. It is mainly used on larger, more powerful workstations and is more often used in engineering and scientific settings.

In the United States, two major vendors currently have the lion's share of the Linux market: Red Hat, at `http://www.redhat.com` (see Figure 23.3) and Caldera, at `http://www.calderasystems.com` (see Figure 23.4).

FIGURE 23.3

The home page of Red Hat, one of the major Linux distributors in the United States.

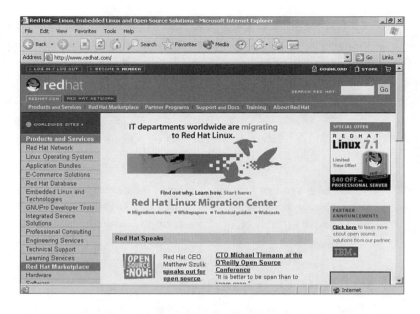

FIGURE 23.4

Caldera, another major Linux distributor in the United States.

Even though both companies (and many others) will sell you a copy of Linux, Linux is not actually owned by either company. Linux follows the Open Source model, which means that the program and its source code are available to anyone who wants them and who wants to download them from any of several hundred Internet sites. This means that if you are a skilled and talented computer programmer, you can not only obtain a copy of Linux but also change it to your heart's content. What Red Hat and Caldera are selling you are versions of Linux that are much easier to install than to download off the Internet. Both companies also include additional applications and utilities that make Linux easier to get up and running, including Internet applications and utilities such as Netscape Navigator.

Linux will run on a lot less hardware than will Windows 2000/Me/XP. If you have an old 486 lying around that you have (hopefully!) discarded, you can dust it off add new life to it by installing Linux on it. Although Linux, like most other operating systems, will run better on Pentium-based PCs, it will run satisfactorily on an older 486.

Both companies include utilities to install Linux on your everyday PC provided that you have enough free disk space. The companies also include utilities to allow you to dual-boot to both Linux and whatever version of Windows you are running. A typical installation of Linux requires around 500MB of disk space. If you don't have this much free disk space, that's another reason to go back and reread Hour 10, "Replacing, Upgrading, or Adding a Hard Disk Drive."

The installation procedures are different for each vendor, but a beginner or novice can install either and have Linux up and running in about an hour (see Figure 23.5).

FIGURE 23.5

Caldera's version of the Linux operating system.

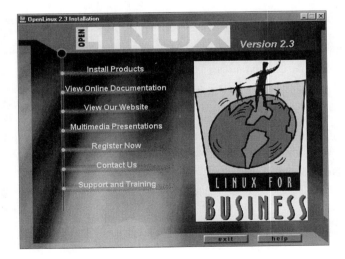

Even though you may have heard that Linux is a lot harder to use than Windows, it's actually not. It's just different, so expect a learning curve. If you use Linux from the command line (like you used to do with DOS) you will notice that a lot of the DOS commands you learned are very similar under Linux, such as MKDIR to make a directory and RMDIR to remove a directory. To make that learning curve a little less steep, both companies include one or more Windows-like GUIs (Graphical User Interfaces) to help shield you from an unfamiliar OS.

Summary

In the past hour, you learned about upgrading your operating system and especially why you should upgrade if you are still using the DOS/Windows 3.1 combination or Windows 95. You also learned about some of the features in Windows 98 and Windows 2000/Me/XP, which should help you decide which of these operating systems you should select, whether you are mainly a home or corporate user. You also learned about Linux, a viable alternative to Windows that offers much if not all of the same functionality provided by the various Windows operating systems.

Q&A

Q You've mentioned a lot of advantages in upgrading to Windows 2000/Me/XP but what are the disadvantages to upgrading to any of these operating systems?

A Well, obviously there is a learning curve. The interfaces for newer versions of Windows are somewhat different than those of the older versions. This is probably the biggest disadvantage, but like anything else on your PC, you start out learning the basics and then advance to the more difficult areas. In the long run, you will see that the advantages far outweigh the disadvantages.

Q Does this also apply to Linux?

A Yes, even more so. Some versions of Linux offer you more than one Windows-like GUI interface. There are numerous other "differences" despite the similarities. As with any new OS, take it slow and learn as you go.

HOUR 24

How to Purchase PC Components on the Internet

In the past 23 hours, you have learned a considerable amount about how to upgrade the various components in your PC. You also should have picked up a few tips about how to select the upgrade items. In this hour, you will learn how to go about purchasing those items over the Internet.

During this hour, you will learn:

- The pros and cons of purchasing online
- How to locate companies and components
- What you need to know about Internet security to safely purchase PC components (or anything else) over the Internet

Purchasing Over the Internet

All the PC components mentioned throughout this book can very readily be purchased directly over the Internet and delivered right to your front door. Although many computer users continue to purchase items through mail order, not as many are purchasing over the Internet despite the fact that most of the companies selling mail order are also selling over the Internet. As expected, you have to make a few tradeoffs when purchasing over the Internet.

On the plus side:

- No sales reps will bother you by trying to sell you additional items you don't want or need.

- Most companies place their entire inventory on their Web sites, but place only a fraction of it in magazines and catalogs. This allows you to locate the exact model of whatever item you are looking to purchase.

- You have instant access to current pricing and inventory status. The key phrase here is "inventory status." If you are ready to purchase, you can instantly see who is ready to ship you the item you need.

- It's very easy to do comparison shopping (pricing) online and many, if not most, items can be purchased cheaper online as compared to purchasing in-store.

However, purchasing over the Internet also has a down side:

- You must know exactly what you want to purchase, which usually means manufacturer and model.

- You must purchase using a credit card. Because you are in effect purchasing from a computer system and not a person, you cannot pay with a check, a money order, or a company purchase order.

- You have to trust Internet security. This still seems to be the biggest turnoff for most potential online customers, but as you will see later in this hour, it shouldn't be.

Locating Companies

Locating computer companies and computer supply companies who do business over the Internet is relatively easy. Look in any computer magazine, and you will see ads for dozens of companies—most will include a Web address of where you can find their online storefront.

You can also locate computer companies on the Internet by using the Internet. One of the best places to start looking is at Yahoo! (`http://www.yahoo.com/`). On the Yahoo! home page, you will see a link for Shopping. Click this link to enter the Yahoo! Shopping section (see Figure 24.1).

FIGURE 24.1

The Yahoo! Shopping section.

There are several other links you can try on this page. In this example, you'll see how to go shopping for a new active matrix LCD monitor. Select the Computer link, and then select the Monitor link. Finally, select the ViewSonic link to open the page listing ViewSonic monitors, both LCD and CRT varieties (see Figure 24.2).

FIGURE 24.2

ViewSonic monitors available on the Yahoo! Shopping page.

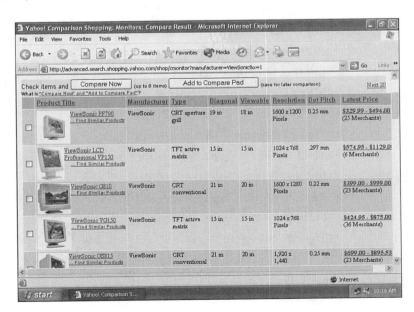

24

Select the price range to the right of the model you're interested in to see the prices offered by various online merchants (see Figure 24.3).

FIGURE 24.3

Various online merchants offering LCD monitors for sale on the Yahoo! Shopping site.

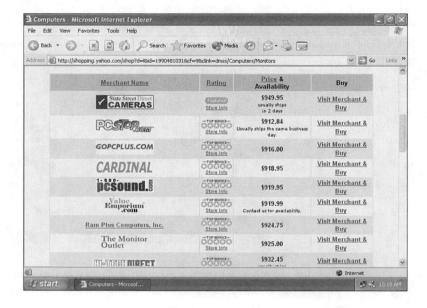

If you're in the market for something other than a new LCD monitor, here are a few other online shopping sites you might want to visit:

- **Computer Discount Warehouse**—http://www.cdw.com/
- **PC Connection**—http://www.pcconnection.com/
- **Internet Shopping Network**—http://www.isn.com/
- **Micro Center**—http://www.microcenter.com/
- **PC Mall**—http://www.pcmall.com/
- **Micro Warehouse**—http://www.microwarehouse.com/
- **The PC Zone**—http://www.pczone.com/
- **Insight**—http://www.insight.com/
- **Buy.Com**—http://www.buy.com/
- **PCToday**—http://www.pctoday.com/
- **TigerDirect**—http://www.tigerdirect.com/

After you locate a few companies you think you might want to do business with, you should look at a few other things before you place your first order:

- *How does the company ship the order and what do they charge?* Some companies advertise what appear to be lower-than-competitive prices and then turn around and charge you exorbitant shipping and handling charges to make their profit. Find out what carriers the company ships with and find out whether they ship overnight delivery, 2nd day delivery, or 3–5 day ground delivery. For most computer components, shipping charges should be minimal considering that most computer components are rather small and lightweight. The exception, however, is computer monitors. If you opt for a 17-inch or larger monitor, bear in mind that the shipping weights can be 60 lbs. and up; and you will often see shipping charges in the neighborhood of $60–$80 (see Figure 24.4). When comparison shopping on monitors, keep this shipping charge in mind and weigh it against possibly paying a state sales tax at a local computer store.

24

FIGURE 24.4

An example of shipping charges for a computer monitor.

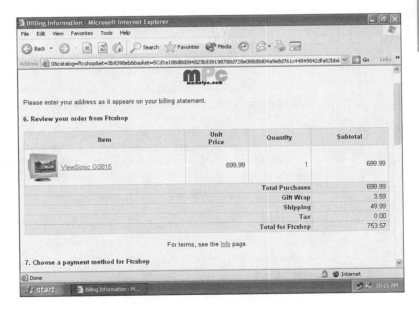

- *What are the company's return policies?* If you order the wrong part or if the item you order does not work with your computer, can you return it? Some companies will charge a 5–15 percent restocking fee for returned items.
- *Will you be charged sales tax for the item?* In most cases, you will not be charged sales tax for your state (assuming that your state has a tax) for the items you purchase unless the company has a physical presence in your state. If your state does have sales tax and you are not charged sales tax, in many states you are required (by your state) to pay what is often called a merchandise tax.

- *Do any of the companies offer lowest price guarantees?* Some companies will guarantee that theirs is the lowest price and will meet or beat a competitor's price. It never hurts to ask.

Internet Security

For online purchases, does the company use a secure Web site? A secure Web site is a way of conducting your transaction by establishing an encrypted connection between your computer and the Web site computer so that no one can tap into the communication session and see information you want to keep private, such as your credit card number. If the company is not using a secure site, make your transaction over the telephone using the company's 800 number.

The question of Internet security is probably the single most important factor still limiting online commerce. The main problem is not that the Internet commercial transactions are not secure. The main problem is that the Internet commercial transactions are not *perceived* as being secure.

> Every time someone asks me if I'm worried about making purchases over the Internet and giving out my credit card number, I turn around and ask them if they have ever eaten out in a restaurant. I ask them if they worried when they gave the waiter their credit card and watched him disappear into a back room. I then point out to them that I am probably safer giving my credit card number out over a secure Internet connection than they are giving their credit card to a waiter they've never met before.

You can very easily identify when you have a secure connection by two visible signs in your Web browser. The first sign is the address of the Web page you are viewing. A normal or unsecured Web page address begins http://, but a secure Web page address usually begins https://.

The second sign is some symbol or indicator from your Web browser that the Web site is secure. In Netscape, you will see an icon of a closed lock (see Figure 24.5).

In Internet Explorer, a secure Web site is illustrated by a lock icon displayed on the status bar at the bottom of the screen (see Figure 24.6).

FIGURE 24.5

In Netscape, you see a lock icon like this one, which indicates a connection with a secure Web site.

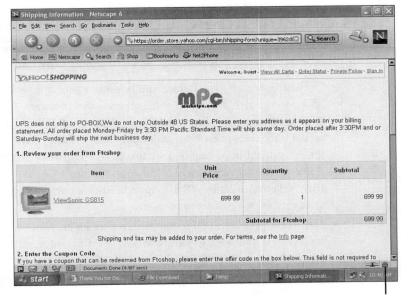

Netscape's secure site indicator

24

FIGURE 24.6

In Internet Explorer, you see this indicator informing you that you have established a connection with a secure Web site.

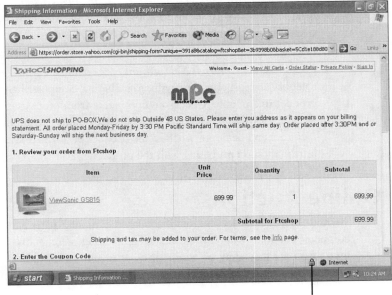

Internet Explorer's secure site indicator

Tips on Buying PC Components

Finally, let me offer a few tips on buying computer components whether you purchase them over the Internet, call an 800 number, or simply walk into a computer store.

- *Do your research first.* Before you buy any item for your PC, read a few product reviews comparing the item from several manufacturers. For example, if you are thinking about upgrading your CD-ROM to a CD-RW drive, look through some recent issues of some of the major computer industry journals and see what features are considered important and what type of comparison testing has been done. Some product reviews include either an "Editor's Choice" selection or a "Best Buy" recommendation. CNET has a hardware comparison Web site you can check at `http://www.computers.com`.

- *Get recent information.* Product reviews are an excellent way of getting information on products you want to purchase, but not if the information is two years old. Remember, an old product review is about as useful as last week's *TV Guide*. Computer products change rapidly. Don't bother with reviews that are more than six to eight months old. If you can't find a recent review, wait a few weeks and there will be another one.

- *Make friends with the "computer guru" in your company.* Every company usually has one person who seems to know just about everything there is to know about computers. Seek out this person and become friends. Often, much of the information you need is available simply for the asking.

- *Check Usenet (Internet Newsgroups) for comments from other users.* Usenet has a category for just about everything, including computer hardware and every software product imaginable. Check out comments from other users on specific brands and models. Look for comments on customer relations with various companies (manufacturers and dealers), whether the product performed as advertised, and any information on problems with the product.

Online Auctions

Another source for checking out discounted computer parts and peripherals is online computer auctions. Many of these sites are selling merchandise from dealers or manufacturers who are disposing of excess or older inventories. Some are also selling used merchandise, which by law they must identify as used equipment.

Here are a few online auction sites where you can shop for computer equipment:

- **DealDeal.Com**—`http://www.dealdeal.com/`
- **OnSale**—`http://www.onsale.com/atauction/computers/computers.htm`

- **CNET Auctions**—http://auctions.cnet.com/
- **eBay**—http://www.ebay.com/

On some auction sites, you buy from the site and on other auction sites, you buy from a third-party seller. Check the rules of the site before you bid. Be sure to check all merchandise at the manufacturer's site before you bid to know exactly what you are bidding on, how old it is, and approximately how much it is worth.

Some sights will also list a history of the seller's previous auctions and whether there have been problems or complaints from other buyers. Be sure to check this information if it is available.

Is it safe to buy from online auctions? The vast majority of the time, it is. But when in doubt, use one of the many escrow services available for auction buyers.

> An escrow service is a service that will hold your payment until you verify that you have received the item and that it is OK.

Summary

In this hour, you learned about purchasing upgrade components for your PC over the Internet. You learned about some of the security precautions you should be aware of to maintain a secure connection with the company you are purchasing from. And finally, you learned a few tips on purchasing computer products whether you buy them online or in a computer store.

Q&A

Q What should I usually pay for shipping?

A That's a hard question to answer because most online computer stores set their own shipping policies. Some charge by weight, with a minimum charge for very small items like SIMMs. Some charge by distance and weight, and some charge you a flat rate for all items under a certain weight limit. Keep in mind that shipping charges vary according to when you want to receive your purchase. Overnight delivery is the most expensive, and what is called "surface transit" typically is the least expensive. Shop around though. Some retailers (or e-tailers as some are now called) will discount products and then jack up their shipping charges to make up for the discount.

Q Are there any other shopping concerns I should have?

A If the price on an item looks too good to be true, make sure that you are not
purchasing a refurbished item when you think you are purchasing a new item.
It is not uncommon for manufacturers to offer refurbished items, but they must be
identified as such. However, an individual seller can list a used item as new, and
your recourses for grievance are few. Also, if you do purchase a refurbished item,
check what type of warranty is supplied with the item, if any, and whether you can
return the item if it does not meet your needs. Check also to see whether the dealer
charges you a re-stocking fee for returned items.

APPENDIX A

Glossary

Following is a list of terms used throughout this book.

16-bit and 32-bit   Technical terms you will hear whenever the discussion turns to operating systems and/or programming, among other things. Quite simply, they refer to how computer instructions and data are processed by your computer, either in 16-bit units or in 32-bit units. Because a 32-bit unit is twice as large as a 16-bit unit, the assumption is that 32-bit programs and operating systems are twice as fast as their 16-bit counterparts. "Twice as fast" may be stretching it a bit, but the basic underlying assumption is generally true. 32-bit programs and operating systems are faster than 16-bit programs and operating systems.

ADSL   Asynchronous Digital Subscriber Line. See *DSL*.

Analog   *See* **Digital and analog**.

BIOS   The acronym for Basic Input Output System. The BIOS is a set of instructions built in to your computer to control how information and data flow in and out of your computer.

Bit   A plus or minus electrical charge (more commonly understood as 1 or 0). Eight bits equal one *byte*.

Boot, warm and cold   The terms describe two methods of rebooting or restarting your PC. As the names imply, a *warm boot* is a reboot with the power on and a *cold boot* is a reboot with the power off. The difference between the two booting methods is more than just the presence of electrical power. A cold boot is a more thorough, or complete, boot up process because it also releases any data that might still be in several system caches or memory holding areas. A cold boot runs a more thorough POST—the Power On Self Test. A warm boot is less stressful on your electrical components.

Bps   Bits per second. Usually used to describe a digital communications speed.

Broadband   A type of communications, either digital or analog, in which one wire multiple signals. Cable TV is an example of broadband communications along with cable modem Internet service and DSL (Digital Subscriber Line) service.

Bus   The bus in your PC is the connecting electronic pipeline among your processor, memory, and the PC's peripherals, such as drives and interface cards.

Bus speed   Refers to how fast data and instructions are able to move among the CPU, memory, and your PC's peripherals. Part of bus speed is controlled by how wide the bus is and the speed of the bus. Bus width refers to how many bits of data can be passed at one time—8 bits, 16 bits, or 32 bits of data. Obviously, a bus that can pass data 32 bits at a time can operate faster than a bus that can pass data only 8 bits at a time. To put this analogy into a more real-world scenario, think of a water pipe that is 1 inch in diameter versus a water pipe that is 4 inches in diameter. The 4-inch pipe allows more water to pass every second than does the 1-inch pipe.

CD-RW   A rewritable CD-ROM drive.

Centronics parallel cable   A simple communications cable with a 36-pin Centronics connector on one end and a 25-pin female connector on the other. You can purchase a Centronics parallel cable in most computer stores in lengths ranging from 6–15 feet. And don't believe that myth about parallel cables having to be less than 10 feet in length. If you need a 15-foot cable, go ahead and purchase one. Many stores now carry printer cables in lengths of 25 feet and longer.

Clock speed   A measurement of how fast (its maximum speed) a particular CPU is set to operate. The speed is the measurement in megahertz (MHz) of an oscillating timing crystal used to control how fast the CPU can perform internal operations. Although the term "maximum" implies that there is also a minimum speed, that is no longer the case. It was true with some early 286 and 386 processors for which you could adjust the speed (why anyone would ever want to use anything but the maximum speed is beyond me), but since the 486, the stated clock speed is the speed at which the CPU should be operating, according to the manufacturer.

Digital and analog These are terms used quite freely and have taken on several popular meanings. In the context of computer communications, *analog* refers to communicating by means of converting the signal in your computer to a measurable frequency and modulation, which happens to be sound waves. *Digital* refers to communicating by means of transmitting your message using a representation of the binary symbols 0 and 1 just as they are created in your PC.

DIMMs Dual Inline Memory Modules. Memory modules used in newer Pentium II and Pentium III PCs. Sizes usually range from 32–256MB.

Disk controller The interface that connects your disk drives to your motherboard. The controller can either be built in to the motherboard, as are most IDE controllers in most PCs built in the last few years, or they can come in the form of an interface card that is installed into one of the slots on your motherboard.

dpi dots per inch.

DSL Digital Subscriber Line. A digital communications line for connecting to the Internet. Speeds can vary, but are usually between 720Kbps and 7.1Mbps for downloading. It's called asynchronous because upload speeds are considerably slower than download speeds.

DVD Digital Versatile (originally "Video") Disk. A digital technology very similar to CD-ROM technology. DVDs differ in that they can store several times the capacity of CD-ROM disks (CD-ROMs can store approximately 650MB).

Ergonomics The study of the relationship between people and their work environments. In simpler terms, it means producing tools in the workplace—such as chairs, desks, keyboards, and so on—that conform more to the way human bodies are designed and how they function rather than making human bodies conform to workplace tools. The idea is to increase comfort and reduce the possibility of injuries or stress.

FAT16 The original disk file organizational structure used by DOS and Windows 3.1. Maximum partition size is 2048MB.

FAT32 The disk file organizational structure released with Windows 98 (and Windows 95 OSR2 version). FAT32 eliminated many of the limitations of FAT16 such as the 2048MB partition size—the maximum partition size under FAT32 is two terabytes. FAT32 also offers more efficient use of hard disk drives.

Firewall A system—hardware, software, or both—used to prevent unauthorized access to or from a computer or a private computer network.

FireWire™ A very fast, external bus standard, designated as the IEEE 1394 standard, that supports data transfer rates of up to 400Mbps (400 million bits per second) originally developed by Apple Computer Company. Apple also has trademarked the name *FireWire*.

A

Firmware   Software that has been embedded into certain chips in your computer and that runs automatically without intervention on your part. The distinction is usually made between programs you can easily change, erase, and delete—software—and programs you cannot easily alter—firmware.

Gigabyte (GB)   A thousand megabytes or a billion bytes.

IDE   Integrated Drive Electronics. An interface that enables up to two devices to be attached to each port. Originally, IDE enabled data to pass to its connected devices at the rate of only 2Mbits/sec, but newer Enhanced IDE Ultra ATA/66 interfaces and devices can transfer data at the rate of 66Mbits/sec.

ISDN   Integrated Services Digital Network. An early proposal for upgrading the telephone system from analog to digital. ISDN never progressed very far for replacing the telephone system, but it did make some headway for providing Internet access despite its high costs. It is now being supplanted by DSL and cable.

Kilobyte (KB)   1024 bytes (2^{10} bytes).

Main system board or motherboard   These terms are often used interchangeably and refer to the same component: the main electronic circuit board in a PC.

Megabyte (MB)   One million bytes.

MHz   The abbreviation for *megahertz* (millions of hertz per second), used as a measurement for the oscillating timing frequency used by processors. In simpler terms, it is an indication of the relative speed of a processor.

MIDI   Musical Instrument Digital Interface. An interface and a file format that enables you to connect a musical instrument to a computer and store musical instrument data. The musical instrument data can then be enhanced, edited, and played back.

Modem   **MO**dulate **DEM**odulate. A communications device that converts a digital computer signal into an analog signal (sound) that can be transmitted over standard telephone lines. A modem at the other end of the signal demodulates the analog signal back to a digital computer signal. Communications speeds for modems range up to 56,000bps.

MPEG-2   An international graphics standard established by the Motion Picture Entertainment Group (MPEG) for audio and video compression and playback.

Multitasking   This term means that several programs or tasks are capable of running simultaneously. In Windows 98/NT/2000/Me/XP, the operating system controls the amount of CPU time allotted to each running procedure or application.

Network   Two or more computers connected together so that files, peripherals, and resources can be shared.

Optical Character Recognition (OCR)   A way of using your scanner and special software to scan a page of text, such as a newspaper or magazine article, and convert what is being scanned into a text file. Some OCR programs can also convert the scanned document into several popular word-processing formats, such as Microsoft Word and Corel WordPerfect. Keep in mind that several good OCR programs are on the market, and even the best is not 100% perfect.

Plug and Play   A combination hardware-and-software feature that enables an operating system such as Windows 95/98/2000/Me/XP to identify and configure hardware you add to your PC. To work, the hardware item has to have special chips built in that identify the hardware item. The operating system has to be Plug and Play enabled so that it can read those chips and use the information they contained to configure the hardware.

RAM and memory   Often used interchangeably. RAM is short for Random Access Memory and is the electronic memory (the chips) your computer uses for running programs and storing temporary data. RAM is not the permanent storage area for files.

SCSI   Small Computer System Interface. Enables you to connect up to seven devices to the interface. Since the original SCSI standard was released, it has been updated several times and now includes SCSI-2 and SCSI-3, and can achieve data transfer speeds up to 80Mbits/sec.

SIMMs   Single Inline Memory Modules. SIMMs are electronic modules about 10 1/2 centimeters long that sit in slots, usually located on your main system board.

UNIX   An operating system for mid-sized computers created in the 1970s and eventually made available for PCs ranging from PCs to mainframes. It is still in use today and was the design basis for Linux.

USB   Universal Serial Bus. An external bus standard that supports data transfer rates up to 480Mbps. A single USB port can connect up to 127 peripheral devices, such as mice, modems, and keyboards.

Video cards   Also referred to as *video adapters*, *graphic adapters*, and *graphic cards*. These terms all refer to the same device: the interface card installed in your computer that controls and produces video on your monitor. Although the term "video card" mostly applies to separate interface cards installed in your PC, it can also refer to the video display circuitry built in to the motherboard.

Wireless   A way of connecting computers to a network using radio frequency waves as the transmission medium instead of coax, twisted-pair, or fiber-optic cables.

A

Appendix B

Manufacturers' Reference

Following are lists of the manufacturers and vendors who make many of the products mentioned in this book. Also included is the information you need to contact each manufacturer.

BIOS

- Award BIOS—http://www.award.com/
- BIOS Guide—http://www.pcmech.com/bios/index.htm
- BIOS Setup Information Guide—http://www.sysopt.com/bios.html
- Micro Firmware—http://www.firmware.com/index.htm

CD-ROM/CD-RW and DVD Drives

- Creative Labs—http://www.americas.creative.com/home.html
- Hewlett Packard—http://www.hp.com/storage/surestore/
- NEC—http://www.nectech.com/cdrom/index.htm
- Samsung—http://samsungelectronics.com/products/odd/odd.html
- Plextor—http://www.plextor.com/home.html

CPU

- AMD—http://www.amd.com/
- Cyrix—http://www.cyrix.com/
- Intel—http://www.intel.com/

Hard Disk Drives and Peripherals

- Adaptec—http://www.adaptec.com/
- Fujitsu—http://www.fujitsu.com/harddisk.html
- IBM—http://www.storage.ibm.com/
- Maxtor—http://www.maxtor.com/
- NEC—http://www.nectech.com/storage/index.htm
- Samsung—http://samsungelectronics.com/products/hdd/hdd.html
- Seagate—http://www.seagate.com/disc/disctop.shtml
- Western Digital—http://www.westerndigital.com/

Home Networks

- D-Link— http://www.dlink.com/products/DigitalHome/Ethernet/
- Intel—http://www.intel.com/anypoint/index.htm?iid=update+010829&
- Linksys—http://www.linksys.com/
- NetGear—http://www.netgear.com/

Keyboards and Mice

- Logitech—http://www.logitech.com/us/keyboards/index.html
- Microsoft—http://www.microsoft.com/catalog/
  display.asp?site=10078&subid=22&pg=1

Memory

- Crucial—http://www.crucial.com/
- Kingston—http://www.kingston.com/

Modems

- 3-Com—`http://www.3com.com/`
- Creative Labs—`http://www.americas.creative.com/home.html`

Monitors

- Compaq—`http://www.compaq.com/athome/monitors/`
- Fujitsu—`http://www.fujitsu.com/plasma.html`
- Hewlett Packard—`http://www.hp.com/desktops/products/monitors/`
- IBM—`http://www.pc.ibm.com/us/accessories/monitors/index.html`
- Mitsubishi—`http://www.mitsubishi-display.com/default.html`
- NEC—`http://www.nectech.com/monitors/index.htm`
- Nokia—`http://www.nokia.com/americas/displays/index.html`
- Sony—`http://www.ita.sel.sony.com/products/displays/`

Motherboards

- ABIT—`http://www.abit.com.tw/english/index.htm`
- ASUS—`http://www.asus.com/Products/Motherboard/index.html`
- BCM Advanced Research—`http://www.bcmgvc.com/`
- BioStar—`http://www.biostar.com.tw/English02/default.htm`
- FIC—`http://www.fic.com.tw/`
- Gigabyte—`http://www.giga-byte.com/gigabyte-web/newindex.htm`
- Intel—`http://www.intel.com/`
- Soyo—`http://www.soyousa.com/`
- Tyan—`http://www.tyan.com/`
- Motherboard Homeworld Vendor Site—`http://www.motherboards.org/vendors.html`

B

PC Cases

- Addtronics—`http://www.addtronics.com/`
- Antec—`http://www.antec-inc.com/products/enclos/enclos.html`
- Case Outlet—`http://www.caseoutlet.com/case/case.htm`

Phoneline Network Manufacturers

- NetGear—`http://www.netgear.com/categories.asp?xrp=9&yrp=21`
- D-Link—`http://www.dlink.com/products/DigitalHome/Hpna/`
- Intel—`http://www.intel.com/anypoint/phoneline.htm`

Printers

- Compaq—`http://www.compaq.com/athome/printers/`
- Epson—`http://www.epson.com/northamerica.html`
- Hewlett Packard—`http://www.pandi.hp.com/pandi-db/home_page.show`
- IBM—`http://www.printers.ibm.com/`
- NEC—`http://www.nectech.com/printers/index.htm`
- Okidata—`http://www.okidata.com/`

Removable Media

- Castlewood Systems—`http://www.castlewood.com/`
- Iomega—`http://www.iomega.com/`
- Sony HiFD— `http://www.ita.sel.sony.com/jump/hifd/index.html`
- SyQuest—`http://www.syquest.com/`

Scanners and Digital Cameras

- Agfa—`http://www.agfa.com/`
- Epson—`http://www.epson.com/northamerica.html`
- Fujitsu—`http://www.fujitsu.com/scanners.html`
- Hewlett Packard—`http://www.pandi.hp.com/pandi-db/home_page.show`
- Kodak—`http://www.kodak.com/`
- Nikon—`http://www.nikon.co.jp/main/index_e.htm`
- Sony—`http://www.ita.sel.sony.com/products/imaging/`
- Umax—`http://www.umax.com/`

Soundcards and Speakers

- Altec Lansing—`http://www.altech.com/`
- Bose—`http://www.bose.com/multimedia/`
- Cambridge Soundworks—`http://www.cambridgesoundworks.com/index.htm`
- Sony—`http://www.ita.sel.sony.com/products/av/`
- Creative Labs—`http://www.americas.creative.com/home.html`
- Speechworks—`http://www.altech.com/`
- Turtle Beach—`http://www.voyetra-turtle-beach.com/site/default.asp`

Video Cards

- 3dfx Interactive—`http://www.3dfx.com/view.asp`
- ASUS—`http://www.asus.com/Products/Addon/Vga/index.html`
- ATI Technologies—`http://www.ati.com/`
- Creative Labs—`http://www.americas.creative.com/graphics/`
- Diamond Multimedia—`http://www.diamondmm.com/`
- Elsa—`http://www.elsa.com/AMERICA/WELCOME.HTM`
- Matrox—`http://www.matrox.com/`

Wireless Products

- D-Link—`http://www.dlink.com/products/DigitalHome/Wireless/`
- Intel—`http://www.intel.com/anypoint/index.htm?iid=update+010829&`
- Linksys—`http://www.linksys.com`
- NetGear—`http://www.netgear.com/categories.asp?xrp=11&yrp=31`

B

INDEX

G-H

GB (gigabyte), 123, 342
glossary, 339-343
graphics cards. *See* **video**
cards
grounding straps, 59

hackers, 222
handheld scanners, 308
hard drives, 23, 123-124
backing up, 127
defragmenting, 141-142
deleting files from,
142-143
disk controllers, 125
displaying information
about, 32-34
FireWire, 139-140
formatting, 138-139
IDE (Integrated Drive
Electronics) drives
advantages and
disadvantages,
124-126, 144
installing, 126-127
multiple drives,
130-131
replacing, 129-130
UltraATA/66, 127
UltraATA/100, 127
IDE (Integrated Drive
Electronics) parameters,
135
installing operating
systems on, 139
manufacturers, 346
monitoring, 47-49

multiple drives, 25
partitioning
FDISK utility, 136-137,
144
Partition Magic utility,
137-138
removable hard drives
Castlewood Systems
ORB drive, 185
installing, 190-194
Iomega Jaz drives,
182-183
Iomega Zip drives,
180-182
LS-120 drive, 186
optimizing perfor-
mance of, 194
Sony HiFD, 185
SyQuest EZFlyer, 183
SyQuest SparQ, 183
SyQuest SyJet, 183
replacing, 129-130
SCSI (Small Computer
System Interface) drives
advantages and disad-
vantages, 124-126,
144
installing, 132-135
multiple drives, 136
terminators, 132-133
upgrading, 10
when to replace, 124
hardware-based firewalls.
See **cable/DSL firewall**
routers
heat buildup problems, 49,
21, 81, 118-119
heat sinks, 21, 81
HiFD drive, 185

high-speed Internet con-
nections
cable modems, 208,
211-214
Cat5 cables, 213
CMTS (Cable Modem
Termination
System), 213
compared to DSL
(Digital Subscriber
Line), 215
connecting to home
networks, 235
costs, 226
DOCSIS (Data Over
Cable Service
Interface
Specifications), 214
installation, 217-221
obtaining, 216-217
security, 222-223
software firewalls,
223-225
DSL (Digital Subscriber
Line), 211-215
cable/DSL firewall
routers, 235-237
Cat5 cables, 213
compared to cable
modems, 215
connecting to home
networks, 235
defined, 341
distance limitations,
215
DMT (Discrete
Multitone) standard,
215
installation, 217-221

X-Z